A YEAR OF DELICIOUS
LOW-FAT
DIET DESSERTS

A YEAR OF DELICIOUS
LOW-FAT
DIET DESSERTS

365 Quick and Easy Low-Calorie Recipes

by Joan Bingham

CAMINO BOOKS, INC.
Philadelphia

Manufactured in the United States of America

1 2 3 4 5   99 98 97 96

Library of Congress Cataloging-in-Publication Data

Bingham, Joan
  [Year of diet desserts]
  A year of delicious low-fat diet desserts: 365 quick and
easy low-calorie recipes / by Joan Bingham
      p. cm.
  Reprint. Originally published in 1987 under title: A year
of diet desserts.
  Includes Index.
  ISBN 0-940159-35-X (pbk)
  1. Desserts. 2. Low-calorie diet—Recipes. 3. Low-fat diet—
Recipes. I. Title.
TX773.B52 1996   96-1567
641.8'6—dc20

This book is available at a special discount on bulk purchases
for promotional, business and educational use.

For information, write to:

Publisher
Camino Books, Inc.
P.O. Box 59026
Philadelphia, PA 19102

with love to
Heather and Jason Batchelder,
Evan Bolin, and Wendy and Peter Gorman
(and to Don)

Contents

Introduction ix

JANUARY: Think Thin—The Mind-Body Connection to Dieting xvi

FEBRUARY: Spicing Up Desserts 22

MARCH: Beverages to Diet With 44

APRIL: Diet and Exercise 66

MAY: Selecting Fresh Fruit, the Dieter's Ally 86

JUNE: Tips on Successful Dieting 112

JULY: Calorie-Controlled Cakes 132

AUGUST: Make Your Diet Desserts Ahead 154

SEPTEMBER: Diet Ideas for Puddings and Piecrusts 174

OCTOBER: The Proper Care, Storage, and Freezing of Desserts . . . 192

NOVEMBER: Decorating Desserts with Diet in Mind 212

DECEMBER: Dessert Parties—How to Show Off
             Your Low-Calorie Specialties 236

Index 255

Introduction

Almost everyone is on a diet or watching calories, and that's no fun — especially when it means foregoing desserts, and there's a rumor among dieters that you can't eat your dessert and lose weight, too. I guess that's true if you make desserts with large amounts of the common dessert ingredients that are fattening and aren't good for you. But I think of dessert as food for the body as well as the spirit, and as with all food, I believe it should add nutrition, not just calories, to your meals. My desserts satisfy more than just your sweet tooth. I cut way down on ingredients such as egg yolks, butter, and cream that, while nutritious, are also high in fat. This means the desserts are both low calorie and wholesome. In fact, this book is proof you can enjoy a different dessert every day of the year and still stay on a diet. You probably won't want to make dessert every single day. There'll be leftovers to use, and some days you may not feel like having a sweet. But isn't it comforting to know you can have a different dessert if you want to? In a few instances, you'll notice that my servings are a bit on the small side; that is so you can enjoy a dessert that's slightly richer than most.

Nutritionally, you get out of any recipe what you put into it. I use whole grain flours for the most part, adding some unbleached white flour when it's necessary for the lightness of a cake or the flakiness of a pastry. Whole grain flours contain fewer calories than white flour. Whole wheat flour, for instance, has 400 calories per cup while a cup of all-purpose white flour contributes 455 calories to a recipe.

Handling the High-Calorie Ingredients Wisely

Sugar is a dieter's downfall: it's high in calories, and it has no nutritional benefits. Honey is the sweetener I use most often. While it's slightly higher in calories than sugar (spoon for spoon), it's also twice as sweet, so I use half the amount I would if I were sweetening with sugar. Honey isn't a very nutritious food, but it does contain small amounts of vitamins and minerals.

There are many types of honey, each with its own distinct flavor. My favorites are the readily available clover honey, wildflower honey, and orange blossom honey. I don't care for raw honey in desserts. Its strong flavor and dark color aren't compatible with delicate flavors. You'll find that desserts made with honey stay fresh and moist longer than those made with sugar.

In many of the recipes in this book, there's no sweetener added. The wonderfully natural sweetness of fruit provides all that's needed to make the dessert delicious.

Cream and even whole milk make the calories in desserts soar. I occasionally use these products in small quantities when they really are needed to achieve the results I want in a specific recipe. But as a rule, I substitute skim milk, nonfat dry milk, or plain low-fat yogurt. In most desserts the difference is barely discernible, and the calorie count and fat content are drastically reduced. These foods are excellent sources of bone-building calcium, too.

In some recipes, cream cheese takes the place of butter. With this simple substitution, you can reduce calories by 160 for every ¼ cup of cream cheese you use. And you're introducing only half as much cholesterol using cream cheese as you would with butter. In some recipes where I do use butter, the amount isn't critical. When I make sweet quick breads, for instance, I use about half of the butter a recipe ordinarily calls for, adding skim milk to obtain the proper consistency. And you can reduce the amount of shortening called for in a cake. It's surprising how little difference you'll notice in the finished product.

Yogurt, that wonderful food that's gained recognition in the past few years, can be substituted for sour cream in many desserts. This produces a dessert with substantially fewer calories. Yogurt is also a fine, low-calorie dessert topping to use in place of whipped cream. Add vanilla or almond extract and a touch of honey for flavor.

I make scrumptious cheesecakes that a dieter can eat with an easy conscience. Replacing cream cheese with the less fattening cottage cheese (or part-skim ricotta cheese) makes it possible to enjoy many variations of this popular dessert. And while these low-fat cheeses have fewer calories than their counterpart, they're still delicious, high-protein foods.

Eggs are a wonderful food. But the yolks contain the lion's share of the calories and the fat. Whenever possible, I use two egg whites in place of each whole egg called for in a recipe.

I seldom use flour as a thickener for desserts anymore, opting instead for cornstarch, tapioca, and, on occasion, eggs to provide just the desired density. And the dieter's friend, gelatin, is a frequent thickener for my recipes.

It's small wonder many people find they can't control their weight and eat desserts too. So many sweets are made with chocolate, and chocolate is over 50 percent fat and high in calories. I never use it in any form. I use carob instead. Some people don't think carob tastes like chocolate, but I maintain that when correctly used, it's difficult to tell the difference between the two. And this low-calorie chocolate taste-alike is only 2 percent fat. Its assets don't stop there. Carob contains no caffeine as chocolate does, and, because it has its own natural sweetness, you don't have to use as much sweetener in a recipe as you do with chocolate, which is quite bitter in its natural state. The secret to successful use of carob is a light touch. Its flavor is much stronger than chocolate's. I never use more than half the amount of carob I would if I were using chocolate.

Most of my cakes are so tasty in their own right, I serve them sans frostings. Others are enhanced by simple frostings or toppings, or decorated without being iced.

Sherbets, ices, and ice milks replace ice cream in the frozen desserts section of this book. I just love them! But since they're homemade and don't contain the stabilizers used in commercial ice creams, they tend to get very hard in the freezer. Removing a homemade frozen dessert from the freezer to the refrigerator an hour or two before serving time solves this problem. The time varies depending on the recipe and on the temperature of the freezer. You may have to experiment a bit.

Fruits Are a Fabulous Resource for Dieters

Most fruits are low in calories, high in fiber, rich in nutrients, and naturally, that makes them heavenly ingredients for diet desserts. Fiber has received a great deal of positive press in recent years, and it's sadly lacking in the average American diet. Fruits with edible seeds, such as figs and raspberries, are especially endowed with fiber.

Many fresh fruits are seasonal, and I try to take advantage of this by using these fruits when they're plentiful. But with modern freezing methods, frozen fruits offer a viable substitute with almost-as-good-as-fresh quality. So when I have a craving for peaches in February, I use frozen. Fresh pineapple isn't always easy to get and it doesn't work well with gelatin, so I use unsweetened canned pineapple in many of my desserts. Some fruits, such as apples, bananas, oranges, lemons, and an array of dried fruits, are in abundance year round.

This book features a fruit each month at the time that fruit is most plentiful and at its succulent best. These fruits are so delicious in their natural form that I recommend enjoying each one by itself for dessert at least once a month so you can appreciate its pure flavor.

A dessert treat I usually reserve for busy days is quickly made by folding a puree of fruit, such as peaches, into a well-beaten egg white. It's light, quick, and oh, so good. Also it's very low in calories!

Shopping Tips for the Weight-Conscious

The first rule for the weight-conscious is to be a smart shopper. Never shop when you're hungry. (You've no doubt heard that before. But it's important and so it's repeated often.) You'll be tempted by an array of foods your stomach will tell you to purchase that you know in your heart you should pass by. And always approach the market armed with a well-thought-out shopping list.

If you're buying any prepared foods, be cautious. Read the labels carefully. Ingredients are listed according to the amounts used, in descending order.

Curtail salt or sodium in any form since it causes water retention. It's abundant in prepared foods, including many where you might not expect to find it. A product marked "Low Sodium" must contain less sodium per serving than is regularly used in the same food. If the package is marked "No Salt," "No Salt Added," or "Salt Free," it has been prepared without adding any sodium. *But* that doesn't necessarily mean it's a food you should eat when you're dieting, since the food itself may have a high sodium content.

The supermarkets now boast all sorts of diet foods. Most of them contain chemicals I'd rather not use in my cooking, so I don't buy them. But it's wise to be aware of the packaging lingo. If a product is marked "Lo-Cal," it must offer no more than 40 calories per serving. And if the label reads "Calorie Reduced," the law requires that the contents be at least one-third lower in calories than the food would be normally. Of course, that still can be pretty high! The term "Sugar Free" is also misleading. While it does mean the package contains no sugar, it may contain any number of sugar substitutes. Some of them are questionable, healthwise, and others are no lower in calories than the sugar they're replacing. Even when you're shopping for honey, read the label carefully. I always select a honey that's marked "pure." If it doesn't have that word on the bottle, honey may be up to 19 percent sugar or corn syrup.

Judicious selection of dairy products to use in your desserts is a big calorie saver, indeed. The fat content is the all-important consideration here. Whole milk contains between 3.25 and 4.0 percent butterfat and at least 8.25 percent milk solids. It's a great source of protein, but it's not a diet food. "Low-fat milk" may have a range of fat from 0.5 to 2.0. Of course, the 0.5 milk is a better choice for anyone who's watching his or her weight. Low-fat milk, too, must contain at least 8.25 percent nonfat milk solids, and it still has as much protein as whole milk. But, while a glass of whole milk adds 150 calories to a recipe, a cup of skim or nonfat milk only contributes 80 calories.

Although buttermilk sounds fattening, it has only 88 calories per cup. What's sold in the markets today, however, has little resemblance to the wonderful buttermilk of years ago and I rarely use it.

Nonfat dry milk fills a variety of needs for the cook who's making low-calorie desserts. Look for "U.S. Extra Grade" on the shield. Most nonfat dry milk has been fortified with 2,000 international units of vitamin A and 400 international units of vitamin D per reconstituted quart. I always use *instant* nonfat dry milk as it dissolves much more readily than the noninstant. An added plus of nonfat dry milk is its price. It's an aid to the pocketbook as well as the waistline.

Cream is loaded with fat—light cream contains 18 to 30 percent milk fat and heavy cream has over 36 percent. I use it only very occasionally and in small quantities—to make a dessert that can't be made without it—or to adorn a dessert that's very low in calories and is much improved with just a dab of cream. I never buy ultrapasteurized cream. It does keep longer, but it also contains additives, and I find it doesn't whip properly.

Yogurt is better—dietwise—than sour cream, but it can't always be substituted for it. Yogurt has all the nutritional properties of whole milk only in *higher* amounts. I prefer to make my own yogurt, but occasionally I do buy it. Most of the yogurt in the supermarket is made from fresh, partially skimmed milk and nonfat dry milk. If the container says "low-fat yogurt," it has anywhere from 0.5 to 2.0 percent milk fat. But if it reads "nonfat yogurt," the milk fat is no more than 0.5 percent. Keep unopened yogurt stored upside down on the door of your refrigerator which is warmer than other parts of the refrigerator. Extreme cold destroys some of the good bacteria of this food.

Whether you're buying ricotta, cream cheese, or cottage cheese, check the dates on the packages in your market and select the freshest product.

I do use some butter in my dessert recipes, and I always buy the sweet, unsalted variety. When you're shopping for butter, look for the words "U.S. Grade AA" or "U.S. 93 Score."

Margarine isn't an ingredient I use, but if you prefer it, you can use it interchangeably with butter in the recipes in this book.

I'm happy to report that carob is being stocked by more and more markets. I buy both powdered carob and carob chips for use in desserts. The chips come in dark carob and milk carob flavors. The latter have a milder flavor and are my favorites. They're a little more difficult to find, but many natural foods stores stock them or will order them if you request it.

I rely heavily on spices to flavor desserts. I don't recommend buying the giant-size bottles or tins, although they may seem like a bargain, since spices lose their freshness and zing rather quickly.

Snacks

No wonder diets fail when so many of them rule out snacks. Imagine looking foward to three meager meals a day for the rest of your life! What a bleak thought. Snacks shouldn't be forbidden. In fact, they should be encouraged as an alternative to that horrible empty feeling that results in indiscriminate overeating when meal-time finally comes around. It's difficult to use restraint when you're ravenous.

There are good, acceptable snacks, and there are those that should be avoided because they're fattening. The purpose of a snack is, after all, to take the edge off your appetite. I try to keep my snacking to under 100 calories, and I prefer a sweet snack.

Once you attain your desired weight, it's easy to maintain and you don't have to starve. If you eat good nutritious foods and make meals special occasions, you'll be less apt to overeat. Don't eat on the run. Savor every mouthful, and eat sitting down at an attractively appointed table.

I find life more complete since I've found I can eat dessert as often as I like and still stay at my desirable weight. I hope you enjoy the year's recipes as much as I do.

Some Satisfying Under-100-Calorie Snacks

When hunger pangs won't quit, and you just *have* to eat something right away, choose a treat from this list of satisfiers.

1 medium-size papaya	1 succulent pear
½ cup applesauce	1 cup fresh blackberries
1 large apple	1 cup fresh or frozen
½ medium-size	blueberries
cantaloupe	1 cup fresh sweet
2 cups lush ripe	cherries
fresh strawberries	4 dates (eat slowly and
2 cups plain popcorn	savor)
½ dozen walnut meats	2 figs
1 large, juicy orange	½ grapefruit
½ cup plain or vanilla	¾ cup grapes (any type)
yogurt	1 nectarine
½ dozen dried apricots	2 peaches
1 medium-size, ripe	1 cup fresh pineapple
banana	10 damson plums (a real
10 crisp unsalted	bonus at only 7
almonds	calories each)
1 medium-size wedge of	1 cup fresh raspberries
watermelon	2 tangerines

DON'T LIMIT YOUR PLEASURES!

The recipes for desserts listed on each month's calendar are contained in the chapter immediately following, although the order may change. They are arranged to provide daily variety and take advantage of seasonal fruits. But you might want to enjoy April's fancies in July or December's treats in May. Scan all the monthly calendars to become familiar with the indulgences in store throughout the year. Maybe you'd like the Saint Paddy's Day Mint Treat in February or the New Year's Day Holiday Ice Cream Bombe in August. This book was born to bring some joy into calorie control. Make the most of it!

JANUARY

Think Thin—The Mind-Body Connection to Dieting

FRUIT OF THE MONTH: **APPLES**

DESSERT OF THE MONTH: **APPLE RAISIN PIE**

DRINK OF THE MONTH: **APPLE-GRAPE DRINK**

				New Year's Day 1	2	3
				HOLIDAY ICE CREAM BOMBE	PEANUT PEAR PIE	BLUEBERRY COBBLER
4	5	6	7	8	9	10
CHEESE COOKIES	MAPLE PEAR TORTE	TANGY BANANA FLUFF	LIGHT LEMON GELATIN	APPLE-FILLED GERMAN PANCAKES	BLUEBERRY RICE PUDDING	COFFEE GRANITA WITH CREAM
11	12	13	14	Martin Luther King's Birthday 15	16	17
ONE SHINY, RED APPLE	PEACHY SCALLOP	MOCK DOUGHNUT HOLES	FRUITED ORANGE CUPS	DREAM PIE	APPLE PEAR BAKE	MIXED FRUIT WITH RASPBERRY RUM SAUCE
18	19	20	21	22	23	24
APPLE AND SPICE CAKE	JELLY SHAKES	BANANA COCONUT ICE MILK	PEACH NUT BAVARIAN	STRAWBERRY FRENCH TOAST	GRAPEFRUIT ORANGE PIE	COCONUT THUMB PRINTS
25	26	27	28	29	30	31
PEARS À LA CRÈME	BEAUTIFUL BAKED ALASKA	PEARS WITH RASPBERRY SAUCE	DELECTABLE CAROB CAKE	APPLE RAISIN PIE ★	LITE SURPRISE PUDDING	EASY BAKED PEAR RINGS

It's January! What a wonderful time to start a diet. There's a brand new year ahead and you're full of resolve to be better, look better, and feel better. You intend to let bad eating habits die and replace them with healthy ones. And, of course, that means shedding those extra pounds. More diets probably begin on January first than any other day of the year. But by February first most have been abandoned. One major reason for this is the negative approach so many dieters take. They expect to fail; they see themselves as failures.

Wonderful You

You're going to be successful, so the first thing you need is a good self-image. You are you. You may be overweight, but that doesn't mean you're a bad person. We all know people who are perpetually starting diets that will never last or succeed. They try every new fad diet that comes along. One month their refrigerators overflow with grapefruit, another month it's cottage cheese and pineapple. These people may lose weight for awhile, but they *always* put it back on. Most of them hate themselves for being fat. They think of themselves as losers — not of weight, but at life. They have a poor self-image.

Dr. Barbara Sternberg, a psychological consultant for Weight Watchers, says that many people actually dislike themselves so much for being overweight that they think they don't deserve to be thin. When they diet, they program themselves to fail. In order to lose weight and keep it off, you have to will yourself to succeed. You may never be a size five, but you can attain and maintain your ideal weight. That is, you can if you think you can — and then take the steps necessary to do it. But don't take on a diet that promises you will become a feather-weight overnight. That's exactly the type of diet that leads to failure. You're an okay person right now. And as you lose weight gradually, eating the right foods, along with exercise, you're going to feel better and better about yourself.

Program your subconscious to help you. If you're wishy washy about your diet and reinforce it only with thoughts of "I'll try to diet," or

"I know I should diet," your subconscious receives a weak signal. Instead say to yourself, "I will be successful at changing my eating habits to include only those foods that are good for me and will help me to attain my perfect weight." Then change your eating habits—permanently!

Does this mean you can never again enjoy all those wonderful foods you look forward to? No, it does not! I think diets in which all tempting foods are absolutely forbidden are bound to fail. There's nothing as enticing as something you are ordered to avoid forever. Most dishes that are classically made with fattening ingredients can be made in a lighter, better-for-you version. This book offers many examples of that—recipes for desserts that taste wonderful but substitute ingredients such as evaporated skim milk instead of cream, egg whites instead of whole eggs, and yogurt instead of sour cream.

Of course, substitution doesn't apply just to desserts. Light versions of most of the things you crave can be worked into your new eating program. The few dishes that just can't be made without high-calorie ingredients can be enjoyed occasionally, too. But first ask yourself, "Is this a food I really love and don't want to give up?" If you feel you can't forego it, don't abandon your diet; simply eat half as much of the treat as you would ordinarily. Eat slowly. Savor every bite. Remember this is special. As long as you don't consider any foods *absolutely* off limits, you should be able to stick to your weight loss plan.

Don't be too hard on yourself if you put on a few pounds from time to time. Be objective. You want to lose weight, your clothes are getting tight and unattractive. Proceed with a reasonable plan to remedy the situation.

In your new way of eating, it's very important to avoid letting yourself get really hungry. (No one can stick to a diet for long if it means feeling starved all the time.) And, of course, your diet must be well balanced so you'll be eating for health as well as slenderness. All of the basic food groups must be represented.

One common trait among people who have trouble losing weight is that they continue to eat when they've actually had enough, and the additional food makes them feel bloated and uncomfortable. It's essential to listen to the inner voice that says, "You've had enough." Adding bulk to your diet is a good way to make yourself feel full faster, and because fiber doesn't stay in your system as long as other substances and isn't readily absorbed, you'll get the fullness without the added weight.

Remember, dieting seldom goes smoothly. Most people have set-backs. If you binge, don't feel defeated and give up. You're entitled to stray now and then. So what, if for one meal, or one day, or even one week you reverted to your old eating habits. Forgive yourself, and go back to good, nutritional, nonfattening meals. You can regain the ground you've lost and lose the weight you've gained.

The Mental Advantages of Exercise

Exercise is important to weight loss. It not only firms your muscles and burns calories, it helps you attain self-confidence by giving you control over your body. You'll be reluctant to surrender this new sense of self, and weight control will be easier.

Auto Suggestion

Auto suggestion is a helpful tool for dieters. There are many ways you can utilize it. For instance, you can cut out a picture of a slender model—one who has a similar bone structure to yours. Paste a photograph of your face on the face in the picture and put it on the refrigerator door. Every time you go to the refrigerator, look at the picture and see yourself thin.

Another way to use auto suggestion is to buy stylish jeans, or a bathing suit in the size you aspire to. Hang it in a visible place and every time you look at it tell yourself, "It fits me perfectly."

Something for Nothing

The reward system is my favorite! Every time I put on a few extra pounds, I promise myself a special present for taking them off. The reward is never food, of course. But I might get a pair of earrings that I've been admiring, a pretty dress in my new size, or tickets to a show I've been wanting to see.

A new hobby is a great help to many dieters because it's distracting. Select something you really want to do—something you can get lost in. I found when I first took up crocheting, I would actually forget to eat.

The simple message I want to impart is: everything starts with a thought, so guard against the kind of thinking that can lead you to eating when you're not hungry. Include nonfattening foods in your diet. You can make real headway toward reaching your desired weight by adopting these two basic measures. And you don't even have to give up desserts—just use the ones in this book.

Blueberry Cobbler

3 cups unsweetened frozen blueberries, thawed
¼ cup honey
1 tablespoon cornstarch
¼ cup water
½ cup whole wheat pastry flour
½ cup unbleached white flour
1½ teaspoons baking powder
2 tablespoons butter
½ cup skim milk

Preheat oven to 375°F.

In a medium-size saucepan, combine blueberries and honey. Dissolve
cornstarch in water and add to blueberries. Cook over medium heat, stirring
constantly, until mixture thickens.

In a medium-size bowl, whisk together whole wheat pastry flour, unbleached white flour, and baking
powder. Cut butter into pieces. Add to
flour mixture and cut in with pastry
blender or 2 knives. Stir in skim milk.

Turn blueberries into a 1½-quart
casserole. Drop batter in 8 equal spoonfuls on top of blueberries. Bake on middle shelf of oven until batter is lightly
browned, 25 to 30 minutes.

Makes 8 servings
(160 calories per serving)

Cheese Cookies

*While these cookies aren't sweet, my
family loves them for dessert served
with a piece of fresh fruit.*

⅓ cup butter, softened
⅓ cup grated cheddar cheese
1 egg, beaten
2 tablespoons skim milk
¾ cup whole wheat pastry flour
¼ teaspoon ground cinnamon

Preheat oven to 350°F. Spray 2 baking sheets with vegetable spray.

With the back of a wooden spoon,
cream together butter and cheese in a
medium-size bowl. Add egg and mix in
well. Add skim milk, stirring to blend.
Mix in flour and cinnamon.

Fill pastry bag fitted with a large
star tip with dough. Pipe in 2-inch rounds
on prepared baking sheets and bake
each batch on middle shelf of oven until
golden, 12 to 15 minutes.

Remove to wire racks to cool.

Makes 30 cookies
(45 calories per cookie)

Skinny Piecrust

Rolling this dough out takes a little practice.

2 tablespoons butter
¼ cup whole wheat pastry
   flour

¼ cup unbleached white flour
4 to 8 teaspoons ice water

In a medium-size bowl, combine whole wheat pastry flour and unbleached white flour. Cut butter into flour with a pastry blender until crumbly. Add water, a teaspoon at a time, until dough clings together when pressed against the sides of the bowl. Form into a flat round, wrap in plastic wrap, and chill well.

Roll out lightly floured dough to paper thinness on cool surface between 2 pieces of waxed paper. Remove top piece of waxed paper.

For bottom crust only: Invert crust, paper side up, over pie plate. Remove second piece of paper and press crust against bottom and sides of plate. (There will be no ridge of crust as in a conventional pie.) To bake blind, prick bottom and sides with a fork and bake on bottom shelf of preheated 425°F oven until lightly browned, about 10 minutes.

For top crust only: Place crust over filling, paper side up. Remove second piece of paper. Press edges against edge of pie plate. Cut vents.

Makes 1 bottom or 1 top crust
(10   43-calorie servings)

Maple Pear Torte

1   recipe for Heavenly Angel Food
      Cake (page 38)
4   fresh pears
1½   teaspoons cornstarch
2   tablespoons maple syrup
½   teaspoon vanilla extract
1   cup Slim Pastry Cream
      (page 246)
16   pecan halves, optional

Bake angel food cake according to directions.

Halve, peel, and core pears. Place them cut side down in a large skillet. Cover with water. Cover pan and bring to a boil. Reduce heat and simmer for 5 minutes.

Remove pears with a slotted spoon and set them aside to cool.

Pour ⅓ cup of the liquid from pears into a small saucepan. Stir in cornstarch until it dissolves. Add maple syrup and heat, stirring constantly, until mixture thickens. Remove from heat, add vanilla, and set aside.

Cut cake in half crosswise. Place one layer on serving plate, reserving second layer for future use. Spread top with pastry cream. Arrange pears around edge, cut side down. Arrange pecan halves around pears, if desired. Drizzle maple glaze over pears and chill cake.

Makes 16 servings
(100 calories per serving)

Holiday Ice Cream Bombe

I use crumbs from Heavenly Angel Food Cake for this. But any cake crumbs will do.

3   cups French Carob Ice Milk
      (page 180) softened
½   cup Heavenly Angel Food Cake
      crumbs (page 38), divided
2½   cups Frozen Peach Brandy
      Supreme (page 115)
2   cups Banana Strawberry Freeze
      (page 110)
16   fresh strawberries

Line an 8-cup bombe mold with softened French Carob Ice Milk, pushing it against sides and leaving an even indentation in center. Sprinkle with ¼ cup cake crumbs. Cover mold with plastic wrap and freeze until firm, about 1 hour.

While French Carob Ice Milk is hardening, allow Frozen Peach Brandy to soften. Then form a layer of Frozen Peach Brandy inside the layer of French Carob Ice Milk, leaving an even indentation in center. Sprinkle with remaining cake crumbs. Cover mold with plastic wrap and freeze until firm, about 1 hour.

While Frozen Peach Brandy is hardening, allow Banana Strawberry Freeze to soften. Fill in indentation left in mold. Smooth top, cover with plastic wrap, and return to freezer until ready to serve.

To unmold, quickly dip bottom of mold in warm, not hot, water, and invert on a platter. Surround with strawberries.

Makes 15 servings
(119 calories per serving)

Tangy Banana Fluff

This tart, light dessert is ideal when you want a finale that's not too sweet.

1 envelope unflavored gelatin
1 cup freshly squeezed orange juice
3 tablespoons honey
1 cup plain low-fat yogurt
2 egg whites
⅛ teaspoon cream of tartar
1 medium-size ripe banana
6 mandarin orange sections, optional

In a small saucepan, sprinkle gelatin over orange juice. Set aside for 3 minutes to soften. Heat over low heat, stirring constantly, until gelatin dissolves. Remove from heat.

In a medium-size bowl, stir gelatin mixture, honey, and yogurt together. Chill until thickened but not set, stirring occasionally so edges won't set.

In a medium-size bowl, beat egg whites until foamy. Add cream of tartar and continue beating until stiff peaks form.

Cut banana into quarters, lengthwise. Cut quarters crosswise into small pieces. Fold into yogurt mixture. Fold in beaten egg whites and divide among 6 dessert glasses. Decorate with mandarin orange sections, if desired, and chill until set.

Makes 6 servings
(77 calories per serving)

Light Lemon Gelatin

⅓ cup freshly squeezed lemon juice
1½ cups water, divided
1 envelope unflavored gelatin
¼ cup honey
¼ teaspoon lemon extract
about 6 drops natural yellow food coloring

In a medium-size bowl, combine lemon juice and 1 cup of the water.

In a small saucepan, sprinkle gelatin over remaining water. Set aside to soften for 2 minutes. Add honey and heat over medium heat, stirring until gelatin dissolves. Add to juice mixture. Mix in lemon extract and food coloring and chill until set.

Makes 4 servings
(75 calories per serving)

Blueberry Rice Pudding

1¼ cups skim milk
 3 tablespoons honey
 2 eggs, beaten
1½ teaspoons vanilla extract
 1 teaspoon ground cinnamon
 2 cups cooked rice
 ¾ cup unsweetened frozen blue-
     berries, thawed

Preheat oven to 325°F. Spray a 1½-quart casserole with vegetable spray.

In a large bowl, whisk together skim milk, honey, eggs, vanilla, and cinnamon. Fold in rice and blueberries gently so berries won't break. Bake on middle shelf of oven until set near (but not in) center, 45 to 50 minutes.

Remove from oven and allow to cool slightly.

Makes 8 servings
(125 calories per serving)

Apple-Filled German Pancakes

The middle of this oven-cooked treat sinks and the edges rise as it bakes.

 3 eggs
 ½ cup skim milk
 2 teaspoons honey
 ¼ cup whole wheat pastry flour
 ¼ cup unbleached white flour
 1 cup Applesauce (page 81)
 ½ teaspoon ground cinnamon

Preheat oven to 425°F. Spray a 9-inch pie plate with vegetable spray.

In a medium-size bowl, beat eggs with a whisk until foamy. Beat in skim milk and honey.

In a small bowl, sift together whole wheat pastry flour and unbleached white flour, whisking to blend. Beat into egg mixture until just mixed. Pour into prepared pan and bake on middle shelf of oven until lightly browned, 15 to 20 minutes.

Remove from oven and fill indentation with Applesauce. Sprinkle with cinnamon, slice, and serve immediately.

Makes 8 servings
(83 calories per serving)

Mock Whipped Cream

This keeps well in the refrigerator for about a day.

1½ teaspoons unflavored
gelatin
¼ cup boiling water
1½ teaspoons honey

1 cup ice water
½ cup instant nonfat dry milk
2 teaspoons vanilla extract

Chill a large bowl and beaters.
Dissolve gelatin in boiling water.
Stir in honey.

In chilled bowl, beat together ice water, nonfat dry milk, and vanilla until very frothy. Gradually add gelatin mixture and continue beating until quite stiff. Chill for at least 1 hour before using.

Makes about 4 cups
(3 calories per tablespoon)

Coffee Granita with Cream

The correct way to treat a granita is to freeze it until it's quite solid, then shave it into dessert dishes at serving time. But it can be served in scoops like a sherbet or ice.

1 quart boiling water
2 tablespoons decaffeinated
instant coffee (3 if you want
a strong coffee taste)
⅓ cup honey
½ cup Mock Whipped Cream
(page 9), divided

In a medium-size bowl, mix together all ingredients except whipped cream and let mixture cool.

Process mixture in an ice cream maker according to manufacturer's instructions, or turn mixture into a large pan and freeze until thick but not solid. Remove from freezer, beat to break down ice crystals, and then return to freezer. Repeat this procedure twice.

At serving time top each portion with 1 tablespoon of the Mock Whipped Cream.

Makes 8 servings
(46 calories per serving)

Peachy Scallop

4   cups unsweetened frozen sliced
    peaches, thawed
¼   cup water
2   tablespoons honey
1   teaspoon vanilla extract
¾   teaspoon ground cinnamon
¼   teaspoon ground nutmeg

Preheat oven to 350°F.

Mix peaches with other ingredients in a 1½-quart casserole. Bake on middle shelf of oven until peaches are tender, about 20 minutes. Serve warm.

Makes 4 servings
(97 calories per serving)

Fruited Orange Cups

2   large oranges
½   cup unsweetened frozen
    cherries, thawed
½   cup unsweetened crushed
    pineapple
2   tablespoons raisins, plumped
8   seedless green grapes, quartered

Cut oranges into halves. Carefully cut out pulp, leaving shells intact. Chop orange pulp, removing seeds and pith. Combine with remaining ingredients in a medium-size bowl and chill to blend flavors.

To serve, mound fruit in orange shells.

Makes 4 servings
(97 calories per serving)

Peanut Pear Pie

1   recipe for Skinny Piecrust
    (page 5)
5   cups peeled fresh pear chunks
3   tablespoons honey
2   tablespoons freshly squeezed
    lemon juice
2   tablespoons chopped raisins
2   tablespoons chopped peanuts
1   teaspoon ground cinnamon
1   tablespoon whole wheat pastry
    flour

Preheat oven to 350°F. Line a 9-inch pie plate with pastry and bake blind according to directions.

In a large bowl, toss pears with remaining ingredients, mixing well. Turn into prepared piecrust and bake on bottom shelf of oven until crust is golden and fruit is tender, about 40 minutes.

Makes 10 servings
(130 calories per serving)

Easy Vanilla Frosting

1   egg white
¼   teaspoon cream of tartar
2   tablespoons honey

1   teaspoon vanilla extract
½   cup instant nonfat dry milk*

In a small bowl, beat egg white until foamy. Add cream of tartar and continue to beat, adding honey and vanilla. Gradually add nonfat dry milk, beating constantly.

*Makes about 1 cup
(20 calories per tablespoon)*

*Use a very fine-textured nonfat dry milk for this recipe.

Apple and Spice Cake

The sweeter and juicier the apples you select for this cake, the more delicious the finished product will be.

4   eggs
½   cup honey
½   cup vegetable oil
1½ teaspoons vanilla extract
¾   cup whole wheat pastry flour
¾   cup unbleached white flour
2   teaspoons baking powder
2   teaspoons ground cinnamon
½   teaspoon ground nutmeg
2   medium-size apples
1   cup Delicious Diet Cream
      (page 109), **divided**
    ground cinnamon for sprinkling

Preheat oven to 325°F. Spray a 9 × 9-inch pan with vegetable spray.

In a large bowl, beat together eggs, honey, oil, and vanilla.

Sift together whole wheat pastry flour, unbleached white flour, baking powder, cinnamon, and nutmeg and add to beaten ingredients. Mix together thoroughly.

Peel, core, and chop apples. Stir into batter and turn into prepared pan. Bake on middle shelf of oven until a cake tester inserted into center comes out clean, 30 to 35 minutes.

Serve warm or cold. Top each serving with a tablespoon of the diet cream and a sprinkle of cinnamon.

*Makes 16 servings
(170 calories per serving)*

Apple Pear Bake

⅓ cup water
2 tablespoons freshly squeezed
   lemon juice
½ teaspoon ground ginger
1 teaspoon ground cinnamon
2 apples
2 fresh pears

Preheat oven to 350°F.

In a small bowl, mix together water, lemon juice, ginger, and cinnamon.

Peel and core apples and pears and cut into halves. Place in a casserole in a single layer. Pour water mixture over all, cover, and bake on middle shelf of oven until fruit is tender, about 30 minutes.

Put apple half and pear half in each of 4 dessert dishes.

Makes 4 servings
(99 calories per serving)

Jelly Shakes

4 envelopes unflavored gelatin
4 cups grape juice, divided

Sprinkle gelatin over 2 cups of the grape juice.

In a small saucepan, heat remaining juice to boiling. Add gelatin mixture and heat until gelatin dissolves, stirring constantly. Pour into a 9 × 13-inch pan and chill until set.

Cut into 1-inch squares.

Makes 117 squares
(6 calories per square)

Dream Pie

½ cup whole wheat pastry flour
½ cup unbleached white flour
1½ teaspoons baking powder
3 eggs
⅓ cup honey
1 teaspoon vanilla extract
¼ cup skim milk
1 cup Tangy Lemon Filling
   (page 222)
½ cup Easy Vanilla Frosting
   (page 11)

Preheat oven to 350°F. Spray 2 8-inch layer cake pans with vegetable spray.

Sift whole wheat pastry flour, unbleached white flour, and baking powder together into a small bowl.

In a large bowl, beat eggs until thick and light colored, about 7 minutes. Drizzle in honey and vanilla, beating for another minute.

Scald skim milk in a small pan.

Sift flour mixture into egg mixture, folding in. Add hot milk all at once, mixing in well. Turn batter into prepared pans and bake on middle shelf of oven until cake layers spring back when pressed lightly, 15 to 20 minutes.

Cool in pans inverted on wire racks.

Spread lemon filling on one cake layer. Place second layer on top and spread with vanilla frosting.

Makes 10 servings
(136 calories per serving)

Banana Coconut Ice Milk

2 large, ripe bananas
1 cup water
1 cup skim milk
¼ cup nonfat dry milk
3 tablespoons maple syrup
2 teaspoons vanilla extract
1 teaspoon lemon juice
1 cup plain low-fat yogurt
½ cup unsweetened flaked coconut

Cut bananas into chunks. Puree in food processor. Add water, skim milk, nonfat dry milk, maple syrup, vanilla, and lemon juice, processing until smooth. Add yogurt and process just until blended.

Process mixture in an ice cream maker according to manufacturer's instructions. When processed, fold in coconut before putting in freezer. If you're not using an ice cream maker, turn mixture into a bowl and freeze until mushy. Remove from freezer, beat to break down ice crystals, and then return to freezer. Repeat this procedure twice, folding in coconut and spooning into a 1-quart, covered container the last time. Freeze until ready to serve.

Makes 8 servings
(86 calories per serving)

Peach Nut Bavarian

1¼ cups skim milk
2 eggs, separated
2 envelopes unflavored gelatin
¼ cup honey
1½ teaspoons vanilla extract
⅛ teaspoon cream of tartar
½ cup evaporated skim milk, chilled
1 cup chopped unsweetened frozen peaches, thawed and well drained
¼ cup chopped walnuts

In the top of a double boiler, beat together skim milk and egg yolks. Sprinkle gelatin over mixture and allow to soften for 2 minutes. Add honey, set over hot, not boiling, water and cook, stirring constantly, until gelatin is dissolved. Remove from heat and mix in vanilla. Chill until thickened but not set, 25 to 30 minutes. Whisk briefly until smooth.

In a medium-size bowl, beat egg whites until foamy. Add cream of tartar and continue beating until stiff peaks form. Fold egg whites into gelatin mixture.

In a chilled, medium-size bowl, beat evaporated skim milk to the consistency of whipped cream. Fold peaches and nuts into gelatin mixture, then fold in whipped milk. Turn into a wet 8-cup mold and chill until set.

Unmold on platter at serving time.

Makes 12 servings
(78 calories per serving)

Mixed Fruit
with Raspberry Rum Sauce

12 seedless green grapes, divided
 2 ripe pears
 2 cups unsweetened frozen sliced
      peaches
 ½ teaspoon rum extract
 1 cup Ruby Raspberry Sauce
      (page 127)

Halve 8 grapes. Peel, core, and coarsely chop pears. Mix together grapes, pears, and peaches in a medium-size bowl.

Mix rum extract into raspberry sauce and toss with fruit. Divide among 4 dessert glasses. Decorate each with a whole grape.

Makes 4 servings
(113 calories per serving)

Coconut Thumb Prints

4 ounces low-fat creamed cottage cheese
6 tablespoons butter, softened
3 tablespoons honey
1 teaspoon vanilla extract
½ cup whole wheat pastry flour
½ cup unbleached white flour
⅓ cup Coconut Sugar (page 60)
  about 2 tablespoons red currant jelly, divided

In a food processor, process cheese, butter, honey, and vanilla.

In a large bowl, mix whole wheat pastry flour and unbleached white flour together with a wire whisk. With a wooden spoon, mix in cheese-butter mixture. Chill until firm enough to hold shape.

Spray 2 baking sheets with vegetable spray.

Preheat oven to 350°F.

Roll bits of dough (about 1 teaspoon) between palms of your hands into 1-inch balls. Roll balls in Coconut Sugar and place about 1 inch apart on prepared baking sheets, flattening slightly with back of spatula. With back of spoon, make a small indentation in each cookie. Put ⅛ teaspoon jelly in each indentation. Bake, 1 sheet at a time, on middle shelf of oven until coconut is lightly browned, 15 to 20 minutes.

Remove to wire racks to cool.

Makes 3 dozen cookies
(44 calories per cookie)

Strawberry French Toast

Usually thought of as breakfast fare, this version of French toast makes a marvelous dessert.

1 egg
½ cup skim milk
½ cup unsweetened frozen strawberries, pureed
¼ teaspoon vanilla extract
4 slices whole grain bread
¼ cup Mock Whipped Cream (page 9), divided
4 whole unsweetened frozen strawberries, thawed, divided

Spray a large griddle with vegetable spray. Heat to medium.

In a medium-size bowl, beat egg. Whisk in skim milk, strawberry puree, and vanilla extract. Soak bread on both sides in mixture. Cook on griddle until lightly browned on both sides, turning once.

Serve each slice topped with 1 tablespoon of the Mock Whipped Cream and a strawberry.

Makes 4 servings
(100 calories per serving)

Coconut Crust

1½ cups unsweetened flaked
   coconut

1½ tablespoons butter,
   softened

Preheat oven to 325°F.
In a medium-size bowl, combine coconut and butter. Whirl briefly in a blender. Line a 9-inch pie plate with mixture and bake on middle shelf of oven until coconut is golden, about 15 minutes.

Cool before using. Crust will firm up as it cools.

Makes 1 piecrust
(8   65-calorie servings)

Mock Doughnut Holes

If you want these to look festive, add a drop or two of natural food coloring to the frosting.

reserved cut-out cake from
   Discovery Cake (page 201)
½ cup freshly made Easy Vanilla
   Frosting (page 11)
skim milk
⅓ cup Coconut Sugar (page 60)

Between the palms of your hands, lightly roll cake into 12 balls. Quickly roll each ball in frosting. (If frosting becomes too thick or stiff, work in just enough skim milk to make it loose.) Roll frosted balls in Coconut Sugar before frosting dries.

Makes 12 doughnut holes or 6 servings
(174 calories per serving)

Beautiful Baked Alaska

1 quart Raspberry Rum Sherbet
   (page 150), softened
1 Lazy Day Loaf Cake (page 183)
10 egg whites
¼ teaspoon cream of tartar
1 tablespoon honey
1½ teaspoons vanilla extract

Line a round 2-quart bowl with plastic wrap. Pack softened sherbet into it, smoothing top. Cover with plastic wrap and return to freezer until very firm.

Cut cake lengthwise into 4 pieces. Fit together side by side, and cut into a circle 1½ to 2 inches larger than the top of bowl containing sherbet. Place cake on baking sheet.

Unmold sherbet on top of cake. Cover and return to freezer until very firm.

Just before serving, preheat oven to 450°F.

In a large bowl, beat egg whites until foamy. Add cream of tartar and continue beating, drizzling in honey and vanilla, until stiff peaks form. Working quickly, frost sherbet and cake with meringue, making peaks of meringue. Bake on middle shelf of oven until meringue is golden, about 4 minutes. Serve immediately.

Makes 14 servings
(197 calories per serving)

Apple-Grape Drink

½ cup unsweetened frozen white
    grape juice concentrate
1½ cups club soda
1 cup apple juice

Dissolve grape juice concentrate in
club soda. Stir in apple juice and serve
over crushed ice.

Makes 4 servings
(95 calories per serving)

Lite Surprise Pudding

3 cups Carob Chip Pudding
    (page 183), **divided**
8 Carob Thins (page 50)
½ cup Ruby Raspberry Sauce
    (page 127)

Put 1½ cups Carob Chip Pudding
into a 2-quart casserole. Top with Carob
Thins. Spread Raspberry Sauce over
cookies. Top with remaining pudding
and chill until serving time.

Makes 8 servings
(108 calories per serving)

Delectable Carob Cake

*You don't have to bake all angel cakes
in tube pans. This one is thin enough to
cook evenly in a 9-inch springform pan.*

⅓ cup whole wheat pastry flour
⅓ cup unbleached white flour
3 tablespoons carob powder
10 egg whites
¼ teaspoon cream of tartar
¼ cup honey
1 teaspoon vanilla extract

Preheat oven to 350°F.
Sift together whole wheat pastry
flour, unbleached white flour, and carob
powder 3 times. Re-measure to equal ⅔
cup plus 3 tablespoons.
In a large bowl, beat egg whites until
foamy. Add cream of tartar and continue
beating, drizzling in honey and vanilla,
until stiff peaks form. Fold flour mixture
gently into egg whites, turn into 9-inch
springform pan and bake on bottom shelf
of oven until top springs back when
lightly pressed, 35 to 40 minutes.
Cool completely upside down. Cut
with serrated knife.

Makes 12 servings
(51 calories per serving)

Grapefruit Orange Pie

The fruit for this pie should be well drained before it's added to the other ingredients.

1 recipe for Coconut Crust
   (page 16)
¼ cup cornstarch
1¼ cups skim milk
⅓ cup honey
¾ cup freshly squeezed orange
   juice
½ cup fresh grapefruit sections
½ cup fresh seedless orange
   sections

Bake Coconut Crust according to directions. Cool.

In a medium-size saucepan, dissolve cornstarch in skim milk. Add honey and bring to a boil, stirring constantly, until thickened. Remove from heat and stir in orange juice. Heat again, stirring until thickened. Remove from heat and fold in fruit. Allow to cool, stirring occasionally. Turn into piecrust and chill well before serving.

Makes 10 servings
(121 calories per serving)

Pears with Raspberry Sauce

¾ cup water
2 tablespoons honey
½ teaspoon vanilla extract
8 medium-size fresh pears, peeled,
   halved, and cored
1 cup Ruby Raspberry Sauce
   (page 127), divided

In a large saucepan, bring water and honey to a boil. Stir in vanilla. Add pears, cover, and reduce heat to simmer, cooking until pears are soft, 6 to 8 minutes.

Drain and chill pears. Divide pear halves among 8 bowls, placing sides with indentations up. Fill each indentation with 1 tablespoon of the raspberry sauce and serve immediately.

Makes 8 servings
(114 calories per serving)

Pears à la Crème

1½ teaspoons cornstarch
½ cup unsweetened pineapple
    juice
½ teaspoon ground cinnamon
2 tablespoons honey
2 fresh pears
1 cup evaporated skim milk,
    chilled

In a medium-size saucepan, dissolve cornstarch in pineapple juice. Stir in cinnamon and honey.

Peel, core, and coarsely chop pears. Add to saucepan and bring to a boil, stirring constantly. Reduce heat, cover, and let simmer until pears are fork tender, about 10 minutes. Remove from heat and chill.

Just before serving, beat evaporated skim milk in a medium-size bowl until soft peaks form. Fold in pear mixture. Turn into 8 dessert glasses and serve immediately.

Makes 8 servings
(73 calories per serving)

Apple Raisin Pie

1 recipe for Skinny Piecrust
    (page 5)
5 apples
½ cup raisins, plumped
1 teaspoon ground cinnamon
1 teaspoon vanilla extract
2 teaspoons freshly squeezed
    lemon juice
2 tablespoons cornstarch

Preheat oven to 425°F. Line a 9-inch pie plate with pastry according to directions. Chill.

Peel, core, and thinly slice apples into a bowl of cold water, to which 1 teaspoon of lemon juice has been added. Drain apple slices well and toss with remaining ingredients. Turn into prepared pie shell, cover with foil, and bake on bottom shelf of oven until crust is golden, 35 to 40 minutes.

Makes 10 servings
(110 calories per serving)

Easy Baked Pear Rings

4 firm, ripe pears
2 tablespoons butter, melted
2 teaspoons honey
   ground cinnamon for sprinkling

Preheat oven to 350°F. Spray a baking sheet with vegetable spray.

Peel, core, and slice pears into rounds about ½ inch thick. Arrange rounds on prepared baking sheet. In a small bowl, mix together butter and honey. Brush mixture on top of pear rings. Sprinkle with cinnamon and bake on middle shelf of oven for about 15 minutes, or until pears are fork tender.

Makes 6 servings
(108 calories per serving)

FEBRUARY

Spicing Up Desserts

FRUIT OF THE MONTH: **BANANAS**

DESSERT OF THE MONTH: **BANANA LEMON TORTE**

DRINK OF THE MONTH: **TOMATO ZIP**

				1	*Ground Hog* 2 *Day*	3
				BANANA LEMON TORTE ★	FRIENDLY HERMITS	VERMONT PUDDING
4	5	6	7	8	9	10
CRUSTLESS COFFEE PIE	FRUITED DESSERT SHAKE	ORANGE SORBET	STRAWBERRY AMBROSIA	ROYAL RED TAPIOCA	PERFECT PEAR CREPES	FROZEN BANANA SQUARES
11	12	13	*Valentine's* 14 *Day*	15	16	17
GORGEOUS GRAPEFRUIT	UPSIDE-DOWN PINEAPPLE PIE	SWEET POTATO PUDDING	BE MY VALENTINE CAKE	AMERICAN APPLE BAKE	LEMON RAZMATAZ	BLACK AND WHITE PUDDING PIE
18	19	20	21	22	*Presidents'* 23 *Day*	24
ONE SMALL. RIPE BANANA	HEAVENLY ANGEL FOOD CAKE	BANANA PUDDING LAYERS	MOCK MOCHA POPS	CHEERY CHERRY PIE	PRESIDENTS' DAY PATRIOTIC PARFAITS	PFEFFERNUSSE
25	26	27	28	29		
FLUFFY BLUEBERRY OMELET	PEAR BREAD PUDDING	BANANA ROYAL	FROZEN STRAWBERRY FLUFF	FRUITY YOGURT PIE		

Spices and extracts are essential ingredients in many desserts, but their role is especially important in diet desserts where they are often relied upon to make up for the reduced sweetening that saves on calories. Vanilla is the single most useful essence for this. With a sweetness of its own, this quintessential extract can be used either as the primary flavoring or to bolster others.

Spices

Derived from the bark, leaves, seeds, stamens, fruit, flowers, or roots of a wide variety of tropical plants, spices come from faraway places with romantic names like the Spice Islands, Madagascar, and Zanzibar. In fact, allspice is the only commonly used spice native to the Western Hemisphere.

I don't use any hard-to-find spices in this book. Most desserts can be improved with the addition of such widely available spices as cinnamon, cloves, ginger, or nutmeg, although occasionally I do use allspice or anise seeds in a dessert.

Whole or Ground Spices

Whole spices, that you plan to grind yourself, will keep much longer than those already ground. Nutmeg is one spice most cooks use frequently that is considerably better when home-ground just prior to use. A small, readily available nutmeg grater will make this an easy chore.

When buying ground spices, don't be lured by large boxes at low prices. Ground spices don't become rancid, but they do lose their potency quickly and should therefore be purchased in very small quantities and used as soon as possible. Date each newly purchased container before storing it, and discard it after about six months. If you're not sure whether a spice has seen its day and should be thrown out, smell it. A musty odor means that the flavor is gone, and the container should be eliminated from your supply.

The spice section of any given market offers an array of spices sold in a variety of containers. Avoid those in cardboard boxes—the flavor leaches into the cardboard and is soon dissipated. And glass jars allow light, an enemy of freshness and long life for spices, into the containers. Select instead small tin boxes of ground spices.

Since both air and light rob spices of their freshness, get into the habit of closing a container immediately after you've measured the necessary amount.

Some cooks grind whole spices with a mortar and pestle. This is time consuming, and it produces a lumpy, uneven powder. The late James Beard, master chef and cookbook author, suggested the use of a small electric coffee mill to grind spices.

The best ground spices (other than home-ground) can be found in spice stores. If there aren't any in your region, you'll find that many sell spices mail order. Here are the names and addresses of a few companies that carry a large variety of spices:

Aphrodisia
282 Bleecker St.
New York, NY 10014
(212) 989-6440

Caprilands Herb Farm
534 Silver St.
Coventry, CT 06238
(203) 742-7244

Balducci's
424 Avenue of the Americas
New York, NY 10011
(212) 673-2600

While stylishly decorative spice shelves with a selection of jars of interesting shapes and sizes may add character to kitchens, they're not recommended for storing spices, as they leave them vulnerable to light and often stove heat. Keep spices secreted away in a cool, dark cabinet.

Spices must, of course, be added to cakes, pies, and cookies when you're making the batter or filling. But when you make pudding or any other loose-textured dessert in which it's possible to add a spice during the cooking process, do so. For best results, add spices about ten minutes before a dessert is finished cooking. The heat of cooking greatly diminishes the strength of spices.

Extracts

While lacking the romance of spices, extracts are nonetheless just as essential for dessert making. A dash of almond, a spoonful of vanilla, or a hint of mint can be either the featured flavoring or play a supporting, but important, role in the production of a dessert.

Spices and Some Other Flavorings for Diet Desserts

One of the most important aspects of making successful desserts is an understanding of flavorings. The following table suggests ways to use some of the best of them in preparing diet desserts.

Allspice	Flavor of cinnamon, cloves, and nutmeg	Cakes, pies, puddings
Almond	Strong, nutlike extract	Cakes, candies, cookies, pies, puddings
Anise seeds	Licorice taste	Candies, cookies
Cinnamon	Aromatic, tangy—very useful in diet desserts	Cakes, cookies, pies, puddings
Cloves	Pungent	Cakes, cookies, pies
Ginger	A bit hot and zesty	Candies, cakes, cookies, gingerbread, puddings
Lemon	Very tart extract	Cakes, cookies, fillings, pies, puddings
Nutmeg	Sharp, nutty—best when ground just prior to use	Cakes, custards, drinks, pies, puddings
Orange	Citrus extract	Cakes, cookies, fillings, frostings, pies, puddings
Vanilla	Sweetish extract	All desserts

Extracts add few calories, but they can make the difference between an uninteresting dessert and a shining success. They can virtually dictate the flavor of a dessert. Using almond extract, for instance, in a cake traditionally made with vanilla extract will make it taste totally different. The recipes can be identical except for that one small difference, but what a difference! Or a small amount of extract can be added to a recipe producing a subtle, but important, change in flavor.

There is a huge array of extracts. I liberally use those I like. In diet desserts, where the object is maximum flavor for minimum calories, they're indispensable. For instance, I may add orange extract to an orange pudding made with fresh orange juice because I want a more pronounced orange taste without the calories of more orange juice.

The extracts I use most, and which I always have on my shelf, are vanilla (which I do buy in a big bottle because I use it so frequently and in quite large amounts), lemon, orange, almond, rum, brandy, and peppermint. Like spices, extracts should be closed tightly immediately after use and kept in a cool, dark place. Brandy and rum extracts make it possible to present more exotic desserts featuring those flavors without adding either alcohol or an appreciable number of calories.

Vanilla works well in tandem with almost any other extract, and combining other extracts, such as lemon and almond, lemon and rum, or brandy and orange, also makes interesting flavorings.

Always buy pure vanilla. The synthetic, called vanillin, while cheaper and stronger, smells like vanilla but has a slightly bitter, off taste that doesn't duplicate the flavor of real vanilla.

Almond is the strongest extract I use, and should be used cautiously at about half the strength of other extracts.

Heat destroys extracts and cold dulls the taste buds to them. Add extracts to a recipe as late as possible (after cooking is through is best). And when making a frozen or chilled dessert, you may need what seems like an incredible amount of extract. I taste a frozen-type dessert before processing or freezing it. When it tastes just about right, I add the same amount of extract that I've already used. Although the flavor is certainly powerful before the dessert is frozen, it turns out to be perfect after processing.

Friendly Hermits

A low-calorie version of an old favorite!

¼ cup raisins
5 tablespoons butter
⅓ cup honey
2 eggs
½ cup plain low-fat yogurt
½ cup whole wheat flour
½ cup unbleached white flour, divided
⅓ cup rolled oats
1 teaspoon ground cinnamon
½ teaspoon ground ginger
½ teaspoon baking powder

Cover raisins with warm water and set aside to plump.

Preheat oven to 350°F. Spray 2 baking sheets with vegetable spray.

In a large bowl, beat butter and honey together until fluffy. Beat in eggs. Fold in yogurt.

In a medium-size bowl, mix together whole wheat flour, ¼ cup of the unbleached white flour, oats, cinnamon, ginger, and baking powder, whisking to blend. Mix gently but thoroughly into moist ingredients.

Drain raisins well, and toss with remaining unbleached white flour. Fold into batter and drop batter by heaping teaspoonfuls onto 1 prepared baking sheet, pulling spoon along each mound of dough to make long cookies. Bake on middle shelf of oven until lightly browned, 15 to 18 minutes. While first batch is baking, repeat process with remaining dough.

Cool cookies on wire racks.

Makes 3 dozen cookies
(49 calories per cookie)

Crustless Coffee Pie

1 envelope unflavored gelatin
½ cup cold water
3 tablespoons honey
¾ teaspoon ground cinnamon, divided
2 teaspoons vanilla extract
1 cup strong, hot decaffeinated coffee
3 eggs, separated
⅛ teaspoon cream of tartar

Spray a 9-inch pie plate with vegetable spray.

In a small saucepan, sprinkle gelatin over cold water. Set aside for 5 minutes to soften.

Stir in honey, ¼ teaspoon of the cinnamon, and vanilla into coffee. Set aside.

In the top of a double boiler set over hot, not boiling, water, beat egg yolks until slightly thickened, about 3 minutes. Gradually stir in coffee mixture. Remove from heat.

Heat gelatin mixture over medium heat, stirring constantly, until gelatin dissolves. Whisk into coffee mixture. Chill until slightly thickened.

In a medium-size bowl, beat egg whites until foamy. Add cream of tartar and continue to beat until stiff peaks form. Fold coffee mixture into egg whites. Turn into prepared pie plate, sprinkle with remaining cinnamon, and chill until set.

Makes 8 servings
(58 calories per serving)

Banana Lemon Torte

1 recipe for Pretty Peach Layer
   Cake (page 117)
1 envelope unflavored gelatin
¾ cup water
2 tablespoons honey
¼ cup freshly squeezed lemon juice
   natural yellow food coloring
1 ripe banana

Bake cake according to directions.
In a small saucepan, sprinkle gelatin over water. Set aside to soften for 5 minutes. Heat, over medium heat, stirring constantly, until gelatin dissolves. Remove from heat and stir in honey and lemon juice. Add a few drops of food coloring. Chill, stirring often, until mixture is thickened but not set.

Wrap and freeze 1 layer of the cake for future use. Place the second layer on a serving plate. Slice banana. Arrange slices on top of cake. Spread gelatin mixture over fruit and chill until set.

Makes 12 servings
(63 calories per serving)

Vermont Pudding

1 envelope unflavored gelatin
½ cup cold water
¼ cup plus 1 tablespoon maple
   syrup, divided
1 teaspoon vanilla extract
1 cup evaporated milk, chilled
1 egg white
⅛ teaspoon cream of tartar
2 tablespoons grape-nuts cereal,
   divided

In a small saucepan, sprinkle gelatin over cold water. Set aside for 5 minutes to soften. Stir in ¼ cup maple syrup. Heat over medium heat, stirring constantly, until gelatin dissolves. Remove from heat and stir in vanilla and evaporated milk. Put in large bowl and chill until slightly thickened.

In a small bowl, beat egg while until foamy. Add cream of tartar and beat until stiff peaks form.

Beat gelatin mixture to the consistency of whipped cream. Fold in egg white and divide among 6 dessert glasses. Sprinkle 1 teaspoon grape-nuts over each pudding. Drizzle ½ teaspoon maple syrup over top. Refrigerate until serving time.

Makes 6 servings
(91 calories per serving)

Fruited Dessert Shake

½ cup unsweetened pineapple juice
½ cup freshly squeezed orange
     juice
½ cup skim milk
½ cup Vanilla Ice Milk (page 72)

In a blender, whirl together pineapple juice, orange juice, skim milk, and Vanilla Ice Milk. Divide between 2 glasses and serve at once.

Makes 2 servings
(144 calories per serving)

Royal Red Tapioca

1¼ cups red grape juice
1¼ cups water
  2 tablespoons honey
 ¼ cup quick-cooking tapioca
  1 teaspoon vanilla extract

In a medium-size saucepan, combine all ingredients. Set aside for 5 minutes to soften tapioca.
Bring to a boil over medium heat, stirring occasionally. Allow to boil 1 minute, stirring constantly. Chill.

Makes 6 servings
(76 calories per serving)

Strawberry Ambrosia

2 seedless oranges, chopped
1 pink seedless grapefruit,
    chopped
½ cup seedless green or red
    grapes, halved
1 cup unsweetened frozen
    strawberries, thawed
1 cup unsweetened flaked coconut
¼ cup freshly squeezed orange
    juice
1 teaspoon freshly squeezed
    lemon juice
1 banana

In a large bowl, combine all ingredients except banana and toss well. Slice banana, add to fruit mixture, and toss again.

Makes 10 servings
(74 calories per serving)

Delicious Diet Crepes

These crepes can be frozen by putting waxed paper between each crepe and wrapping all with plastic wrap, then foil.

2 eggs
1 teaspoon honey
⅔ cup skim milk
1¼ cups water
½ cup whole wheat pastry
   flour

½ cup unbleached white
   flour
½ teaspoon baking powder
½ teaspoon vanilla extract

In a large bowl, beat together eggs and honey. Beat in skim milk and water.

Sift together whole wheat pastry flour, unbleached white flour, and baking powder. Stir into egg mixture just until blended. Stir in vanilla. Cover and let mixture stand in refrigerator for at least 1 hour.

Spray an 8-inch skillet with vegetable spray. Heat over medium heat until a drop of water dropped in the middle of the skillet sizzles. Pour ⅛ cup of batter into pan, moving pan from side to side to distribute it evenly. When bubbles form on surface, about 45 seconds, turn crepe over and cook another 15 seconds. Repeat process until batter is finished.

Makes 16 crepes
(43 calories per crepe)

Be My Valentine Cake

⅓ cup whole wheat pastry flour
¼ teaspoon baking powder
1 egg white
1 egg, separated
⅛ teaspoon cream of tartar
2 tablespoons cold water
3 tablespoons honey
½ teaspoon almond extract
1 teaspoon vanilla extract
 natural red food coloring
½ cup Decorator Frosting
 (page 34)

Preheat oven to 325°F. Line bottom of a heart-shaped 8-inch cake pan with waxed paper cut out in heart shape.

Sift together flour and baking powder into a small bowl. Whisk to blend.

In a medium-size bowl, beat egg whites until foamy. Add cream of tartar and continue beating until stiff peaks form.

In a large bowl, beat together egg yolk and water until foamy. Add honey and extracts and continue beating for 8 minutes. Fold in flour mixture, then beaten egg whites. Turn into prepared pan and bake on middle shelf of oven for 30 minutes.

Run a knife around edges of pan and turn out onto a wire rack. Remove waxed paper and allow to cool before decorating.

Add natural red food coloring to Decorator Frosting. Make stars around edge of cake with star tip. Write on top of cake with writing tip.

Makes 6 servings
(158 calories per serving)

Perfect Pear Crepes

2 cups diced fresh pears
2 teaspoons honey
¼ teaspoon ground cinnamon
⅛ teaspoon ground nutmeg
2 tablespoons ground pecans
8 Delicious Diet Crepes (page 30)
½ cup plain nonfat yogurt, divided

In a blender, puree pears. Turn into a medium-size saucepan. Add honey, cinnamon, and nutmeg and cook over medium heat, stirring constantly, for 5 minutes. Stir in nuts.

Divide among crepes, spooning mixture in a line down the middle of each one. Roll first 1 side over filling, then the other side. Spoon 1 tablespoon of the yogurt on top of each crepe and serve immediately.

Makes 8 servings
(84 calories per serving)

Upside-Down Pineapple Pie

1 20-ounce can unsweetened
   crushed pineapple
1 cup part-skim ricotta cheese
2 eggs
2 tablespoons honey
2 teaspoons vanilla extract

Preheat oven to 325°F. Spray a 10-inch pie plate with vegetable spray.

Drain pineapple thoroughly, reserving juice.

In a blender or food processor, combine reserved juice, ricotta, eggs, honey, and vanilla.

Spread crushed pineapple in prepared pie plate. Pour blended ingredients over pineapple and bake on middle shelf of oven for 50 to 60 minutes, or until a knife inserted near the center comes out clean. Serve warm or chilled.

Makes 12 servings
(43 calories per serving)

Frozen Banana Squares

2 very ripe bananas
1 cup part-skim ricotta cheese
2 tablespoons honey
1 teaspoon vanilla extract
¾ cup evaporated skim milk,
   chilled

In a food processor, puree bananas and ricotta. Add honey and vanilla.

In a large bowl, beat evaporated skim milk to the consistency of whipped cream. Fold in banana mixture. Turn into an 8 × 8-inch pan, cover, and freeze. Cut into 16 2-inch squares. Allow to soften slightly before serving.

Makes 16 squares
(32 calories per square)

Gorgeous Grapefruit

2 seedless pink grapefruits
2 egg whites
⅛ teaspoon cream of tartar
¼ teaspoon vanilla extract
4 fresh sweet cherries, pitted

Preheat oven to 350°F.

Cut grapefruits into halves. Run serrated knife between skins and pulp, then run knife between membranes and pulp, loosening sections.

In a medium-size bowl, beat egg whites until foamy. Add cream of tartar and vanilla and continue to beat until stiff peaks form. Divide evenly and pile on top of halved grapefruits, bringing beaten egg whites to edges of fruit. Place in a pan and bake on middle shelf of oven 12 to 15 minutes, or until meringue browns.

Cool and top each meringue with a cherry.

Makes 4 servings
(53 calories per serving)

Black and White Pudding Pie

1 recipe for Skinny Piecrust
    (page 5)
1 cup Very Vanilla Pudding
    (page 76)
1 cup Creamy Carob Pudding
    (page 160)
2 tablespoons ground walnuts,
    optional

Line a 9-inch pie plate with pastry and bake according to directions. Allow to cool thoroughly.

Spread cooled vanilla pudding in pie shell. Top with a layer of cooled carob pudding, spreading it to cover vanilla pudding. Sprinkle with nuts, if desired, and refrigerate until serving time.

Makes 8 servings
(124 calories per serving)

Decorator Frosting

This frosting must be used as soon as it is made. However, if you're using frosting in several colors, you can quickly put each color in a plastic decorating bag, folding down the top to prevent exposure to the air. If the frosting gets too hard, try beating in a bit of skim milk—a few drops at a time. Only fine-textured dry milk will work for this recipe!

2   egg whites
½   teaspoon cream of
     tartar
3   tablespoons honey
2   teaspoons vanilla extract

2   cups instant nonfat
     dry milk
     natural food coloring,
     optional

In a medium-size bowl, beat egg whites until foamy. Beat in cream of tartar, honey, and vanilla. Slowly add nonfat dry milk, beating until stiff and glossy. If you're using food color-ing, beat in a few drops until you reach desired shade.

Makes about 1¼ cups
(49 calories per tablespoon)

Banana Pudding Layers

3 cups Very Vanilla Pudding
    (page 76), divided
12 Light Lemon Cookies (page 121),
    divided
1 ripe banana, divided

Put 1 cup of the pudding into a
1½-quart casserole. Top with 6 cookies.
Thinly slice banana and put half of the
slices on top of cookies. Top with 1 cup
of the pudding, the remaining cookies,
and the rest of the banana slices. Spread
remaining pudding on top and chill until
serving time.

Makes 8 servings
(163 calories per serving)

Mock Mocha Pops

3 tablespoons Versatile Carob Syrup
    (page 148)
1 tablespoon strong decaffeinated
    coffee
1 envelope unflavored gelatin
2 cups water

In a small saucepan, combine carob
syrup and coffee. Sprinkle gelatin over
mixture and set aside for 5 minutes to
soften. Add water and heat over medium
heat, stirring constantly, until gelatin
dissolves. Pour into 8 2-ounce pop molds
and freeze until very firm.

Makes 8 pops
(24 calories per pop)

American Apple Bake

4 baking apples
¼ cup water
1 teaspoon freshly squeezed
    lemon juice
2 tablespoons honey, warmed
¼ teaspoon ground nutmeg
½ cup grated cheddar cheese
1 tablespoon whole wheat pastry
    flour
½ teaspoon ground cinnamon

Preheat oven to 350°F.
Peel, core, and slice apples. Turn into
an 8 × 8-inch baking dish.
In a small bowl, combine water, lemon
juice, honey, and nutmeg. Drizzle over
apples. Cover and bake on middle shelf
of oven until apples are fork tender, about
40 minutes.
In a medium-size bowl, toss together
cheese, flour, and cinnamon. Sprinkle
over apple slices. Return, uncovered, to
oven until cheese melts, about 4 minutes.

Makes 8 servings
(95 calories per serving)

Lemon Razzmatazz

½ cup freshly squeezed lemon
  juice, strained
1½ cups water
1 10-ounce package unsweetened
  frozen raspberries, thawed
1½ envelopes unflavored gelatin
¼ cup honey
¼ teaspoon lemon extract

In a medium-size bowl, mix together lemon juice and water.

Drain raspberries, reserving juice. Strain reserved juice into a small saucepan. Sprinkle gelatin over top and set aside to soften for 2 minutes. Add honey and heat over medium heat, stirring constantly, until gelatin dissolves. Remove from heat, mix in lemon extract, and stir into lemon juice in bowl. Chill until thickened but not set, about 45 minutes. Fold in raspberries and turn into 6 decorative molds or 6 dessert glasses. Chill until set.

If using decorative molds, dip bottoms in warm water for about 30 seconds and unmold before serving.

Makes 6 servings
(99 calories per serving)

Sweet Potato Pudding

1 pound sweet potatoes
⅓ cup skim milk
3 tablespoons honey
1 teaspoon vanilla extract
1 teaspoon ground cinnamon
6 tablespoons unsweetened pineapple juice, divided
3 tablespoons Coconut Sugar
  (page 60), **divided**

Peel and quarter sweet potatoes. In a medium-size saucepan, cook sweet potatoes in enough boiling water to cover until tender, about 20 minutes.

In a food processor, puree sweet potatoes with skim milk, honey, vanilla, and cinnamon. Divide among 6 dessert glasses. Top each with 1 tablespoon of the pineapple juice and ½ tablespoon of the Coconut Sugar. Serve immediately.

Makes 6 servings
(123 calories per serving)

Presidents' Day Patriotic Parfaits

This recipe is a tribute to George and Abe as well as all our other presidents — past and present.

- 1½ cups skim milk
- ¼ cup honey
- 2 egg yolks, beaten
- 1 envelope unflavored gelatin
- 1 teaspoon vanilla extract
- 16 ounces part-skim ricotta cheese
- 1½ cups unsweetened frozen blueberries, thawed, divided
- 1½ cups unsweetened frozen raspberries, thawed, divided

In a medium-size saucepan, beat together skim milk, honey, and egg yolks. Sprinkle gelatin over top and set aside for 5 minutes to soften. Heat over low heat, whisking constantly, until gelatin dissolves, about 5 minutes. Mix in vanilla.

In a large bowl, beat ricotta until smooth. Beat in gelatin mixture and chill, stirring occasionally, until thick but not set.

Put a layer of cheese mixture in each of 6 parfait glasses. Top with 2 tablespoons of the blueberries. Add another layer of cheese mixture. Top with 2 tablespoons of the raspberries, another layer of cheese, 2 tablespoons of the blueberries, another layer of cheese, and end with 2 tablespoons of the raspberries. Chill until cheese is set.

Makes 6 servings
(193 calories per serving)

Cheery Cherry Pie

- 3¾ cups unsweetened frozen cherries
- ¼ cup raisins, plumped
- ¼ cup honey
- 1 tablespoon cornstarch
- ¼ cup water
- 1 teaspoon brandy extract
- 1 recipe for Mini Piecrust (page 104)

In a large saucepan, toss cherries, raisins, and honey together.

Dissolve cornstarch in water and stir into cherry mixture. Cook over medium heat, stirring constantly, until mixture thickens. Remove from heat and add brandy extract. Set aside for 15 minutes.

Preheat oven to 400°F. Line a 9-inch pie plate with Mini Piecrust according to directions. Turn cherry mixture into prepared piecrust. Cover with foil tent and bake on bottom shelf of oven until crust is lightly browned, 50 to 60 minutes.

Makes 10 servings
(130 calories per serving)

Heavenly Angel Food Cake

The only trick to making this easy cake is in folding in the flour. To keep the air in the batter, never let the spoon or spatula emerge from the batter during the folding process.

- 10 egg whites
- 1 teaspoon cream of tartar
- ⅔ cup honey
- ½ cup whole wheat pastry flour
- ½ cup unbleached white flour
- 2 teaspoons vanilla extract

Preheat oven to 350°F.

In a large bowl, beat egg whites until foamy. Add cream of tartar and beat until stiff peaks form. Drizzle in honey, beating just to blend.

Sift whole wheat pastry flour and unbleached white flour together 3 times. Measure 1 cup and sprinkle it on top of beaten egg whites. Fold flour in thoroughly but gently. Fold in vanilla extract. Pour batter into a 10-inch tube pan with removable tube and bake for 35 to 40 minutes, or until top springs back when lightly pressed with fingertips.

Invert pan on a wire rack until cake is completely cool. Run a knife around edges and turn out onto plate. Run knife along bottom to release tube.

Makes 16 servings
(87 calories per serving)

Pear Bread Pudding

- 4 slices whole grain bread
- 1½ cups skim milk
- 2 tablespoons honey
- 3 eggs
- ½ teaspoon ground cinnamon
- ¼ teaspoon ground nutmeg
- 2 pears
- ¼ cup raisins, plumped

Preheat oven to 325°F. Spray a 2-quart casserole with vegetable spray.

Toast bread and cut into cubes.

In a medium-size saucepan, scald skim milk. Remove from heat, add toast cubes and honey, and set aside briefly until toast is saturated.

In a medium-size bowl, beat together eggs, cinnamon, and nutmeg. Peel, core, and dice pears. Add, along with raisins, to egg mixture. Stir in bread and milk and turn into prepared casserole. Bake on middle shelf of oven until set, about 45 minutes.

Makes 6 servings
(177 calories per serving)

Pfeffernusse

This is a calorie-trimmed version of the traditional German Pepper Nut. It can be sliced into 1-inch rounds or cut with a small, decorative cookie cutter.

1¼ **cups whole wheat pastry flour**
1¼ **cups unbleached white flour**
 1 **teaspoon ground cinnamon**
 ½ **teaspoon ground nutmeg**
 ¼ **teaspoon ground cloves**
 ¼ **teaspoon white pepper**
 3 **eggs**
 ⅓ **cup honey**
 ½ **teaspoon anise extract or**
     1 teaspoon vanilla extract
 ⅓ **cup walnuts**
 ½ **cup raisins**

In a medium-size bowl, combine whole wheat pastry flour, unbleached white flour, cinnamon, nutmeg, cloves, and pepper, whisking to blend.

In a large bowl, beat eggs until foamy. Drizzle in honey and continue beating until very thick, about 8 minutes. Beat in extract.

In a food processor, finely chop walnuts and raisins with ¼ cup of flour mixture to keep raisins from sticking together. Mix into flour.

Stir flour-raisin mixture into eggs, blending well. Roll dough into a ball, wrap in plastic wrap, and chill until firm enough to roll.

Preheat oven to 325°F. Line 2 baking sheets with parchment paper.

Roll out one quarter of the dough between 2 pieces of waxed paper. Cut into desired shapes and place on pre-pared baking sheets. Repeat process with remaining dough, one quarter at a time. Bake, 1 sheet at a time, on middle shelf of oven until firm, about 15 minutes. Remove to wire racks to cool.

The texture of these cookies will improve if you store them a day or 2 with a piece of bread in a tightly sealed container.

Makes 3 dozen cookies
(61 calories per cookie)

Tomato Zip

6 **ounces tomato juice**
2 **drops Tabasco sauce**
  wedge of lime

Mix together tomato juice and Tabasco in a small bowl. Squeeze a few drops of lime juice into mixture. Pour over ice in a glass and garnish with lime wedge.

Makes 1 serving
(35 calories per serving)

Fruity Yogurt Pie

1 recipe for Skinny Piecrust
       (page 5)
1 8-ounce can unsweetened
       pineapple chunks
1 envelope unflavored gelatin
1½ teaspoons vanilla extract
½ teaspoon ground cinnamon
½ cup plain low-fat yogurt
1¼ cups seedless red grapes,
       halved
1 cup mandarin orange sections

Line a 9-inch pie plate with pastry
and bake blind according to directions.
Cool.

Drain pineapple, reserving juice. Add
enough water to juice to make 1¼ cups
and transfer to small saucepan. Sprinkle gelatin over juice and set aside for 5
minutes to soften. Cook over medium
heat, stirring constantly until gelatin
dissolves. Remove 3 tablespoons of gelatin mixture and set aside. Add vanilla
and cinnamon to remaining gelatin, mixing well, and chill until mixture reaches
the consistency of egg whites, about 30
minutes.

Fold chilled gelatin into yogurt and
turn into prepared piecrust. Chill about
15 minutes to set slightly. Arrange pineapple chunks, grapes, and orange sections on top of yogurt. Brush with
reserved gelatin mixture, heating it briefly
if it has thickened too much to brush on
easily. Cover lightly with plastic wrap
and chill until set.

Makes 10 servings
(77 calories per serving)

Frozen Strawberry Fluff

1 cup unsweetened frozen straw-
       berries, thawed
1 tablespoon honey
2 egg whites, at room temperature
½ cup evaporated skim milk,
       chilled

In a food processor, puree strawberries with honey.

In a medium-size bowl, beat evaporated skim milk to the consistency of
whipped cream.

In a large bowl, beat egg whites until
stiff peaks form. Fold beaten milk and
then strawberry puree into egg whites.
Freeze until ready to serve.

Makes 4 servings
(63 calories per serving)

Fluffy Blueberry Omelet

Folding in beaten egg whites makes this dessert omelet as light as air.

2   teaspoons cornstarch
½   cup freshly squeezed orange juice
½   cup unsweetened frozen blue-
       berries, thawed
2   tablespoons honey, divided
2   teaspoons vanilla extract
2   eggs, separated
2   eggs
⅛   teaspoon cream of tartar

In a jar with a tight-fitting lid, shake together cornstarch and orange juice.

In a small saucepan, mix together blueberries, orange juice mixture, and 1 tablespoon of the honey. Mash berries slightly with a fork to release juice. Simmer over medium heat, stirring constantly, until mixture thickens. Remove from heat. Stir in 1 teaspoon of the vanilla extract and set aside in a warm place.

In a medium-size bowl, beat egg yolks and whole eggs. Beat in remaining honey and vanilla.

In a large bowl, beat egg whites until foamy. Add cream of tartar and continue to beat until stiff peaks form. Fold egg yolks into egg whites.

Spray bottom and sides of a large nonstick skillet with vegetable spray. Heat over medium heat. Pour in egg mixture and cook over medium heat for about 2 minutes. Cover and cook 2 minutes more. Remove from heat.

Spread half of warm blueberry mixture on half of cooked omelet. Fold other half over. Remove to warmed platter and pour remaining sauce over top.

Makes 6 servings
(97 calories per serving)

Orange Sorbet

2   cups freshly squeezed orange
       juice
2   cups water, divided
3   tablespoons honey
1   teaspoon orange extract

Strain orange juice into a large bowl. Add 1½ cups of the water. In a small saucepan, heat remaining water and honey until honey dissolves. Pour into large bowl. Add extract and mix well.

Process mixture in an ice cream maker according to manufacturer's instructions, or turn mixture into a large pan and place in freezer until mushy. Remove from freezer, beat to break down ice crystals, and then return to freezer. Repeat this procedure twice. Freeze until ready to serve.

Makes about 10 servings
(42 calories per serving)

Banana Royal

1 cup freshly squeezed orange
    juice
1 cup water, divided
1 envelope unflavored gelatin
1 tablespoon honey
¼ teaspoon orange extract
1 ripe banana
½ cup seedless red grapes, halved

In a medium-size bowl, mix together orange juice and ½ cup of the water.

In a medium-size saucepan, sprinkle gelatin over remaining water. Set aside for 5 minutes to soften. Add honey and heat over medium heat, stirring constantly, until gelatin dissolves. Add to juice. Mix in orange extract and chill until thickened but not set.

Chop banana and fold into gelatin. Fold in grape halves and chill until set.

Makes 7 servings
(49 calories per serving)

MARCH

Beverages to Diet With

				1	2	3
FRUIT OF THE MONTH: **ORANGES** *DESSERT OF THE MONTH:* **ORANGE MERINGUE CUPS** *DRINK OF THE MONTH:* **GRAPE FIZZ**				CAKE ROLL PRUNEAU	PINEAPPLE CHARLOTTE	CAROB THINS
4 LUSCIOUS CITRUS PIE	**5** RAISIN PEAR BREAD PUDDING	**6** ORANGE MERINGUE CUPS ★	**7** CAROB CHIPPERS	**8** FROZEN PUDDING	**9** PEANUT BUTTER APPLES	**10** BANANA CREAM PIE
11 INDIVIDUAL STRAWBERRY CHEESE PUDDINGS	**12** RING OF PLENTY	**13** LUSCIOUS LEMON CHEESCAKE	**14** SPICY PEARS	**15** HAWAIIAN SNOW BALLS	**16** SQUASH CUSTARD	**17** *Saint Patrick's Day* SAINT PADDY'S DAY MINT TREAT
18 ALMOND COCONUT CHIFFON PIE	**19** ONE SMALL ORANGE, PEELED AND SECTIONED	**20** BRANDY ZABAGLIONE	**21** SUPER SPICE CAKE	**22** STUFFED BAKED PEARS	**23** ORANGE DATE COOKIES	**24** NICE SPICE POPCORN
25 TANGY TANGERINE CREPES	**26** BAKED JUNGLE TREAT	**27** CAROB CHIP PIE	**28** LEMON SORBET	**29** LIGHT CARROT CAKE	**30** RUM-TUM-DIDDLE SOUFFLÉS	**31** TANGERINE BREAD PUDDING WITH PEACH SAUCE

$\mathcal{W}$ater is, of course, the perfect beverage. I always keep a large pitcher of it in my refrigerator — nothing is quite as thirst-quenching. Whether you're dieting or not, you should drink six to eight glasses of this no-calorie super drink every day. Water, like all beverages, tends to make you feel full, so it's an effective alternative to food when you're hungry and know you shouldn't be eating. To make water especially appealing, serve it over ice cubes or crushed ice with a slice of lemon floating in each glass.

Coffee, without milk or sweetener, has only four calories a cup, and plain tea has no calories, so they are options for the dieter. But while the calorie count is tempting, the caffeine both contain isn't. I use decaffeinated coffee and herbal teas.

One of my favorite all-weather drinks is club soda. I find it's an exhilarating pick-me-up alone or when a few drops of lemon juice are added, and a great base for all types of fruit drinks. It's calorie free and adds that finishing sparkle.

Lemon juice is a marvelous flavor enhancer for many types of beverages (including, of course, lemonade, at only 107 calories a cup), so it's worth knowing how to maximize this resource. To get the most juice out of a lemon, allow it to come to room temperature or soak it in warm water before cutting into it. If you need only a very small amount of lemon juice, make a hole in one end of a lemon with a food pick. Squeeze out the juice you need, then stop up the hole with the food pick. Store the lemon in the refrigerator until the next time you need a few drops of lemon juice. A lemon will yield two to three tablespoons of juice. And you can grate about three teaspoons of zest from the skin of an average-size lemon.

Fruit juices do have calories, but they're wholesome and far preferable to the sugar-laden sodas and pops that really don't take care of a thirst and do add pounds. These juices are permissible on most diets and certainly are nutritious. You can make delicious punches by

The Calorie Count of Some Fruit Juices

Juice	Calories per Cup	Juice	Calories per Cup
Apple	116	Grapefruit	96
Apricot	122	Orange	112
Carrot	96	Papaya	120
Cranberry	147	Pineapple	140
Grape	156	Tangerine	108

combining several juices, or mixing them with soda water, herbal tea, or water.

Serve beverages that complement the desserts you make. Don't offer a tart drink with a sweet dessert. Grapefruit juice or combination grapefruit-orange juice would be a good choice with a lemon or lime pie. Apple juice is a perfect companion for a sweet cake.

In making diet drinks, replace milk or cream with skim milk. Yogurt is fine for occasional use as a drink ingredient. Homemade skim milk yogurt has fewer calories than the commercial low-fat yogurt.

Teas Are Easy and Offer Varied Choices

Herbal teas offer an opportunity to experiment with a variety of flavors. You can make them from either fresh or dried herbs. But since dried herbs are concentrated, you need to use only about half the amount you would when using fresh herbs. Although herbs differ in strength, when in doubt, figure one teaspoon of dried, or two teaspoons of fresh herbs for every cup of boiling water.

Herbs used to make teas come from the flowers, leaves, seeds, or bark of plants. Lemon verbena and lemon balm teas, my favorites, are delicious alone, hot or cold, or in combination with other herbs. The lovely lemon flavor enhances almost any other herb.

Because herbal teas have no calories, you can feel free to add a bit of sweetener if you wish. As an added bonus, soothing, even curative, properties are traditionally attributed to herbal teas.

Herbs to Use for Making Teas

A tea made from any of these herbs serves as a tasty distraction from high-calorie snacks.

Agrimony	Calamint	Dill	Marigold petals	Rue
Balm	Chamomile	Hyssop	Parsley	Sage
Bergamot	Costmary	Lemon verbena	Peppermint	Savory
Betony	Dandelion	Lovage	Rosemary	Sweet cicely

Cake Roll Pruneau

1 recipe for Jelly Roll Cake
  (page 49)
1 cup pitted prunes
2 cups water
¼ cup honey
½ teaspoon ground cinnamon
1 slice lemon
½ cup part-skim ricotta cheese

Bake Jelly Roll Cake according to directions.

In a medium-size saucepan, combine prunes, water, honey, cinnamon, and lemon. Bring to a boil. Reduce heat, cover, and simmer for 45 minutes.

Remove from heat and strain, reserving juice. Discard lemon. Set aside to cool. In a food processor, puree prunes. Add ricotta and process until smooth. If mixture is too thick to be spreadable, add reserved juice, a tablespoon at a time, until desired consistency is reached. Spread on cake and roll up. Cover and chill.

Slice to serve.

Makes 12 servings
(151 calories per serving)

Pineapple Charlotte

10 Ladyfingers (page 99)
 2 envelopes unflavored gelatin
½ cup water
1½ cups skim milk
½ cup honey
 3 eggs
1½ cups unsweetened pineapple
  juice
 1 teaspoon orange extract

Spray bottom and sides of a 6-cup mold with vegetable spray. Line with Ladyfingers.

Sprinkle gelatin over water and set aside to soften for 5 minutes.

In a large saucepan, heat together skim milk and honey to scalding.

In a medium-size bowl, beat eggs for 1 minute. Whisk some of the hot milk mixture into eggs. Return to milk in pan and heat over medium heat, stirring constantly, until mixture starts to thicken. Stir in gelatin and continue cooking until it dissolves. Remove from heat and stir in juice and extract. Pour into a medium-size bowl and chill until thickened but not set. Beat until fluffy, turn into prepared mold, and chill until set.

Unmold onto a plate just before serving.

Makes 8 servings
(191 calories per serving)

Jelly Roll Cake

This recipe is the basis for the classic jelly roll cake.
Fill it with any of the filling recipes in the book.

5 eggs, separated
¼ teaspoon cream of tartar
3 tablespoons honey
1 teaspoon vanilla extract

½ cup sifted whole wheat
  flour
½ cup sifted unbleached
  white flour

Preheat oven to 350°F. Line a 15 × 10-inch baking pan with parchment paper.

In a medium-size bowl, beat egg whites until foamy. Sprinkle in cream of tartar and continue beating until stiff peaks form.

In a large bowl, beat egg yolks until light colored. Add honey and vanilla and beat for 7 minutes, or until very thick.

Sift together whole wheat flour and unbleached white flour into a small bowl, whisking to blend. Fold into beaten egg yolks. Fold in beaten whites and spread on prepared pan. Bake on middle shelf of oven for 12 minutes.

Sprinkle a tea towel lightly with flour. Turn cake out onto it. Carefully peel off parchment paper and roll cake and towel together, rolling from the short end of the cake. Allow to cool completely. Unroll and trim edges.

Makes 10 servings
(105 calories per serving)

Carob Thins

This elegantly delicate cookie is one of my favorites.

6 tablespoons butter, softened
¼ cup honey
2 teaspoons vanilla extract
1 cup whole wheat pastry flour
1 cup unbleached white flour
2 tablespoons carob powder
¼ teaspoon ground cinnamon
2 tablespoons water

Preheat oven to 350°F. Line a 12 × 16-inch baking sheet (without sides) with foil (dull side up).

In a large bowl, cream together butter, honey, and vanilla.

Sift together whole wheat pastry flour, unbleached white flour, carob, and cinnamon into a medium-size bowl. Gradually mix into butter mixture, adding water as needed to form a stiff but workable dough. Shape dough into 2 rectangles. Place 1 piece of dough in center of prepared baking sheet. Top with piece of waxed paper the size of the baking sheet. Roll rectangle out to 11 × 14 inches on baking sheet. Remove waxed paper and cut dough into 36 squares. Bake on middle shelf of oven for 10 minutes.

Carefully remove to wire rack to cool. Repeat with other piece of dough on a cold baking sheet.

Makes 6 dozen cookies
(25 calories per cookie)

Luscious Citrus Pie

4 Ladyfingers (page 99)
1½ tablespoons unflavored gelatin
1½ cups freshly squeezed orange juice, strained
⅓ cup honey
2 egg yolks, at room temperature
3 egg whites, at room temperature
⅛ teaspoon cream of tartar
1 teaspoon vanilla extract

Lightly spray a 9-inch pie plate with vegetable spray.

Split Ladyfingers lengthwise. Then cut each piece in half crosswise. Stand pieces around edge of pie plate, scallop side up.

In the top of a double boiler, sprinkle gelatin over orange juice. Set aside to soften for 5 minutes.

In a small bowl, beat honey and egg yolks together until thickened. Whisk into softened gelatin mixture, set over simmering water, and heat for 8 minutes, stirring constantly. Turn into a large bowl and refrigerate until thickened but not set, stirring frequently. (Mixture takes about 45 minutes to thicken.)

In a medium-size bowl, beat egg whites until foamy. Add cream of tartar and vanilla and continue beating until stiff peaks form. Fold into orange mixture and turn into prepared pie plate, smoothing top. Chill until set.

Makes 8 servings
(107 calories per serving)

Banana Cream Pie

1 recipe for Meringue Pie Shell
    (page 107)
2 ripe bananas
3 cups Slim Pastry Cream
    (page 246)
¼ cup unsweetened flaked coconut

Bake pie shell according to directions. Allow to cool.

Thinly slice bananas. In a medium-size bowl, mix them with pastry cream. Turn into pie shell. Sprinkle with coconut and serve at once.

Makes 10 servings
(128 calories per serving)

Light Carrot Cake

⅓ cup whole wheat pastry flour
⅓ cup unbleached white flour
2 tablespoons cornstarch
1 teaspoon baking powder
½ teaspoon ground ginger
½ teaspoon ground nutmeg
3 eggs, separated
¼ teaspoon cream of tartar
⅓ cup honey
1 teaspoon vanilla extract
1 cup grated cooked carrots

Preheat oven to 350°F. Spray a 10-inch tube pan with vegetable spray.

Sift together whole wheat pastry flour, unbleached white flour, cornstarch, baking powder, ginger, and nutmeg into a small bowl. Whisk to blend well.

In a medium-size bowl, beat egg whites until foamy. Add cream of tartar and continue beating until stiff peaks form.

In a large bowl, beat together egg yolks, honey, and vanilla until light colored and thick, about 7 minutes. Fold in dry ingredients. Fold in carrots, then beaten egg whites.

Turn into prepared pan and bake on middle shelf of oven until top springs back when lightly pressed, 20 to 25 minutes.

Invert pan on wire rack and cool completely before removing cake from pan.

Makes 10 servings
(100 calories per serving)

Carob Chippers

½ cup whole wheat pastry flour
½ cup unbleached white flour
2 teaspoons baking powder
¼ cup butter, softened
¼ cup honey
2 tablespoons maple syrup
1 tablespoon vanilla extract
⅓ cup carob chips

Preheat oven to 350°F. Spray 2 baking sheets with vegetable spray.

In a small bowl, whisk whole wheat pastry flour, unbleached white flour, and baking powder together to blend.

In a medium-size bowl, beat together butter and honey until fluffy. Beat in maple syrup and vanilla. Gradually beat in dry ingredients. Fold in carob chips. Drop dough by teaspoonfuls onto 1 prepared baking sheet. Bake on middle shelf of oven until lightly browned, 8 to 10 minutes.

While cookies are baking, drop remaining dough onto second prepared baking sheet. Put in oven when first batch is cooked. Remove cookies from baking sheets and cool on wire racks.

Makes 3 dozen cookies
(41 calories per cookie)

Individual Strawberry Cheese Puddings

1 16-ounce package unsweetened frozen strawberries, thawed
1 envelope unflavored gelatin
1 cup part-skim ricotta cheese
¼ cup honey
¾ cup evaporated skim milk, chilled
¾ cup Perfect Pineapple Sauce (page 55), **divided**

Drain strawberries well, reserving both juice and berries. Pour juice into a small saucepan. Sprinkle gelatin over juice and set aside for 5 minutes to soften. Heat over medium heat, stirring constantly, until gelatin dissolves. Remove from heat and set aside to cool.

In a medium-size bowl, beat ricotta and honey together until fluffy. Beat in cooled gelatin and chill until thickened but not set, about 30 minutes, stirring occasionally, so edges won't set.

In a medium-size bowl, beat evaporated skim milk until fluffy. Fold into gelatin mixture along with strawberries. Divide among 6 small dessert dishes and chill until set.

To serve, unmold and top each pudding with 2 tablespoons of the pineapple sauce.

Makes 6 servings
(118 calories per serving)

Raisin Pear Bread Pudding

4 slices whole grain bread
3 eggs, separated
⅛ teaspoon cream of tartar
2 tablespoons honey
1¾ cups skim milk
1 teaspoon vanilla extract
½ teaspoon ground cinnamon
1 large fresh pear, peeled, cored, and chopped
¼ cup raisins, plumped

Preheat oven to 350°F. Spray a 2-quart casserole with vegetable spray.

Break bread into chunks.

In a medium-size bowl, beat egg whites until foamy. Add cream of tartar and continue beating until stiff peaks form.

In a large bowl, beat together egg yolks and honey briefly. Mix in skim milk, vanilla, and cinnamon, beating just to mix. Add bread, stirring until saturated.

Mix pears and raisins into bread mixture. Fold in beaten egg whites and turn into prepared casserole. Bake on middle shelf of oven for about 1 hour. Serve warm or cold.

Makes 8 servings
(125 calories per serving)

Spicy Pears

A lovely juicy pear dessert.

2 tablespoons honey
1 tablespoon butter
1 teaspoon ground cinnamon
¼ teaspoon ground ginger
1 cup cornflakes
4 large fresh Bartlett pears
2 tablespoons apple juice

Preheat oven to 350°F.

In a small saucepan, heat together honey, butter, cinnamon, and ginger until butter is melted. Mix with cornflakes.

Peel, core, and thinly slice pears into a 9-inch pie plate. Pour apple juice over pear slices. Distribute cornflake mixture evenly over top and bake on middle shelf of oven until pears are tender, about 20 minutes. Serve warm or cold.

Makes 6 servings
(141 calories per serving)

Reduced Calorie Peanut Butter

The use of dry roasted peanuts is what reduces the calories in this diet version of one of America's favorite foods.

2 cups dry roasted peanuts

In a food processor, process nuts until they are the consistency of paste, adding water by tablespoonfuls to make it spreadable. Stop machine occasionally and scrape down sides of bowl and release nuts trapped under blade. Store in refrigerator.

Makes about 1½ cups
(70 calories per tablespoon)

Perfect Pineapple Sauce

1 tablespoon cornstarch
¼ cup freshly squeezed
    orange juice

2 tablespoons honey
1 20-ounce can unsweet-
    ened crushed pineapple

Makes about 2 cups
(15 calories per tablespoon)

Stir cornstarch into orange juice in a small saucepan. Add honey, blending well. Add pineapple and cook over medium heat, stirring constantly, until sauce thickens.

Hawaiian Snow Balls

2 cups Vanilla Ice Milk (page 72)
½ cup unsweetened flaked coconut
½ cup Perfect Pineapple Sauce
    (page 55)

Line a small baking sheet with waxed paper. Make 4 perfectly rounded, ½-cup scoops of vanilla ice milk. Place them on prepared baking sheet and freeze until very firm.

Preheat oven to 350°F. Put coconut in shallow pan, and toast on middle shelf of oven, stirring occasionally, until lightly browned, about 10 minutes. Cool slightly, then roll ice milk balls in toasted coconut. Return to freezer for at least 30 minutes.

Serve with 2 tablespoons of pineapple sauce on each ball.

Makes 4 servings
(179 calories per serving)

Peanut Butter Apples

A wholesome, easy dessert, quick and satisfying.

1 apple
4 teaspoons Reduced Calorie
    Peanut Butter (page 54),
    divided
2 teaspoons Coconut Sugar
    (page 60), divided

Core, but do not peel, apple; then cut it into quarters.

Spread 1 teaspoon of the peanut butter on cut sides of each quarter. Sprinkle each piece with ½ teaspoon of the Coconut Sugar.

Makes 4 servings
(48 calories per serving)

Ring of Plenty

1 recipe for Fresh Orange Gelatin
    (page 225)
1 apple
1 fresh pear
2 tablespoons freshly squeezed
    lemon juice
1 seedless orange
16 unsweetened frozen cherries,
    thawed

Make gelatin according to directions up to the point when it is thickened but not set. Then beat gelatin until foamy. Pour into a lightly oiled 4- or 6-cup ring mold. Chill until set.

Core and slice, but do not peel, apple and pear. Toss with lemon juice in a medium-size bowl. Peel and section orange, removing pith. Toss all fruit together.

Unmold orange ring on platter and fill with fruit. Serve at once.

Makes 8 servings
(64 calories per serving)

Luscious Lemon Cheesecake

A special dessert for a special day.

2 envelopes unflavored gelatin
1 cup freshly squeezed lemon
    juice
16 ounces low-fat cottage cheese
2 tablespoons butter, softened
¾ cup plus 1 tablespoon honey,
    divided
4 eggs, separated
⅛ teaspoon cream of tartar
¼ cup Light Lemon Cookie crumbs
    (page 121)

Spray bottom and sides of a 9-inch springform pan with vegetable spray.

In the top of a double boiler, sprinkle gelatin over lemon juice. Set aside for 5 minutes to soften.

In a blender or food processor, beat together cottage cheese and butter.

Stir ¾ cup of the honey into gelatin mixture. Beat egg yolks slightly and add to gelatin. Heat over hot water, stirring constantly, for 10 minutes. Slowly beat hot mixture into cheese mixture. Chill until thickened but not set, stirring frequently.

In a medium-size bowl, beat egg whites until foamy. Add cream of tartar and continue beating, drizzling in remaining honey, until stiff but not dry. Stir a little egg white into gelatin mixture to lighten. Fold in remaining egg whites and turn into prepared pan. Sprinkle with cookie crumbs and chill until set.

To serve, run knife around edge of cheesecake and release springform.

Makes 12 to 16 servings
(164 to 122 calories per serving)

Squash Custard

2 eggs, separated
⅛ teaspoon cream of tartar
2 tablespoons honey
1 cup cooked pureed winter
   squash
¾ cup skim milk
1 teaspoon ground cinnamon
¼ teaspoon ground nutmeg
¼ teaspoon ground ginger

Preheat oven to 325°F. Spray a 1-quart casserole with vegetable spray.

In a medium-size bowl, beat egg whites until foamy. Add cream of tartar and continue beating until stiff peaks form.

In a large bowl, beat egg yolks and honey. Add remaining ingredients and beat just to mix. Fold in beaten egg whites and turn into prepared casserole. Bake on middle shelf of oven until a cake tester inserted into center comes out clean, about 45 minutes. Serve warm or cold.

Makes 6 servings
(75 calories per serving)

Almond Coconut Chiffon Pie

1 recipe for Skinny Piecrust
   (page 5)
1 cup skim milk
3 eggs, separated
3 tablespoons honey
1 envelope unflavored gelatin
1 teaspoon almond extract
⅛ teaspoon cream of tartar
½ cup unsweetened flaked coconut

Line a 10-inch pie plate just to the rim with pastry, and bake according to directions. Set aside to cool.

In a medium-size bowl, beat together skim milk, egg yolks, and honey. Pour into a medium-size saucepan. Sprinkle gelatin over top and heat over medium heat, stirring constantly, for 5 minutes. Stir in almond extract. Turn into a large bowl and chill until thickened but not set, about 1½ hours, stirring every 30 minutes.

In a medium-size bowl, beat egg whites and cream of tartar until stiff peaks form. Fold egg whites into gelatin mixture. Fold in coconut and turn into prepared piecrust. Chill until ready to serve.

Makes 10 servings
(110 calories per serving)

Orange Meringue Cups

3 large seedless oranges
2 egg whites
⅛ teaspoon cream of tartar
3 tablespoons unsweetened flaked coconut
6 seedless green or red grapes, divided

Preheat oven to 350°F.

Cut oranges into halves. With a serrated knife, cut between skins and pulp. Run knife between pulp and membranes, loosening sections. Place orange halves in a muffin tin, pulp side up.

In a medium-size bowl, beat egg whites until foamy. Add cream of tartar and continue beating until stiff peaks form. Fold in coconut and pile mixture on orange halves. Bake on bottom shelf of oven until meringue browns, about 10 minutes.

Cool and top each with a grape.

Makes 6 servings
(42 calories per serving)

Saint Paddy's Day Mint Treat

This is a delightfully refreshing dessert that makes a beautiful presentation.

2 envelopes unflavored gelatin
1½ cups skim milk
2 egg yolks
¼ cup honey
1 tablespoon vanilla extract
1½ teaspoons peppermint extract
3 drops natural green food coloring, optional

4 egg whites
⅛ teaspoon cream of tartar
⅔ cup instant nonfat dry milk
⅔ cup ice water
1 cup Creamy Carob Sauce (page 186)

In a small saucepan, sprinkle gelatin over skim milk. Set aside for 5 minutes to soften.

In a small bowl, whisk egg yolks until thick and yellow.

Add honey to milk mixture and heat over medium heat, stirring until mixture is scalding (150°F on a candy thermometer). Remove from heat and whisk a little hot milk into beaten yolks. Return yolk mixture to saucepan, whisking constantly. Cook over low heat, stirring constantly, until mixture reaches 175°F on a candy thermometer. Turn into a large bowl, and mix in extracts and food coloring, if desired.

In a medium-size bowl, beat egg whites until foamy. Add cream of tartar and continue beating until stiff peaks form.

In a large bowl, beat together instant nonfat dry milk and ice water until soft peaks form.

Fold instant nonfat dry milk into egg mixture, then fold in egg whites. Rinse a 6-cup mold with cold water. Turn mixture into it, smoothing top. Refrigerate until set.

To unmold, dip mold briefly in hot water. Place serving dish on top of mold and invert. Serve with Creamy Carob Sauce.

Makes 8 servings
(190 calories per serving)

Stuffed Baked Pears

These pears are equally delicious warm or chilled.

   ¾ cup water, divided
   ½ cup grape juice
   ½ teaspoon ground cinnamon
   ⅛ teaspoon ground cloves
   4 fresh pears
   2 tablespoons raisins
   2 tablespoons chopped walnuts
   1 tablespoon cornstarch

Preheat oven to 350°F.

In a small saucepan, bring ½ cup of the water, grape juice, cinnamon, and cloves to a boil. Reduce heat and cook for 1 minute. Remove from heat.

Cut tops, about 1 inch down, off pears and reserve. Peel and core pears, leaving bottoms intact.

In a small bowl, mix together raisins and walnuts and stuff pears with them. Replace tops. Stand pears up in a casserole. Pour grape sauce over them. Cover and bake until fruit is soft, about 1 hour.

Pour sauce from casserole into a small saucepan. In a jar with a tight-fitting lid, shake together the remaining water and cornstarch. Stir into sauce and heat, stirring constantly, until thickened. Pour over pears and set aside to cool.

Makes 4 servings
(167 calories per serving)

Frozen Pudding

   2 egg whites
   ⅛ teaspoon cream of tartar
   2 cups Very Vanilla Pudding
       (page 76), cooled slightly but
       not set
   1 banana
   ¼ cup raisins, plumped
   8 seedless red grapes

Line 8 cups of a muffin tin with paper liners.

In a medium-size bowl, beat egg whites until foamy. Add cream of tartar and continue beating until stiff peaks form. Fold into cooled pudding.

Chop banana. Fold along with raisins into pudding. Divide among paper liners and freeze.

When frozen, remove pudding-filled liners from tin and store in a plastic bag in freezer.

To serve, decorate each serving with a grape.

Makes 8 servings
(95 calories per serving)

Coconut Sugar

This easy decoration can be used to dust cakes, candies, or fruits.

1¼ cups unsweetened flaked coconut

In a food processor, process coconut until it is the consistency of powdered sugar.

Makes 1 cup
(20 calories per tablespoon)

Super Spice Cake

You can add zip to a recipe with spices, and the number of calories you add is almost negligible.

½ cup sifted whole wheat pastry
    flour
½ cup sifted unbleached white
    flour
2 teaspoons baking powder
2 teaspoons ground cinnamon
1 teaspoon ground nutmeg
1 teaspoon ground ginger
5 egg whites
¼ teaspoon cream of tartar
3 egg yolks
1 tablespoon vegetable oil
1 teaspoon vanilla extract
½ teaspoon orange extract
¼ cup honey
1 tablespoon molasses

Preheat oven to 350°F.

Sift together whole wheat pastry flour, unbleached white flour, baking powder, cinnamon, nutmeg, and ginger into a medium-size bowl. Stir with wire whisk to blend well.

In a large bowl, beat egg whites until foamy. Add cream of tartar and continue beating until stiff peaks form.

In a small bowl, beat together egg yolks, oil, extracts, honey, and molasses with same beaters. Add to dry ingredients, mixing well. Add a small amount of egg whites, stirring to lighten. Fold in remaining whites and turn into an 8 × 8-inch pan with a nonstick surface. Reduce heat to 325°F. Bake on middle shelf of oven for 40 to 45 minutes, or until a cake tester inserted near center comes out clean. Cool before serving.

Makes 12 servings
(98 calories per serving)

Rum-Tum-Diddle Soufflés

This easy, light-as-air dessert should be served warm.

    3 egg whites
    ¼ teaspoon cream of tartar
    3 tablespoons honey, divided
    1 teaspoon vanilla extract
    ½ cup evaporated skim milk,
        chilled
    ½ teaspoon rum extract
    8 tablespoons Ruby Raspberry
        Sauce (page 127), divided

Preheat oven to 350°F. Spray 8 8-ounce ovenproof custard cups or dishes with vegetable spray.

In a medium-size bowl, beat egg whites until foamy. Add cream of tartar, 2 tablespoons of the honey, and vanilla and continue beating until stiff peaks form.

In a large bowl, beat evaporated skim milk until foamy. Add remaining honey and rum extract and continue beating until soft peaks form. Fold beaten egg whites into beaten milk mixture. Turn into prepared custard cups or dishes and bake on bottom shelf of oven until soufflés have risen and are lightly browned.

Serve hot with a tablespoon of the Ruby Raspberry Sauce on each soufflé.

Makes 8 servings
(49 calories per serving)

Brandy Zabaglione

This dessert must be served as soon as it's made as it tends to separate on standing.

    4 eggs, separated
    2 tablespoons honey
    1 teaspoon brandy extract
    ¼ teaspoon cream of tartar
    1 teaspoon red currant jelly,
        divided

In the top of a double boiler set over simmering water, beat together egg yolks, honey, and brandy extract until mixture is thick and light colored, about 7 minutes.

In a medium-size bowl, beat egg whites until foamy. Sprinkle in cream of tartar and continue beating until stiff peaks form. Fold egg yolk mixture into beaten egg whites. Divide among 4 dessert glasses. Top each with ¼ teaspoon of the jelly and serve immediately.

Makes 4 servings
(118 calories per serving)

Tangy Tangerine Crepes

½ cup part-skim ricotta cheese
1 tablespoon skim milk
¼ teaspoon almond extract
8 Delicious Diet Crepes (page 30)
¼ cup butter
2 tablespoons honey
1 tablespoon cornstarch
1 cup freshly squeezed orange
    juice
1 tangerine, peeled, sectioned and
    pith removed

In a medium-size bowl, beat together ricotta, skim milk, and almond extract until fluffy. Divide among 8 crepes and spread the mixture down the center of each. Fold 1 side over filling, then the other side.

In a large skillet, melt butter. Stir in honey.

Dissolve cornstarch in orange juice. Add to skillet and stir constantly until thickened. Carefully place crepes in hot sauce. Cover, and heat for 5 minutes. Remove from heat. Decorate with tangerine sections and serve immediately.

Makes 8 servings
(146 calories per serving)

Lemon Sorbet

1 cup freshly squeezed lemon
    juice
3 cups water, divided
⅔ cup honey
1 teaspoon lemon extract
    natural yellow food coloring,
    optional

Strain lemon juice into a large bowl. Mix in 2½ cups of the water.

In a small saucepan, heat remaining water and honey until honey dissolves. Add to lemon juice in bowl. Mix in lemon extract and a few drops of food coloring, if desired.

Process mixture in an ice cream maker according to manufacturer's instructions, or turn mixture into a large pan and place in freezer until mushy but not solid. Remove from freezer, beat to break down ice crystals, and then return to freezer. Repeat this procedure twice. Freeze until ready to serve.

Makes about 10 servings
(58 calories per serving)

Tangerine Bread Pudding with Peach Sauce

Be sure to remove all the pith from the tangerine or the pudding will be bitter.

3 eggs, separated, at room temperature
⅛ teaspoon cream of tartar
2 tablespoons honey
1⅔ cups evaporated skim milk
1 teaspoon vanilla extract
½ teaspoon almond extract
½ teaspoon ground cinnamon
4 slices whole wheat bread (with crusts), broken into chunks
1 tangerine
½ cup Peach Sauce (page 120), divided

Preheat oven to 350°F. Spray a 2-quart casserole with vegetable spray.

In a medium-size bowl, beat egg whites until foamy. Add cream of tartar and continue beating until stiff peaks form.

In a large bowl, beat together egg yolks and honey just to blend. Mix in evaporated skim milk, extracts, and cinnamon, beating briefly. Add bread, stirring until it is saturated.

Peel tangerine and separate into sections, removing pith. Cut each section into fourths, removing seeds. Stir into bread mixture. Fold in beaten egg whites and turn into prepared casserole. Bake on middle shelf of oven for 45 minutes.

Serve warm or cold. Top each serving with 1 tablespoon of the Peach Sauce.

Makes 8 servings
(134 calories per serving)

Orange Date Cookies

½ cup whole wheat flour
½ cup unbleached white flour
1 teaspoon baking powder
¼ cup butter, cut into pieces
⅓ cup unsweetened flaked coconut
½ cup freshly squeezed orange juice
2 tablespoons honey
1 teaspoon vanilla extract
1 teaspoon orange extract
1 egg, beaten
9 dates, quartered

Preheat oven to 350°F. Spray 2 baking sheets with vegetable spray.

In a medium-size bowl, mix together whole wheat flour, unbleached white flour, and baking powder with a whisk. Cut butter into flour mixture with pastry blender until mixture resembles crumbs. Mix in coconut.

In a small bowl, combine orange juice, honey, and extracts. Thoroughly stir into flour mixture. Mix in egg. Drop batter by teaspoonfuls onto prepared baking sheets. Put a piece of date on top of each portion of batter. Bake each batch on middle shelf of oven for 10 minutes.

Cool on wire rack.

Makes 3 dozen cookies
(40 calories per cookie)

Grape Fizz

¼ cup crushed ice
½ cup grape juice
⅓ cup club soda

Put ice into an 8-ounce glass. Add grape juice and club soda. Stir.

Makes 1 serving
(84 calories per serving)

Baked Jungle Treat

2 ripe bananas
2 teaspoons butter, melted
¼ cup Coconut Sugar (page 60)

Preheat oven to 400°F. Spray a baking sheet with vegetable spray.
Cut bananas into halves, lengthwise. Brush all surfaces with melted butter and roll bananas in Coconut Sugar. Place, cut side down, on prepared baking sheet and bake on middle shelf of oven until lightly browned, 5 to 7 minutes. Serve immediately.

Makes 4 servings
(78 calories per serving)

Carob Chip Pie

1 recipe for Meringue Pie Shell
   (page 107)
2 cups Carob Chip Pudding
   (page 183)
4 whole fresh strawberries,
   optional

Bake pie shell according to directions. Cool.
Fill meringue shell with thoroughly cooled Carob Chip Pudding.
Cut strawberries into halves lengthwise and decorate pie, if desired. Chill until serving time.

Makes 8 servings
(92 calories per serving)

Nice Spice Popcorn

A handy sweet you can carry away from the table as a low-cal nibble for a later time.

2 tablespoons butter
1 tablespoon honey
1 teaspoon ground cinnamon
¼ teaspoon ground nutmeg
¼ teaspoon ground ginger
8 cups hot popcorn

In a small saucepan, melt butter and honey. Add spices and stir until dissolved. Toss with popcorn and serve immediately, 1 cup per person.

Makes 8 servings
(48 calories per serving)

APRIL

Diet and Exercise

FRUIT OF THE MONTH: **STRAWBERRIES**

DESSERT OF THE MONTH: **GOOD OLD STRAWBERRY SHORTCAKE**

DRINK OF THE MONTH: **STRAWBERRY FIZZ**

April Fools' Day 1 PEAR SURPRISE	2 STRAWBERRY BANANA CREAM	3 COFFEE BAVARIAN CREAM
4 ORANGE PINEAPPLE SHERBET	5 OLD-FASHIONED CUSTARD	6 CAROB CONFECTIONS
7 GOOD OLD STRAWBERRY SHORTCAKE ★	8 BANANA MINT TREATS	9 VANILLA ICE MILK
10 FLUFFY ALMOND TAPIOCA	11 PEANUT BUTTER DROP COOKIES	12 STRAWBERRY GRAPE PIE
13 PEACH SOUFFLÉ	14 APRICOT BRANDY ICE	Easter 15 HAPPY EASTER BASKETS
16 CAROB CRUMB APPLES	17 VERY VANILLA PUDDING	18 PIÑA COLADA PIE
19 STRAWBERRY BREAD PUDDING	20 ALMOND YOGURT	21 APPLESAUCE FLUFF
22 YOGURT-TOPPED GINGERBREAD	23 COOL STRAWBERRY SOUP	24 SENSATIONAL FRUIT PIE
25 FROZEN BANANAS	26 MELLOW MERINGUES	27 ½ CUP SLICED STRAWBERRIES
28 PINEAPPLE FROMAGE	29 MANGO STRAWBERRY CREPE STACKS	30 COTTAGE CHEESE PIE

If you weren't interested in being slender and healthy, you probably wouldn't be reading this book. Eating correctly is certainly a large part of total fitness, but it is only part. Firming up completes the picture. Although you need exercise year round, I've selected April as exercise month. With summer on the horizon and the winter blahs but a memory, it's an excellent time to begin an exercise program. After all, the time for bathing suits and other light clothes that don't always cover trouble spots is right around the corner.

Do get your doctor's permission before embarking on any exercise program. But whether you're eight or eighty-eight, there are many benefits to be derived from physical activity, and whatever your age or physical condition there's some kind of exercise that's right for you. Even a program of moderate exercise, done on a regular basis, will burn up small amounts of calories and help with weight control.

When you're firming up, the idea is to stretch your muscles just a little beyond what they're accustomed to. Your muscle tone will increase as you continue to exercise over the weeks and months. Since I've started doing specific exercises three times a week and walking daily, I not only feel better physically, but my outlook on life is wonderful. And I sleep better, too. This isn't just coincidence. Exercise relieves stress by causing certain chemical changes in the body. After exercising you should feel full of energy and "high" on life.

Many people avoid exercise in the mistaken belief that it increases appetite. The truth is that it decreases your desire for food. You're burning off fat, and so that fat no longer needs calories on which to run.

Always warm up before you do any strenuous exercise. Your muscles need to stretch gently before a workout. Failure to take this simple step has resulted in many a strained or torn ligament. It's also vital to the cardiovascular system to warm down after exercise.

The proper attire may put you in an exercise mood. Select an outfit that's loose fitting, comfortable, and absorbent . . . one that will bend and stretch easily with your body.

Music makes exercising seem easier, keeping motion constant and rhythmic. It's more fun to move to a beat. If you're not used to exercise, start with a slow, steady tune. You'll be surprised at how soon you're ready for a fast-paced piece. Television offers several lively exercise programs. They make it almost like having a friend right there to exercise with you.

An exercise session should be uninterrupted, not only for the sake of convenience, but also so you won't lose the benefits of your warm-ups. Take the phone off the hook, or tell your family and friends not to call you during your exercise time.

Exercise at your own pace. It's all right to start slowly and build up to whatever you're comfortable doing. You should feel your muscles working, but real pain or very hard, rapid breathing are indications you're overdoing it.

I've often heard that for every inch taller you sit, you look five pounds thinner. So include an exercise to strengthen your back and improve your posture in your program.

Walking is a gold star exercise that almost anyone can do. You won't lose a great deal of weight this way, but it's a fantastic way to maintain weight loss if you do it correctly. Hold in your stomach, stand tall, and walk briskly with your arms swinging. Start with a half mile and work up. You can add a half mile to your walking program every week or so until you build it up to a distance that's comfortable for you and fits into your time schedule.

There's no medical evidence to back up the idea that you shouldn't walk after eating, providing you're in good health and not suffering from a coronary insufficiency.

Walking offers many benefits other than maintaining weight. It strengthens the heart, tightens the stomach muscles, and reduces tension. And walking seems to be something most people can stick to. There are fewer drop-outs than in other more strenuous exercise programs. There are also very few injuries.

Coffee Bavarian Cream

1¼ cups skim milk
2 eggs, separated
2 envelopes unflavored gelatin
⅓ cup honey, divided
1 tablespoon decaffeinated
   instant coffee
1½ teaspoons vanilla extract
⅛ teaspoon cream of tartar
1 cup evaporated skim milk,
   chilled
12 mandarin orange sections,
   optional

In the top of a double boiler, beat together skim milk and egg yolks. Sprinkle gelatin over mixture and set aside for 5 minutes to soften. Add 2 tablespoons of the honey and coffee, set over hot, not boiling, water and cook, stirring constantly, until gelatin is dissolved. Remove from heat and mix in vanilla. Chill until thickened but not set, no longer than 30 minutes. Whisk briefly until smooth.

In a medium-size bowl, beat egg whites until foamy. Add cream of tartar and drizzle in remaining honey. Continue to beat until stiff peaks form. Fold egg whites into gelatin mixture.

In a chilled, medium-size bowl, beat evaporated skim milk to the consistency of whipped cream. Fold into gelatin mixture. Turn into a wet 8-cup mold and chill until set.

Unmold and decorate with orange sections, if desired.

Makes 12 servings
(76 calories per serving)

Pear Surprise

2 cups water
3 fresh pears
⅓ cup Light Lemon Cookie crumbs
   (page 121)
1 4 ½-ounce jar strained plums
¼ teaspoon rum extract
1 tablespoon butter

In a large saucepan, bring water to a boil. Add pears, reduce heat, and poach for 10 minutes. Remove with a slotted spoon and set aside to cool.

Preheat oven to 350°F. Spray a 9-inch pie plate with vegetable spray.

In a small bowl, mix together cookie crumbs, plums, and rum extract.

In a small saucepan, melt butter.

When pears are cool enough to handle, peel, halve, and core them. Place, hollow side up, in prepared pie plate. Fill each indentation with crumb mixture. Lightly brush pears and filling with melted butter. Place on middle shelf of oven and bake until fruit is soft, about 10 minutes.

Makes 6 servings
(150 calories per serving)

Orange Pineapple Sherbet

1 envelope unflavored gelatin
½ cup water
⅓ cup honey
1 6-ounce can unsweetened
   frozen orange juice
   concentrate
1 6-ounce can unsweetened
   frozen pineapple juice
   concentrate
2½ cups skim milk

In a small saucepan, sprinkle gelatin over water. Set aside for 5 minutes to soften. Place over low heat. Add honey and stir until gelatin is dissolved.

In a large bowl, mix together juice concentrates and skim milk. Stir in gelatin mixture.

Process mixture in an ice cream maker according to manufacturer's instructions, or turn mixture into a large pan and place in freezer until thickened but not solid. Remove from freezer, beat to break down ice crystals, and then return to freezer. Repeat this procedure twice, turning mixture into 2 1-quart containers the last time. Freeze until ready to serve.

Makes 8 servings
(184 calories per serving)

Cool Strawberry Soup

This cooling summer dessert is so delicious, I sometimes make it my entire lunch.

3 cups unsweetened frozen strawberries, thawed
⅓ cup white grape juice
½ cup freshly squeezed orange
   juice
1 tablespoon cornstarch
2 tablespoons honey
¼ teaspoon ground cinnamon
1 teaspoon vanilla extract
1 cup plain low-fat yogurt

In a food processor, puree strawberries. Turn into a medium-size saucepan.

In a jar with a tight-fitting lid, shake together grape juice, orange juice, and cornstarch. Add to strawberries. Stir in honey and cinnamon, and cook over medium heat, stirring constantly, until thickened, 5 to 10 minutes. Remove from heat and mix in vanilla. Cool, then whisk in yogurt just until blended. Chill before serving.

Makes 6 servings
(94 calories per serving)

Banana Mint Treats

½ teaspoon peppermint extract
¼ cup Creamy Carob Sauce
     (page 205), divided
2 cups Vanilla Ice Milk (page 72),
     divided
1 ripe banana

In a small bowl, mix peppermint extract into carob sauce.

Put ¼ cup Vanilla Ice Milk into each of 4 dessert dishes. Slice 2 banana rounds into each dessert dish. Top with ¼ cup of the Vanilla Ice Milk. Repeat banana layer and top each serving with 1 tablespoon of the carob sauce. Serve immediately.

Makes 4 servings
(187 calories per serving)

Yogurt-Topped Gingerbread

1 cup plain nonfat yogurt
2 tablespoons freshly squeezed
     lemon juice
1 tablespoon honey
1 banana
     Gingerbread Squares, uncut
     (page 184)

In a small bowl, mix together yogurt, lemon juice, and honey. Chop banana and add to yogurt. Spread mixture on top of Gingerbread. Cut into 9 pieces and serve immediately.

Makes 9 servings
(152 calories per serving)

Strawberry Banana Cream

2 cups skim milk, divided
⅔ cup nonfat dry milk
2 medium-size ripe bananas
1 teaspoon freshly squeezed
     lemon juice
2 tablespoons cornstarch
1½ tablespoons honey
1½ teaspoons vanilla extract
1 cup sliced fresh strawberries

In the top of a double boiler, whisk together 1½ cups of the skim milk and nonfat dry milk.

In a small bowl, thoroughly mash together bananas and lemon juice, whisking briskly to blend. Whisk bananas into milk in top of double boiler. Shake together remaining skim milk and cornstarch in a tightly covered jar. Whisk into milk-banana mixture, set over boiling water, and cook, stirring constantly, until mixture thickens, about 8 minutes. Remove from heat and stir in honey and vanilla. Mix in strawberries and chill well before serving.

Makes 8 to 10 servings
(86 to 68 calories per serving)

Skinny Shortcakes

These are wonderful for making fruit shortcakes.

½ cup whole wheat pastry
   flour
½ cup unbleached white flour
1 teaspoon baking powder

3 tablespoons chilled
   butter
6 to 8 tablespoons skim
   milk, divided

Preheat oven to 425°F. Spray a baking sheet with vegetable spray.

In a medium-size bowl, whisk together whole wheat pastry flour, unbleached white flour, and baking powder. Cut in butter with a pastry blender until mixture is crumbly.

With a wooden spoon, stir in ¼ cup of the skim milk. Add more milk, 1 tablespoon at a time, until dough clings together. Divide dough into 6 pieces and drop onto prepared baking sheet. Bake on middle shelf of oven for 10 minutes.

Remove to wire racks to cool.

Makes 6 servings
(132 calories per serving)

Vanilla Ice Milk

⅓ cup honey
1 vanilla bean
1 tablespoon vanilla extract
1 quart low-fat milk, divided

In a medium-size saucepan, mix together honey, vanilla bean, vanilla extract, and 1 cup of the low-fat milk. Add remaining low-fat milk and heat to scalding, stirring occasionally. Remove from heat and let stand 20 to 30 minutes. Remove vanilla bean.

Process mixture in an ice cream maker according to manufacturer's instructions, or turn mixture into a large pan and place in freezer until partially frozen. Remove from freezer, beat to break down ice crystals, and then return to freezer. Repeat this procedure twice, turning mixture into 2 1-quart containers the last time. Freeze until ready to serve.

Makes about 8 servings
(115 calories per serving)

Good Old Strawberry Shortcake

4 cups fresh strawberries,
   quartered
1 tablespoon maple syrup
6 Skinny Shortcakes (page 72)
¾ cup plain low-fat yogurt, divided

Combine strawberries with maple syrup in a large bowl and chill for 2 hours. Toss again after 1 hour to coat all berries.

Split shortcakes crosswise. Divide berries among shortcakes, piling them on bottom halves. Put tops of shortcakes over berries. Top each with 2 tablespoons of the yogurt. Serve immediately.

Makes 6 servings
(197 calories per serving)

Old-Fashioned Custard

4 eggs
3 tablespoons honey
2 cups skim milk
1½ teaspoons vanilla extract
   ground nutmeg for sprinkling

Preheat oven to 325°F. Spray 6 custard cups or a 6-cup glass casserole with vegetable spray.

In a large bowl, beat together eggs and honey until light colored. Beat in remaining ingredients. Divide among prepared custard cups, or pour into casserole. Put into a shallow pan on middle shelf of oven. Pour hot water into pan until it almost reaches the tops of the custard cups or casserole. Bake until a knife inserted into centers of custards comes out almost clean, 45 to 60 minutes.

Sprinkle with nutmeg and serve warm or chilled.

Makes 6 servings
(116 calories per serving)

Carob Confections

⅓ cup butter
¼ cup carob chips
2 eggs
¼ cup honey
1 teaspoon vanilla extract
¼ cup whole wheat pastry flour
¼ cup unbleached white flour
½ cup Easy Vanilla Frosting
     (page 11)
2 tablespoons unsweetened flaked
     coconut

Preheat oven to 350°F.

In the top of a double boiler set over boiling water, melt together butter and carob chips. Set aside to cool.

In a medium-size bowl, beat together eggs, honey, and vanilla. Stir in carob mixture. In a small bowl, mix whole wheat pastry flour and unbleached white flour together with a whisk and then stir into carob mixture with a spoon until well blended. Turn into an 8 × 8-inch pan with a nonstick surface and bake on middle shelf of oven for 20 to 25 minutes, or until batter pulls away from sides of pan. If bubbles form in the middle, push them down with the back of a spatula.

When cool, spread frosting on top and sprinkle with coconut. Cut into 32 pieces.

Makes 16 servings
(100 calories per serving)

Peanut Butter Drop Cookies

⅔ cup whole wheat pastry flour
⅓ cup unbleached white flour
1 teaspoon baking powder
3 tablespoons butter, softened
¼ cup Reduced Calorie Peanut
     Butter (page 54)
2 tablespoons maple syrup
2 tablespoons honey
1 teaspoon vanilla extract
1 egg

Preheat oven to 350°F.

In a medium-size bowl, sift together whole wheat pastry flour, unbleached white flour, and baking powder. Whisk to blend well.

In a large bowl, beat together butter and peanut butter until fluffy. Beat in maple syrup, honey, vanilla, and egg. Mix dry ingredients into peanut butter mixture, blending well. Drop by tablespoonfuls onto 2 nonstick baking sheets and bake each batch on middle shelf of oven for 8 minutes.

Makes 3 dozen cookies
(36 calories per cookie)

Apricot Brandy Ice

There's something really refreshing about a fruit ice on a hot day.

2 cups water
3 cups peeled, pitted fresh
    apricots
½ cup honey
1½ teaspoons brandy extract

In a large saucepan, bring water to a boil. Add apricots, reduce heat, and poach until soft, about 10 minutes. Drain well, reserving juice, and set aside to cool.

In a food processor, puree apricots. Add 2 cups of the reserved apricot juice and remaining ingredients and process until blended.

Process mixture in an ice cream maker according to manufacturer's instructions, or put mixture into a large, shallow pan and place in freezer until thickened but not solid. Remove from freezer, beat to break down ice crystals, and then return to freezer. Repeat this procedure twice, spooning mixture into a container the last time. Freeze until ready to serve.

Makes 8 servings
(94 calories per serving)

Happy Easter Baskets

Both children and adults love these festive dessert baskets.

2 recipes for Meringue Shells
    (page 76)
2 cups Raspberry Rum Sherbet
    (page 150)
2 cups French Carob Ice Milk
    (page 180) or Vanilla Ice Milk
    (page 72)
1½ cups Slim Pastry Cream
    (page 246), divided
½ cup unsweetened flaked
    coconut, divided

Bake Meringue Shells according to directions.

Line a baking sheet with waxed paper. With the large end of a melon baller, scoop out balls of Raspberry Rum Sherbet and put them on prepared baking sheet. Do the same with French Carob Ice Milk or Vanilla Ice Milk. Place in freezer until serving time.

Put 2 tablespoons of the pastry cream into each meringue shell. Top with 2 of each kind of frozen balls. Sprinkle each with 1½ teaspoons of the coconut and serve immediately.

Makes 16 servings
(129 calories per serving)

Meringue Shells

*These shells make a wonderful base for many desserts,
and they always add a note of elegance.*

4 egg whites
¼ teaspoon cream of tartar

2 teaspoons maple syrup
1 teaspoon vanilla extract

Preheat oven to 250°F. Butter and lightly flour a large baking sheet.

In a large bowl, beat egg whites until foamy. Add cream of tartar and continue beating, drizzling in maple syrup and vanilla, until stiff peaks form.

Divide beaten egg whites into 6 mounds, evenly spacing them on prepared baking sheet. With the back of a spoon, flatten mounds slightly and make large indentations in centers. Bake on middle shelf of oven until golden, 40 to 50 minutes.

Carefully remove from baking sheet with a spatula and cool on wire racks.

Makes 6 servings
(15 calories per serving)

Very Vanilla Pudding

2 cups skim milk, divided
3 tablespoons cornstarch
2 tablespoons honey
1 teaspoon butter
1 egg, beaten
1 tablespoon vanilla extract

In the top of a double boiler set over boiling water, heat 1½ cups of the skim milk.

Shake remaining skim milk and cornstarch together in a jar with a tight-fitting lid. Add gradually to milk, mixing well. Stir in honey and continue to cook, stirring constantly, until mixture thickens. Stir in butter until melted. Mix a small amount of hot mixture into egg. Pour back into hot mixture and continue cooking, stirring constantly, for another 2 minutes. Remove from heat and stir in vanilla.

Makes 4 servings
(127 calories per serving)

Applesauce Fluff

2 cups unsweetened Applesauce
  (page 81), **divided**
2 egg whites
⅛ teaspoon cream of tartar
1 tablespoon honey
½ teaspoon ground cinnamon

Preheat oven to 425°F.

Put ½ cup of the applesauce in each of 4 custard cups.

In a medium-size bowl, beat egg whites until foamy. Add cream of tartar, honey, and cinnamon. Beat until stiff peaks form.

Divide among custard cups, spreading to cover Applesauce. Bake on middle shelf of oven until meringue is golden brown, about 5 minutes.

*Makes 4 servings
(75 calories per serving)*

Peach Soufflé

2 envelopes unflavored gelatin
½ cup cold water
1 20-ounce package unsweetened
  frozen peaches, thawed
¼ cup maple syrup
2 tablespoons honey
2 teaspoons vanilla extract
3 egg whites
¼ teaspoon cream of tartar
1 cup evaporated skim milk,
  chilled
2 tablespoons currant jelly

Fit a 2-quart soufflé dish with a soufflé collar.*

In a small saucepan, sprinkle gelatin over cold water. Set aside for 5 minutes to soften. Heat over medium heat, stirring constantly, until gelatin dissolves. Remove from heat.

In a food processor, puree peaches with maple syrup, honey, vanilla, and gelatin. Chill until thickened but not set. Whisk until smooth.

In a medium-size bowl, beat egg whites until foamy. Add cream of tartar and continue beating until stiff. Fold in peach mixture.

In a large bowl, beat evaporated skim milk to the consistency of whipped cream. Fold into peach mixture. Turn peach mixture into soufflé dish and chill until firm.

In a small saucepan, melt jelly. Drizzle over soufflé and return to refrigerator. Remove collar before serving.

*Makes 16 servings
(94 calories per serving)*

*To make a soufflé collar, cut a piece of foil 10 inches wide and long enough to encircle the soufflé dish plus 2 inches. Fold lengthwise. Tie collar around dish with string, allowing the foil to extend 3 inches above the rim. Tape the seam together. Butter or oil inside of collar.

Carob Crumb Apples

I like this dessert. It's an unlikely delightful blending of flavors.

4 apples, peeled, cored, and chopped
2 teaspoons freshly squeezed lemon juice
¼ cup honey
⅓ cup plus 3 tablespoons whole wheat pastry flour, divided
1 teaspoon ground cinnamon
½ cup carob chips
2 tablespoons butter
⅓ cup unbleached white flour

Preheat oven to 350°F. Spray a 9-inch pie plate with vegetable spray.

In a large bowl, toss apples with lemon juice, honey, 3 tablespoons of the whole wheat pastry flour, and cinnamon. Turn into prepared pie plate and bake on middle shelf of oven for 25 minutes.

In the top of a double boiler set over hot water, melt together carob chips and butter. Remove from heat.

In a small bowl, whisk remaining whole wheat pastry flour and unbleached white flour to blend. Stir into carob mixture. The mixture will separate into crumbs. Distribute crumbs evenly over top of apple mixture and return to oven for 25 minutes. Serve warm.

Makes 10 servings
(159 calories per serving)

Strawberry Grape Pie

3 cups fresh strawberries, quartered
2 cups seedless white grapes, halved
¼ cup cornstarch
1 teaspoon vanilla extract
½ teaspoon brandy extract, optional
2 tablespoons honey
1 recipe for Skinny Piecrust (page 5)

Preheat oven to 400°F. Spray a 9-inch pie plate with vegetable spray.

In a large bowl, toss together strawberries, grapes, cornstarch, vanilla, and brandy extract, if desired. Add honey and toss to coat. Turn into prepared pie plate.

Roll out piecrust into a 10 × 6-inch piece. Cut into 4 1½-inch strips and make a spoke pattern on top of filling. Bake on middle shelf of oven until pastry is browned and filling bubbly, about 30 minutes.

Allow to cool before serving.

Makes 10 servings
(105 calories per serving)

Piña Colada Pie

1 tablespoon cornstarch
2 cups skim milk, divided
2 envelopes unflavored gelatin,
   divided
2 tablespoons honey, divided
½ teaspoon vanilla extract
1 teaspoon rum extract, divided
½ cup unsweetened flaked coconut
1 20-ounce can unsweetened
   crushed pineapple

Spray a 9-inch pie plate with vegetable spray.

In a medium-size saucepan, dissolve cornstarch in 1 cup of the skim milk. Sprinkle 1 envelope of the gelatin over milk and set aside for 5 minutes to soften. Add 1 tablespoon of the honey and heat over medium heat, stirring constantly, until mixture thickens and gelatin dissolves. Stir in vanilla, ½ teaspoon of the rum extract, remaining skim milk, and coconut. Pour into prepared pie plate and chill until set, about 2 hours.

Drain pineapple, collecting juice in a small saucepan. Sprinkle remaining gelatin over juice and set aside for 5 minutes to soften. Heat over medium heat, stirring constantly, until gelatin dissolves. Remove from heat and stir in remaining honey and remaining rum extract. Mix into pineapple and let cool slightly. Spread over coconut mixture and chill until set.

Makes 8 servings
(144 calories per serving)

Almond Yogurt

1 envelope unflavored gelatin
½ cup water
1 cup plain low-fat yogurt
¼ cup honey
2 teaspoons vanilla extract
1 teaspoon almond extract
¾ cup evaporated skim milk,
   chilled
1 kiwi fruit, sliced

In a small saucepan, sprinkle gelatin over water and set aside for 5 minutes to soften. Heat over medium heat, stirring constantly, until gelatin dissolves.

In a medium-size bowl, combine yogurt, honey, and extracts. Fold in gelatin and refrigerate until thickened but not set, about 30 minutes.

In a large bowl, beat evaporated skim milk to the consistency of whipped cream. Fold in yogurt mixture and divide among 8 dessert glasses. Chill until set.

Decorate with kiwi slices and serve.

Makes 8 servings
(84 calories per serving)

Strawberry Bread Pudding

Fresh strawberries produce a firmer, more satisfactory dessert, but the recipe will work with frozen berries if they're drained well.

2   cups skim milk
⅓   cup honey
1   teaspoon butter
2   eggs
1   teaspoon vanilla extract
1   tablespoon brandy extract
2   cups cubed fresh whole grain bread (4 or 5 slices)
1   cup coarsely chopped fresh strawberries
2   egg whites
⅛   teaspoon cream of tartar

Preheat oven to 325°F. Spray a 1½-quart casserole with vegetable spray.
In a large saucepan, heat skim milk and honey together to scalding. Remove from heat, mix in butter, and set aside to cool slightly.
In a small bowl, beat eggs. Whisk into cooled milk along with extracts. Stir in bread and strawberries.
In a medium-size bowl, beat egg whites until foamy. Add cream of tartar and continue beating until stiff but not dry. Fold into other ingredients.
Turn into prepared casserole and place in a pan of hot water on middle shelf of oven. Bake until a knife inserted about 1 inch from center comes out clean, 50 to 60 minutes. Center will cook after pudding has been removed from oven. Serve warm or cold.

*Makes 8 servings
(141 calories per serving)*

Fluffy Almond Tapioca

3   tablespoons quick-cooking tapioca
3   tablespoons honey, divided
2   cups skim milk
1   egg, separated
½   teaspoon vanilla extract
½   teaspoon almond extract

In a medium-size saucepan, combine tapioca, 2 tablespoons of the honey, and skim milk. Beat egg yolk, add to mixture, and set aside for 5 minutes to soften tapioca.
In a small bowl, beat egg white until stiff peaks form, drizzling in the remaining honey and extracts.
Bring softened tapioca mixture to a boil, stirring constantly. Reduce heat and continue cooking, stirring constantly, for 6 minutes. Set aside to cool for about 10 minutes and then fold in beaten egg white. Serve warm or cold.

*Makes 5 servings
(121 calories per serving)*

Applesauce

**4 apples, peeled, cored,
and quartered**

1 cup water, divided
1 tablespoon honey*

In a food processor, puree apples with ½ cup of the water and honey.

Pour into a large saucepan and simmer for 20 minutes, adding more water as needed, stirring often.

Makes 4 servings
(112 calories per serving)

*To make unsweetened applesauce, omit honey.
(96 calories per serving)

Sensational Fruit Pie

This lovely pie brightens up any meal with its cheerful colors.

1 recipe for Skinny Piecrust
(page 5)
½ 20-ounce package unsweetened frozen strawberries, thawed
1 20-ounce can unsweetened crushed pineapple
3 tablespoons cornstarch
½ teaspoon ground cinnamon
24 seedless green grapes, halved, divided

Line a 9-inch pie plate with pastry and bake blind according to directions.

Drain strawberries and pineapple well, reserving juices. Mix juices together and pour 1½ cups into a medium-size saucepan. Discard remaining juice. (If there are not 1½ cups of juice, add water to make up the difference.) Mix in cornstarch and cinnamon. Heat, stirring constantly, until mixture thickens and boils.

In a large bowl, combine strawberries, pineapple, and 20 grapes (40 halves). Mix in thickened juice and refrigerate until slightly cooled.

Turn into baked piecrust. Arrange remaining grape halves evenly around edge of pie. Refrigerate until thoroughly chilled.

Makes 10 servings
(115 calories per serving)

Mellow Meringues

These cookies are simple to make but a bit tricky to remove from the baking sheet. Allow them to cool on the baking sheet for 10 minutes, then carefully run a knife under each cookie and lift it onto a wire rack to cool.

- ⅓ cup walnuts
- ¼ cup carob chips
- 2 egg whites
- ⅛ teaspoon cream of tartar
- 2 tablespoons maple syrup
- 1 teaspoon vanilla extract

Preheat oven to 225°F. Butter and flour 2 baking sheets.

In a blender container, finely chop nuts and carob chips.

In a medium-size bowl, beat egg whites until foamy. Add cream of tartar and continue to beat, drizzling in maple syrup and vanilla until mixture is very stiff, about 3 minutes.

Fold in ground walnuts and carob chips, and drop by heaping teaspoonfuls onto prepared baking sheets. Bake each batch on middle shelf of oven until tops of cookies feel firm to the touch, 30 to 40 minutes.

Makes about 3 dozen cookies or 6 servings
(17 calories per cookie)

Pineapple Fromage

- 1½ cups low-fat cottage cheese
- 3 eggs
- ⅓ cup honey
- 1½ teaspoons vanilla extract
- 1 teaspoon ground cinnamon
- 6 unsweetened canned pineapple rings, drained
- 6 unsweetened frozen cherries, thawed

Preheat oven to 325°F. Spray a non-stick 9-inch layer cake pan with vegetable spray.

In a food processor, blend cottage cheese, eggs, honey, vanilla, and cinnamon until smooth. Pour into prepared pan. Bake on middle shelf of oven for 45 minutes.

Put one slice of pineapple in center of cake. Arrange other slices around middle slice, overlapping if necessary. Put one cherry in center of each pineapple slice. Bake another 10 minutes.

Chill. Cut into wedges and serve.

Makes 8 servings
(140 calories per serving)

Cottage Cheese Pie

½ tablespoon butter or margarine
3 tablespoons graham cracker
    crumbs
¼ teaspoon ground cinnamon
16 ounces low-fat, cream-style
    cottage cheese
4 teaspoons cornstarch
¼ cup honey
1½ teaspoons vanilla extract
1 teaspoon freshly squeezed
    lemon juice
2 eggs
10 fresh strawberries, halved

Preheat oven to 350°F.

Rinse an 8½-inch glass pie plate in hot water. Dry well and rub butter on bottom of pie plate until all the butter is used. Sprinkle with graham cracker crumbs and press lightly to make crust.

Put remaining ingredients, except strawberries, into a food processor or blender and blend until smooth. Pour over crust and bake on middle shelf of oven until set, about 30 minutes.

Cool well, then decorate with strawberry halves.

Makes 10 servings
(102 calories per serving)

Strawberry Fizz

1 cup fresh or unsweetened frozen
    strawberries, thawed
2 teaspoons honey
1 teaspoon vanilla extract
½ cup club soda

In a blender, puree strawberries with honey and vanilla. Stir in club soda. Pour over ice in individual glasses and serve immediately.

Makes 2 servings
(48 calories per serving)

Mango Strawberry Crepe Stacks

1 cup evaporated skim milk, chilled
1 tablespoon honey
½ teaspoon vanilla extract
¼ cup Slim Pastry Cream (page 246)
2 cups diced mangoes
2 cups quartered fresh strawberries
8 Delicious Diet Crepes (page 30)

In a large bowl, beat evaporated skim milk until foamy. Drizzle in honey and vanilla and continue beating just until soft peaks form. Fold in pastry cream and fruit.

Place 1 crepe on a large plate. Spread about ⅐th of the fruit mixture on it. Put another crepe on top. Continue making layers, ending with a crepe. Slice, like a cake, with a serrated knife and serve immediately, or whipped milk will lose its volume.

Makes 8 servings
(155 calories per serving)

Frozen Bananas

2 large, firm bananas
1 tablespoon freshly squeezed lemon juice
2 tablespoons honey, warmed
2 tablespoons Coconut Sugar (page 60)

Line a baking sheet with waxed paper.

Cut bananas into halves, crosswise, and brush lightly with lemon juice to prevent darkening. Insert popsicle sticks into cut ends of banana halves. Brush honey on all surfaces of bananas. Roll in Coconut Sugar, place on prepared baking sheet, and freeze until firm. Wrap individually and return to freezer.

Makes 4 servings
(72 calories per serving)

MAY

Selecting Fresh Fruit,
the Dieter's Ally

FRUIT OF THE MONTH: **BLUEBERRIES**

DESSERT OF THE MONTH: **BLUEBERRY ICE MILK**

DRINK OF THE MONTH: **COMPANY PUNCH**

				1	2	3
				BLUEBERRIES WITH MAPLE YOGURT	LIGHT COFFEE SOUFFLÉ	PINEAPPLE SNOW
4	5	6	7	Mother's Day 8	9	10
SKINNY PEACH PUDDING	STRAWBERRY BLISS	BLUEBERRY ICE MILK ★	PRUNE CUPCAKES	CARNATION CASSATA	SPRING DOVE	RUBY RED GRANITA
11	12	13	14	15	16	17
LOVELY LEMON SQUARES	BLUEBERRY TANGERINE PIE	PAPAYA FLUFF	TAPIOCA PARFAITS	ORANGE PUDDING	PURPLE POPS	PEACHY RASPBERRY TORTE
18	19	20	21	22	23	24
LIME CHIFFON PIE	½ CUP FRESH BLUEBERRIES WITH ¼ CUP SKIM MILK	STRAWBERRY PECAN CREPE ROLLS	MANGO YOGURT PUDDING	BANANA SMOOTHIES	LITE MERINGUE KISSES	PRUNE CONFECTIONS
25	26	27	28	29	Memorial 30 Day	31
BANANA STRAWBERRY FREEZE	PAPAYA LAYER CAKE	APPLESAUCE MERINGUE	STRAWBERRY PEACH PIE	PAPAYA BASKETS	CRUSTLESS BLUEBERRY CHEESECAKE	STRAWBERRY RHUBARB PIE WITH MERINGUE CRUST

The beauty of fruit for the dieter is that it's nutritious and mostly low calorie, it makes you feel full due to its high fiber content, and some kinds are available in the markets during every month of the year. Add to all that the natural sweetness it imparts to desserts and you have a near-perfect diet food.

Selecting fruits at their succulent best can mean the difference between creating a superior dessert and one that's just so-so. While some fruits are always abundant, each fruit has a special season, and that's when its quality excels. Happily, when a fruit is truly in season, it is also least expensive.

Choosing fruit is an art you can learn. Your eyes, nose, and fingers are all good indicators of the quality of a piece of fruit—don't be afraid to use them. A superior specimen adds so much to the finished dish, especially when fruit is used raw.

Purchase ripe fruit close to the time you're planning to use it. With few exceptions, such as citrus fruits and apples, fruit is delicate and wilts quickly. If you're buying unripe fruit, you need to know how long it will take to ripen so you can plan its use. Don't be tempted by sale fruit that's past its prime unless you're planning to make jam or preserves. Even then, by the time you've cut out all the bruised and spoiled spots, you may find you've actually paid more per pound than you would have for top quality.

Individual Fruits and
What You Should Know about Them

Here are some fruits I use often in making desserts with tips on how to select, ripen, and store them so they can be enjoyed at top quality.

Apples: One of America's favorite fruits, apples are available year round.
They range from fiery red to the palest of yellows—from sugary sweet to lemony sour. The type of apple you select depends entirely on

how you intend to use it. For instance, those wonderfully sweet, Red Delicious apples are a delight to sink your teeth into, living up to their name, but they're not good for cooking.

Look for apples that have good color for their variety and unbroken, unbruised skins. Bruises indicate that the fruit has been subjected to freezing temperatures, which apples can't withstand. Scald (tan or brown spots so common on apples) affects only the portion of apple where it occurs; just cut out and discard the affected part.

Handle each apple before you buy, if possible. It should feel uniformly firm, not mushy or soft in spots. Soft apples have a mealy texture; you want crispness.

Although there are many wonderful varieties of tart apples for cooking, I usually opt for a sweet apple in cooking desserts. This cuts down on the sweetener necessary to produce a delectable dessert. The bright red Cortland is one of my favorites for pies. The York apple with its light red background speckled with russet is a marvelous all-around cooking apple that, because of its firmness, retains its shape—not disintegrating as some juicier apples do during cooking. The Winesap, while slightly less sweet than the other two, is an excellent pie apple. But use a trifle more thickener than you do with Yorks since Winesaps are very juicy apples. Golden Delicious are also firm, and I favor them for cooking.

Apples that aren't fully mature before picking lack both flavor and color. Don't rely on time to ripen them. It won't happen.

If you're buying apples in the net bags in which they're so frequently sold, avoid any labeled U.S. No. 2—they're a low grade. Instead look for U.S. Extra Fancy, U.S. Fancy, or U.S. No. 1.

Apples will keep in a cool place or in the refrigerator during hot weather. Heat wilts them prematurely. But in the right environment, apples stay useable for several weeks, although they may become rather lackluster after a week or two. Don't store them near vegetables; apples give off ethylene gas which causes many vegetables to spoil.

Apricots: This ancient fruit with a distinctive flavor has been grown in California since 1792 and dates back to before the birth of Christ.

If you've ever bitten into an apricot and found it startlingly sour, you've eaten one that was picked before it had a chance to mature. Immature apricots have a greenish tinge. Avoid them; they'll never be good eating! Plump flesh of golden-orange fruit, yielding to slight pressure without feeling mushy, is the hallmark of an apricot at its best. A yellow rather than golden hue signals an over-mature specimen.

Utah and Washington State now vie with California for the apricot trade. And among them they keep the markets of our country supplied with apricots during June and July. If selected at its peak, this lovely fruit will keep for a couple of days wrapped tightly in plastic and refrigerated.

Avocados: Yes, avocados are high in calories, but they're also delicious and, unlike other fruits, contain iron and protein. So I occasionally use avocado with a mixture of caution and other lower-calorie ingredients—quite sparingly.

There's no readily discernible difference between the flavor of the Fuerte (winter avocado) and the Haas (summer avocado). Black or purple spots are a sign of decay on either variety as are cracked or broken skins. Avocados must be fully ripe before they're used. A ripe avocado is almost squishy soft. Allow firm fruit to ripen for three to five days at room temperature. If you purchase a fully ripe avocado and don't wish to use it immediately, store it, unwrapped, in the refrigerator.

Bananas: There's a lot to be said for bananas: most people like them, they know no season, and they're good diet fare.

While most fruit should be harvested when fully ripe, bananas are always picked green. They do much of their ripening in transit to our markets. As they ripen, bananas turn from green to yellow. When the fruit becomes flecked with brown and softens to the touch, it's perfect for use. Dark brown patches indicate overripe bananas — undesirable for either eating or cooking as the flesh is usually dark brown, too.

Chiquita Banana notwithstanding, to keep a ripe banana from going bad, store it in the refrigerator for a day or so. This may cause the skin to darken, but it will preserve the flesh of the fruit. But an unripe banana must be stored at room temperature—the chill of the refrigerator will halt its ripening process permanently.

Blueberries: May through September is blueberry season. And if you're lucky enough to live in an area where you can go blueberry picking, you know the glorious flavor of freshly picked berries, eaten plain or with a bit of milk or cream. But the rest of us, who rely on the local market or farmstand, must select berries cautiously.

Fresh blueberries picked at their prime, have a dark blue color touched with a silverish coating. The bloom, as this coating is called, isn't a spray, but a natural phenomenon protecting the freshness of the berries. Blueberries should be plump with dry skins, free of slime. No stems or leaves should be in the basket you select. Keep blueberries in the refrigerator for no more than three days lightly covered, so they can breathe.

Cantaloupes (Muskmelons): This familiar low-calorie melon has a strong flavor. Cantaloupes should ripen on the vine; they separate from their stems when fully ripe. Unfortunately, they're often picked prematurely. Look for a small indentation at the stem end that's well-formed and smooth. If a melon is picked too early, the indentation has a ragged appearance, indicating the fruit was ripped from the stem.

The netting on a cantaloupe should stand out from the rest of the surface and be coarse and well defined. The color underneath the netting shouldn't be green, but rather light yellowish, gray, or tan. A green melon won't ripen, but it will rot. If the color under the netting is a bright yellow, the melon is overripe.

Your nose is an invaluable resource in selecting melons. When a cantaloupe reaches its peak of ripeness, it has a strong but pleasant melonlike aroma. Then it's best for eating. A day later it will be overripe. The blossom end of a ripe cantaloupe yields to slight pressure.

Cantaloupes flood the markets from May through September. A ripe one can be kept, tightly wrapped, in the refrigerator for a couple of days, but the aroma is so strong it may taint some of your other foods, so keep it away from butter and like items. Hold unripe cantaloupe at room temperature until the blossom end is soft.

Cherries: Can you bake a cherry pie and stay on a diet? The answer is a definite yes! But while cherry pies are traditionally made with sour cherries, I use the sweeter varieties to avoid having to load the pies with sweeteners.

When you're shopping for cherries keep in mind that the darker fruit is sweeter. Bing, Black Tartarian, Chapman, Lambert, and Schmidt are all acceptable varieties. Cherries should have their stems intact (they help keep the fruit fresh), and the stems should look bright and alive rather than dried out. A healthy cherry is fat and glossy with no signs of brown spots or leaking skin.

In most places you'll find cherries on the market from May through August, but they're best and most plentiful in June and July.

Cherries are highly perishable. They should be stored in a basket or other airy container, uncovered, with stems still on and used as soon as possible—ideally the day of purchase, but certainly within two days.

Cranberries: The little red berry that conjures up visions of Pilgrims, Thanksgiving, and turkey is also a tasty ingredient for desserts. Unfortunately, cranberries are usually sold in sealed plastic bags bearing printed information, which makes it almost impossible to tell what the berries look like. But if you're lucky enough to find berries that aren't packaged this way, look for firm, plump berries with shiny skins. Most varieties are dark red when ripe, but there are some that have a bright red skin. Shun any soft berries. They'll be sour and give your recipe an "off" taste.

Cranberries are plentiful from September through January, although you'll find the supply at its peak during November and December.

Lightly covered and refrigerated, they'll keep for several weeks.

Grapefruits: What experienced dieter isn't familiar with this citrus fruit? It's as much a staple of dieting as cottage cheese.

The pink varieties are sweeter than the more traditional yellow. Whichever color you prefer, look for fruit that feels firm and heavy for its size. Although the fruit should be uniformly firm, it also should have a slightly spongy feeling when pressed. This sponginess indicates a thin skin and a juicy flesh. If the stem end of the grapefruit is pointed, the skin is thick and the fruit won't be as juicy. A mottled skin with uneven color has no bearing on the quality of the fruit inside.

This good source of vitamins A and C is available year round but is in greatest abundance January through May.

Grapefruits keep nicely in the refrigerator for several weeks.

Grapes: Seedless Thompson grapes are the most popular and the ones you'll find in greatest abundance in the markets. They're sweeter and a bit higher in calories than other grape varieties, such as the Concord, so you may wonder why I use them so often in my diet recipes. The answer is simple—they don't need added sweetener as do some other types of grapes.

When selecting grapes, look for healthy-appearing, greenish stems, bearing firm-fleshed fruit. Green grapes should be yellow tinged, while darker varieties should have an even color. Leaking or wrinkled grapes are past their prime so pass them by.

These little gems are available all year. They're quite perishable but will keep, uncovered, in the refrigerator for about three days.

Honeydew Melons: Slightly higher in calories than the cantaloupe, the milder tasting honeydew is nonetheless worthy of a place in the menu of a dieter. The season for honeydews goes from June through October. Although a few can be found in the other months, they'll be of poor quality.

Look for honeydew with smooth, white to yellow skins—never greenish—with only slight netting. Store them as you would cantaloupes.

Kiwi Fruits (Chinese Gooseberries): This Johnny-come-lately to the American marketplace has become a favorite in fruit salads and as a garnish, but it's a useful addition to desserts as well. I've seen kiwis in the local markets all year, but I find the summer fruit far more desirable.

The kiwi's brown, fuzzy surface yields to slight pressure when the fruit is ripe. The bright green flesh, flecked with tiny, black, edible seeds, has a flavor that suggests a mixture of strawberry, pineapple, and papaya. A ripe kiwi will keep in the refrigerator, uncovered, for about three days.

Lemons: From California and Arizona come enough lemons to keep the country supplied year round with this tart, useful fruit. When lemons are their fresh best, they sport smooth, blemish-free, bright yellow skins. A pale yellow or greenish skin holds an acceptable, although slightly inferior, lemon. But dark yellow or hard skins are certain indications the fruit is dried out and tasteless.

Since lemons are so plentiful, there's no reason to settle for inferior fruit, ever.

Lemons keep well for about two weeks when stored in a refrigerator. I always use freshly squeezed lemon juice in my recipes. Even if it's only a tablespoon or two, the difference between fresh and bottled is monumental.

Limes: Used almost interchangeably with lemons by many cooks, the lime is deserving of a place of its own in the culinary world.

Most of the limes commonly found in our markets are Persian or Tahitian limes. At its best this fruit is bright green and glossy. A purplish-brown spot on the skin, scald, is undesirable only in an advanced stage.

Key limes, which are far more difficult to come by in most parts of the country, are greenish yellow and, of course, are the main ingredients of the famous key lime pie. Although you'll find limes year round, during the winter months you may have to search to find respectable ones. They'll keep for about two weeks stored, uncovered, in the refrigerator or in a cool room.

Mangoes: A fairly recent gift to us from the tropics, mangoes are ready for use when their skins are green with yellow or red areas. They will yield to slight pressure. You'll find mangoes in plenty from May through August. You can keep them in the refrigerator for a maximum of three days.

Nectarines: Don't buy nectarines that are shriveled or have cracked skin. The fully ripe, ideal nectarine yields to pressure along the indentation but the skin stays intact. If it's past its prime, you'll find the fruit leaky when pressed.

If you don't intend to use nectarines for a few days, purchase hard ones and allow them to ripen at room temperature. Ripe nectarines will hold their quality for a day or so in the refrigerator.

Although June and July are the best months for nectarines, you'll find them in the markets in August and September as well.

Oranges: What would we do without the sunshine fruit? It adds flavor to pies, cakes, puddings, and the juice is a healthy thirst quencher and useful ingredient in so many desserts. To top it off, the orange is available year round.

Oranges should feel heavy for their size and be firm to the touch. Pineapple and Navel oranges are good eating, while Parson Browns and Hamlins are better juicers.

The skin color of oranges covers the spectrum from greenish orange to a mottled orange with white or golden spots. Russeting, those tan to black spots you see on Florida or Texas oranges, is a sign of thin skin and good quality. Many oranges are dyed an even orange color and should be so labeled.

I never buy oranges in bags, preferring to select each fruit individually, handling it and making sure I have the best there is to offer. Bags are admittedly cheaper, but the few times I've succumbed to the lure of a good buy, I've found at least one rotten orange in the bag.

Oranges keep well for several weeks in the refrigerator.

Papayas: I just love this fruit with its naturally sweet, juicy goodness and flavor that's a cross between a cantaloupe and a peach. But I limit my use of them to May and June when they're most abundant and least expensive. However, if you wish to eat papayas in January, you'll probably find them in your local market.

Whatever season you buy them, look for yellow, greenish yellow, or green and yellow fruit that yields to gentle pressure. Ripe papayas keep for up to two days in the refrigerator.

Peaches: Of the two varieties of peaches, Freestone is what you're more apt to find in the market. Clingstone, the other type, has stones that cling stubbornly to the flesh and is used mostly for canning. The skin of a peach, may be either fuzzy or smooth, although the smooth variety has gained in popularity. A healthy ripe fruit is yellow or cream-colored with red areas. If a peach is green, don't buy it. It was picked before maturity and will never ripen. Bruised peaches are a poor choice no matter how much of a bargain they seem. They spoil very quickly.

July and August are the prime "peachy" months, but this fruit is available May through September.

Keep ripe peaches in the refrigerator and use them within a day or two. Leave unripened peaches at room temperature for a day or two and they'll ripen nicely.

Pears: Among the many varieties of this fruit, Bartletts are the most common. Pears are stubborn about ripening and purchasing them with this expectation is usually doomed to failure. You'll most often end up with rotten rather than ripe fruit. Instead, choose ripe pears that yield to soft pressure and have unblemished skins. They'll keep in your refrigerator for up to three days. Pears are available year round.

Persimmons: The plump persimmon is deep red with black flecks when ripe, but it can be purchased when it's yellowish orange and ripened at home. A ripe persimmon yields to pressure. Once ripe, the persimmon keeps well, uncovered, in the refrigerator for up to four days. This fruit will add to your dessert pleasure from October through November.

Pineapples: A pleasing aroma indicates a good ripe pineapple. If the odor is the least bit off, the pineapple has started to decay. Look for plump heavy fruit. Red Spanish and Smooth Cayeen are the two varieties in most American markets. When unripe they're green. A gorgeous orangy-yellow color emerges as the fruit ripens. A healthy pineapple has slightly separated eyes. Sunken eyes or bruises are signs of inferior fruit. Thanks to good transportation and improved storage, we can now enjoy pineapple year round.

Contrary to common opinion, pineapples should never be stored at room temperature. The Pineapple Growers' Association of Hawaii claims pineapple must be picked when ripe and will quickly ferment at room temperature. It will, however, keep for a week in the refrigerator. I believe they know what they're talking about, so I always keep fresh pineapple refrigerated, and with good success.

Plums: Did you ever bite into an unripe plum? They're so sour they make your lips pucker! Plums sweeten as they ripen, and no plum should be eaten before its time.

Though the color may range from red to purple, the skin should be even in color and unbroken. Leaky fruit is overripe fruit.

You'll find plums in abundance from June through September. What's offered during the winter months is, in my opinion, a poor excuse for the lush plum you'll get in season.

If plums aren't ripe when you buy them, a day or two at room temperature should do the trick. Then it's into the refrigerator, uncovered, where they'll stay fresh for another day or two.

Raspberries: One of the reasons I love summer is that it's raspberry season. From June through August, the luscious red berries are in great supply. But July is really raspberry month — the time when they're most abundant and the best eating.

Good red color and uniform size are indications of sweet eating berries. Although the small cells should look succulent, they shouldn't be leaking or mushy. These most marvelous of berries will keep in the refrigerator for a day or two (if you can resist them for that long).

Strawberries: I was delighted when I learned that strawberries would be available year round. Imagine fresh strawberry pie in January — what decadence! But I have found that the berries marketed in off months are over-large with a great deal of unappetizing white outside and very little juice or flavor inside. They're lifeless imitations of the real berries you'll find only from April to June.

Look for plump, red berries with bright green caps. If the caps are dried out, chances are the berries are too. Avoid leaking strawberries or those with mold. Examine the berries in the bottom of the basket as well.

Strawberries keep, lightly covered, in the refrigerator for up to three days.

Watermelons: I never buy a whole watermelon. It's virtually impossible to tell what secrets the green skin holds without cutting into it. I look for bright red, watery flesh with black or brown seeds and few, if any, white streaks. An immature melon has greenish seeds.

Watermelon, which is available May through September, will keep, covered, in the refrigerator for up to five days.

Unsweetened frozen fruit is a viable alternative when fresh fruit is out of season, and in many recipes the difference between frozen and fresh fruit is hardly discernible.

Most frozen fruit will keep for about ten months. To use it, thaw it in your refrigerator for eight to ten hours. Many people thaw frozen fruit at room temperature for about four hours. I'm not comfortable doing this and prefer the safer refrigerator method. And, of course, I never thaw anything under warm water! I do sometimes thaw fruit in my microwave, carefully following directions. And some recipes facilitate the use of frozen fruit without the bother of thawing it, particularly if the fruit is individually frozen, such as blueberries or strawberries, and can be removed from the package in separate pieces instead of in one large frozen mass.

Store all fresh fruit unwashed. Water hastens the decaying process. But do wash fruit well before using it.

Purple Pops

¾ cup milk
1 cup grape juice
¼ cup honey

Blend all ingredients in a blender. Divide among 8 2-ounce pop molds and freeze.

Makes 8 pops
(68 calories per pop)

Light Coffee Soufflé

This soufflé rises so high, it may push against the oven shelf above it. So I remove all shelves except the one on which the soufflé cooks.

2 tablespoons cornstarch
1½ teaspoons decaffeinated instant coffee
3 tablespoons honey
1 cup evaporated skim milk
2 teaspoons vanilla extract
½ teaspoon orange extract
6 egg whites
¼ teaspoon cream of tartar

Remove all but lower rack of oven. Preheat oven to 375°F. Fit a 2½-quart casserole or soufflé dish with a soufflé collar.*

In a large saucepan, blend together cornstarch and coffee. Mix in honey and skim milk, and cook over medium heat, stirring constantly, until mixture thickens. Remove from heat and stir in extracts.

In a large bowl, beat egg whites until foamy. Add cream of tartar and continue beating until stiff peaks form. Mix a small amount of beaten egg whites into coffee mixture to lighten. Fold in remaining whites and turn into prepared casserole or soufflé dish. (Or you may wish to use individual soufflé cups.) Bake for about 25 minutes (15 minutes for cups), or until soufflé has risen and is golden on top. Serve immediately.

Makes 8 servings
(69 calories per serving)

*To make a soufflé collar, cut a piece of foil 10 inches wide and long enough to encircle soufflé dish plus 2 inches. Fold lengthwise. Tie collar around dish with string, allowing foil to extend 3 inches above rim of dish. Tape seam together. Butter or oil inside of collar.

Skinny Peach Pudding

1½ envelopes unflavored gelatin
½ cup cold water
1 cup skim milk
3 tablespoons honey
4 cups ripe, peeled peaches
1 teaspoon almond extract

In a small saucepan, sprinkle gelatin over cold water and set aside to soften for 5 minutes. Add skim milk and honey and heat, stirring constantly, until milk is scalding.

In a food processor, puree peaches. Turn peach puree into a large bowl. Mix in milk mixture and almond extract. Divide among 8 dessert dishes and chill until set.

Makes 8 servings
(73 calories per serving)

Blueberries with Maple Yogurt

1 cup plain low-fat yogurt
3 tablespoons maple syrup
1 teaspoon vanilla extract
2 cups fresh blueberries

In a medium-size bowl, lightly mix together yogurt, maple syrup, and vanilla. Fold in blueberries and chill.

Makes 6 servings
(76 calories per serving)

Pineapple Snow

1 8-ounce can unsweetened crushed pineapple
2 teaspoons unflavored gelatin
1 tablespoon honey
½ teaspoon vanilla extract
1 egg white

Spray a 4-cup dessert mold with vegetable spray.

Drain pineapple, reserving juice. Add enough water to juice to make 1 cup.

In a medium-size saucepan, sprinkle gelatin over juice. Set aside for 5 minutes to soften. Mix in honey and heat, stirring, until gelatin is dissolved. Add vanilla and chill until thickened but not set, about 35 minutes.

In a medium-size bowl, beat egg white until stiff peaks form, then beat into thickened gelatin. Fold in pineapple and turn into mold.

Makes 4 servings
(103 calories per serving)

Prune Cupcakes

½ cup whole wheat pastry flour, divided
½ cup unbleached white flour
1 teaspoon baking powder
½ teaspoon ground cinnamon
¼ teaspoon ground nutmeg
¼ cup honey
½ cup prune juice
⅓ cup vegetable oil
1 egg
1 teaspoon vanilla extract
¼ cup prunes

Preheat oven to 350°F. Line a 12-cup muffin tin with paper liners.

In a medium-size bowl, sift together all but 2 teaspoons of the whole wheat pastry flour, unbleached white flour, baking powder, cinnamon, and nutmeg. Whisk to blend. Mix in honey, prune juice, oil, egg, and vanilla. Beat for 3 minutes.

In a food processor, finely chop prunes with remaining whole wheat pastry flour. Fold into batter.

Divide among prepared muffin cups and bake on middle shelf of oven until a cake tester inserted into centers comes out clean, 20 to 25 minutes.

Remove from tin and cool on wire racks.

Makes 12 servings
(121 calories per serving)

Ladyfingers

This classic cake is an invaluable ingredient for many desserts.

3 eggs, separated
3 tablespoons honey
½ teaspoon vanilla extract
½ cup sifted whole wheat
    pastry flour

½ cup sifted unbleached
    white flour
1 tablespoon cornstarch
⅛ teaspoon cream of tartar

Preheat oven to 350°F. Line 2 baking sheets with parchment paper.

In a large bowl, beat egg yolks until golden. Add honey and beat for 10 minutes until ribbons form. Mix in vanilla.

Sift together whole wheat pastry flour, unbleached white flour, and cornstarch into a medium-size bowl. Whisk to blend. Fold flour mixture into egg mixture, a little at a time.

In a medium-size bowl, beat egg whites until foamy. Add cream of tartar and beat until stiff peaks form.

Fold beaten whites into batter. Put batter into pastry bag with ¾-inch opening. Squeeze 24 lengths of dough, about 3 inches long and about 1 inch apart, onto prepared baking sheets. Bake each batch on middle shelf of oven for 10 to 12 minutes, or until lightly browned.

Remove carefully with a spatula and cool on wire racks.

Makes 2 dozen fingers
(38 calories per finger)

Lite Meringue Kisses

Be sure to bake these meringues long enough for them to become dry. If they're underbaked they'll be sticky inside.

3 egg whites
⅛ teaspoon cream of tartar
¼ cup maple syrup
1 teaspoon vanilla extract

Preheat oven to 225°F. Line 2 baking sheets with parchment.

In a medium-size bowl, beat egg whites until foamy. Add cream of tartar and continue to beat, gradually adding maple syrup and vanilla, until whites are very stiff and dry.

Drop mixture by teaspoonfuls onto prepared baking sheets. Bake each batch on middle shelf of oven until lightly browned and dry, about 60 to 70 minutes.

Allow to cool before removing from baking sheet.

Makes 90 kisses
(3 calories per cookie)

Crustless Blueberry Cheesecake

2 cups part-skim ricotta cheese
3 eggs
2 tablespoons cornstarch
2 tablespoons honey
1 teaspoon almond extract
1 teaspoon vanilla extract
1½ cups fresh blueberries

Preheat oven to 325°F. Butter a 9-inch pie plate.

In a large bowl, beat ricotta and eggs together until smooth. Add cornstarch, honey, and extracts and beat just until blended. Turn into prepared pie plate and bake on middle shelf of oven for 1 hour.

Chill. Just before serving, top with blueberries.

Makes 8 servings
(160 calories per serving)

 ## Blueberry Ice Milk

3 cups fresh blueberries
⅓ cup honey
2 cups skim milk
1 teaspoon vanilla extract

In a medium-size saucepan, heat blueberries and honey to boiling, stirring constantly. Reduce heat and simmer for 10 minutes. Puree mixture in a blender. Strain pureed berries into a large bowl. Stir in skim milk and vanilla.

Process mixture in an ice cream maker according to manufacturer's instructions, or turn mixture into a pan, cover, and put in freezer until thickened but not frozen solid. Remove from freezer, beat to break down ice crystals, and then return to freezer. Repeat this procedure twice, putting ice milk into a covered container the last time before returning it to freezer. Freeze until ready to serve.

Makes 8 servings
(95 calories per serving)

Banana Smoothies

1 envelope unflavored gelatin
½ cup water
1⅓ cups cold water
⅔ cup nonfat dry milk
1 egg
2 tablespoons honey
2 teaspoons vanilla extract
2 bananas
    ground nutmeg for sprinkling,
        optional

In a small saucepan, sprinkle gelatin over water. Set aside for 5 minutes to soften. Heat over medium heat, stirring constantly, until gelatin dissolves.

Blend together cold water, nonfat dry milk, egg, honey, and vanilla in a blender. Add gelatin mixture and blend.

Cut bananas into small pieces, dividing them among 8 dessert dishes. Pour gelatin mixture on top and chill until set.

Sprinkle with nutmeg before serving, if desired.

Makes 8 servings
(90 calories per serving)

Lovely Lemon Squares

1 recipe for Skinny Piecrust
    (page 5)
2 eggs
⅓ cup honey
¼ cup whole wheat pastry flour
1 teaspoon baking powder
⅓ cup freshly squeezed lemon juice
½ teaspoon lemon extract

Preheat oven to 425°F. Spray an 8 × 8-inch pan with vegetable spray.

Roll piecrust into an 8-inch square. Place on bottom of prepared pan and bake blind on middle shelf of oven until lightly browned, about 10 minutes. Remove from oven and reduce heat to 350°F.

In a large bowl, slightly beat eggs and honey.

Sift together flour and baking powder into a small bowl. Whisk to blend. Beat into egg mixture. Beat in lemon juice and extract and pour over crust. Bake on middle shelf of oven for 20 minutes.

Cool in pan and cut into 9 squares.

Makes 9 servings
(135 calories per serving)

Blueberry Tangerine Pie

1 recipe for Mini Piecrust
    (page 104)
3 cups fresh or unsweetened
    frozen blueberries
2 tangerines, peeled and sectioned
3 tablespoons cornstarch
½ teaspoon ground cinnamon
½ cup honey

Preheat oven to 425°F. Spray a 9-inch pie plate with vegetable spray and line it with pie crust. Partially bake crust blind according to directions.

Put blueberries into a large bowl. Halve tangerine sections and add blueberries. Toss with cornstarch and cinnamon. Add honey and toss again.

Fill prepared piecrust with mixture. Cover with foil but do not let it touch filling. Bake on middle shelf of oven until crust is golden and filling bubbly, about 45 minutes.

Remove foil and allow to cool. Serve warm or cold.

Makes 8 servings
(145 calories per serving)

Spring Dove

1 large, ripe cantaloupe
1 cup fresh watermelon balls
½ cup fresh blueberries
1 cup halved fresh strawberries
½ cup halved seedless green grapes

Carve out cantaloupe dove according to instructions on page 216, using melon baller to remove cantaloupe flesh. Mix together cantaloupe balls and remaining ingredients. Pile into cantaloupe dove and serve.

Makes 8 servings
(32 calories per serving)

Ruby Red Granita

¼ cup honey
3 cups red grape juice
2 cups water
1 teaspoon lemon extract
   kiwi fruit, optional

Mix together honey and grape juice in a large bowl. Stir in water and extract. Turn into a large metal pan and freeze until ice crystals begin to form, about 1½ hours. Beat well to break down crystals. Return to freezer and freeze for another 5 hours, breaking down crystals every 30 minutes. Turn into a lightly oiled, decorative 8-cup mold and return to freezer.

When ready to serve, unmold and decorate with kiwi fruit, if desired.

Makes 10 servings
(76 calories per serving)

Strawberry Bliss

1 pint fresh strawberries
¼ cup honey
1 tablespoon butter
½ teaspoon ground cinnamon
1 teaspoon orange extract
2 cups plain low-fat yogurt

Quarter strawberries. (Cut them into halves if they're small.) Place strawberries, honey, and butter into a medium-size saucepan. Cook over medium heat, stirring constantly, until berries soften a bit and give up some juice, making a pink sauce. Remove from heat and stir in cinnamon and orange extract. Allow to cool.

Serve in 4 dessert dishes topped with yogurt.

Makes 4 servings
(180 calories per serving)

Tapioca Parfaits

1 recipe for Fluffy Almond Tapioca
   (page 80), **divided**
½ cup **Ruby Raspberry Sauce**
   (page 127), **divided**
½ cup **Peach Sauce** (page 120),
   divided

Place ¼ cup of the Fluffy Almond Tapioca into 4 dessert glasses. Top each with 2 tablespoons of the raspberry sauce. Divide remaining tapioca among glasses. Top each with 2 tablespoons of the Peach Sauce.

Makes 4 servings
(130 calories per serving)

Mini Piecrust

This thin piecrust eliminates the crimped edge that contains the lion's share of calories in the average pie while still providing the delicate flavor of pastry with every bite. It is a bit difficult to roll out, but it's well worth the effort.

¼ **cup whole wheat pastry**
   flour
¼ **cup unbleached white**
   flour

2 **tablespoons vegetable oil**
   ice water

In a small bowl, combine whole wheat pastry flour and unbleached white flour with a wire whisk. Sprinkle oil on top and work in with a fork. Add ice water a teaspoon at a time, blending after each addition, just until mixture holds together. Press into a flat round. Wrap in plastic wrap and chill thoroughly.

Roll out lightly floured dough into a circle between 2 pieces of waxed paper. Remove both pieces of waxed paper carefully. Lightly dust 1 side of the crust with flour. Line a 9-inch pie plate with dough, placing flour side down. Dough should come almost to top of pie plate. To bake blind, prick bottom and sides with a fork and bake on bottom shelf of preheated 425°F oven until lightly browned, about 10 minutes.

Makes 1 piecrust
(8   58-calorie servings)

Peachy Raspberry Torte

This is a showy finish for a company meal.

    4 egg whites, at room temperature
    ⅛ teaspoon cream of tartar
    3 tablespoons honey
    1 teaspoon vanilla extract
    2 fresh peaches
    1 cup fresh raspberries
    1 cup Slim Pastry Cream
       (page 246)

Preheat oven to 275°F. Butter and lightly flour a large baking sheet. With a 7-inch saucepan cover, mark 2 circles on baking sheet.

In a large bowl, beat egg whites until foamy. Add cream of tartar. Gradually drizzle in honey and vanilla, beating until stiff peaks form. Divide between circles on baking sheet, spreading mixture to edges of circles. Bake on middle shelf of oven 40 to 45 minutes.

Cool meringues before removing from baking sheet. Just before serving, peel, pit, and chop peaches. In a medium-size bowl, mix them, along with raspberries, into pastry cream. Put half of the fruit mixture on the first meringue, spreading to edges. Place the second meringue on top and spread with remaining fruit mixture.

Makes 8 to 10 servings
(112 to 90 calories per serving)

Lime Chiffon Pie

    1 recipe for Meringue Pie Shell
       (page 107)
    1 envelope unflavored gelatin
    3 tablespoons freshly squeezed
       lime juice
    2 egg yolks
    ⅓ cup honey
    1 teaspoon vanilla extract
    ½ cup evaporated skim milk, chilled
       natural green food coloring,
       optional
    4 thin slices lime, halved, optional

Bake pie shell according to directions.

Sprinkle gelatin over lime juice and set aside for 5 minutes to soften.

In top of a double boiler, beat together egg yolks and honey. Beat in lime-gelatin mixture. Set over hot water and cook over low heat. Continue beating until gelatin dissolves, about 7 minutes. Remove from heat, and beat in vanilla. Allow to cool.

In a large, chilled bowl, beat evaporated skim milk until the consistency of whipped cream. Fold in lime mixture and green food coloring. Turn into pie shell and refrigerate until set.

Before serving, decorate with lime slices, if desired.

Makes 8 servings
(88 calories per serving)

Orange Pudding

This light and luscious pudding is as good warm as it is chilled.

2 eggs, separated
⅛ teaspoon cream of tartar
¼ cup honey, divided
½ cup freshly squeezed orange juice
2 tablespoons cornstarch
1 cup skim milk, divided
1 teaspoon orange extract

Preheat oven to 350°F. Spray a 1½-quart casserole with vegetable spray.

In a medium-size bowl, beat egg whites until foamy. Add cream of tartar and continue beating until stiff peaks form. Drizzle in 1 tablespoon of the honey and beat just until blended.

In a medium-size bowl, beat egg yolks. Beat in orange juice and remaining honey.

Stir cornstarch into ¼ cup of the skim milk. In a medium-size saucepan, heat remaining milk to scalding. Add cornstarch mixture and cook over low heat until thickened. Remove from heat. Add 1 cup hot mixture very slowly to egg yolk mixture, then whisk into remaining hot milk mixture. Cook over low heat, stirring constantly, until thickened. Remove from heat and let cool.

Fold in egg whites and extract. Pour into prepared casserole and place casserole in a pan of hot water. Bake on middle shelf of oven until pudding is well browned, about 45 minutes.

Makes 6 servings
(105 calories per serving)

Papaya Layer Cake

1 recipe for **Heavenly Angel Food Cake** (page 38)
½ recipe for **Papaya Fluff** (page 110), divided
½ ripe papaya, peeled and thinly sliced

Bake angel food cake according to directions.

Cut cake into halves crosswise, making 2 layers. Spread half of the Papaya Fluff on bottom layer. Put second layer over it and spread rest of the fluff filling on top of cake, allowing it to drip down sides a little. Decorate with papaya slices and serve immediately.

Makes 12 servings
(124 calories per serving)

Prune Confections

8 prunes
¼ cup chopped dates
1 tablespoon ground walnuts
1 teaspoon honey

Halve and pit prunes.

Mix together dates, walnuts, and honey in a small bowl. Use mixture to stuff prunes.

Makes 8 servings
(34 calories per serving)

Strawberry Pecan Crepe Rolls

Since these luscious crepes are served cold, they can be made ahead.

  1 cup plain nonfat yogurt
  ¼ cup ground pecans
  2 tablespoons honey
  1 teaspoon vanilla extract
  ½ teaspoon brandy extract
 16 Delicious Diet Crepes (page 30)
  1 cup Strawberry Sauce (page 230)

In a small bowl, mix together yogurt, pecans, honey, and extracts. Spread over crepes to within ¼ inch of edges. Fold crepes into fourths and chill.

Serve each topped with 1 tablespoon of the sauce.

Makes 16 servings
(86 calories per serving)

Mango Yogurt Pudding

  1 envelope unflavored gelatin
  ½ cup boiling water
  2 tablespoons honey
  1 teaspoon orange extract
  1 cup plain low-fat yogurt
  3 ripe mangoes, pureed (about
       1½ cups)
  2 tablespoons graham cracker
       crumbs, divided

Dissolve gelatin thoroughly in boiling water. Mix in honey, then all other ingredients except graham cracker crumbs.

Divide among 4 dessert dishes. Sprinkle top of each with ½ tablespoon cracker crumbs. Chill.

Makes 4 servings
(194 calories per serving)

Meringue Pie Shell

  3 egg whites
  ⅛ teaspoon cream of tartar

  1 tablespoon honey
  ½ teaspoon vanilla extract

Preheat oven to 250°F. Butter and lightly flour a 9-inch pie plate.

In a large bowl, beat egg whites until foamy. Add other ingredients and beat until stiff peaks form. Line bottom and sides of prepared pie plate with beaten whites, spreading mixture high on sides (crust will shrink during baking). Bake on middle shelf of oven for 30 to 35 minutes, or until golden brown.

Makes 1 pie shell
(8   15-calorie servings)

Company Punch

7 cups pineapple juice
2 cups grapefruit juice
5 cups freshly squeezed orange
    juice
2 cups white grape juice
¼ cup honey, warmed

Mix all ingredients together. Chill and serve in a punch bowl over ice cubes.

Makes 32 servings
(80 calories per serving)

Papaya Baskets

2 very ripe papayas
1 cup quartered fresh strawberries,
    divided
¼ cup freshly squeezed orange juice,
    divided
¼ cup Delicious Diet Cream
    (page 109), divided

Halve papayas and scoop out seeds. Pile ¼ cup of the strawberries into each papaya half. Pour 1 tablespoon of the orange juice over each papaya half. Top each serving with 1 tablespoon of the diet cream.

Makes 4 servings
(84 calories per serving)

Applesauce Meringue

This loose, saucy pudding is a splendid dessert either warm or chilled.

2 eggs, separated
3 tablespoons honey, divided
½ cup part-skim ricotta cheese
1 teaspoon vanilla extract
1 teaspoon ground cinnamon
2 cups unsweetened Applesauce
    (page 81)
⅛ teaspoon cream of tartar

Preheat oven to 350°F. Spray a 1½-quart casserole with vegetable spray.

In a large bowl, beat egg yolks and 2 tablespoons of the honey until thick and light colored. Beat in ricotta, vanilla, and cinnamon. Fold in Applesauce and turn into prepared casserole. Bake on middle shelf of oven for 50 to 60 minutes.

Remove from oven and allow to cool slightly.

In a medium-size bowl, beat egg whites until foamy. Add cream of tartar and continue beating, drizzling in remaining honey, until stiff peaks form. Spread on top of pudding, sealing edges with beaten whites. Return to oven and bake until meringue is golden brown, 8 to 10 minutes.

Makes 8 servings
(81 calories per serving)

Delicious Diet Cream

1 20-ounce can evaporated
    skim milk, chilled

1 tablespoon honey
1½ teaspoons vanilla extract

In a large, chilled bowl, beat evaporated skim milk until foamy. Add honey and vanilla and beat to the consistency of whipped cream. Use immediately.

Makes about 6 cups
(3 calories per tablespoon)

Papaya Fluff

1 **very ripe papaya**
⅓ **cup evaporated skim milk, chilled**
1 **tablespoon honey**
½ **teaspoon orange extract**

Peel, seed, and cut papaya into chunks. Puree in a food processor or blender.

In a medium-size bowl, beat evaporated skim milk until foamy. Add honey and orange extract and continue beating until stiff peaks form. Beat in papaya puree until blended.

Makes 4 servings
(63 calories per serving)

Strawberry Rhubarb Pie with Meringue Crust

1 **recipe for Meringue Pie Shell**
   (page 107)
2 **envelopes unflavored gelatin**
1½ **cups water, divided**
2¼ **cups chopped fresh rhubarb**
1½ **cups chopped fresh strawberries**
½ **cup honey**

Bake pie shell according to directions.

In a small bowl, sprinkle gelatin over ½ cup of the water. Set aside for 5 minutes to soften.

In a medium-size saucepan, combine rhubarb, strawberries, honey, and remaining water. Bring to a boil over medium-high heat. Reduce heat and simmer for 5 minutes, stirring often. Add gelatin and stir until dissolved. Pour into a large bowl and refrigerate until thickened but not set.

Pour into pie shell and chill until set.

Makes 10 servings
(80 calories per serving)

Banana Strawberry Freeze

2 **cups halved fresh strawberries**
2 **large ripe bananas, chunked**
3 **tablespoons honey**
1 **cup skim milk**
1 **teaspoon vanilla extract**

Drop strawberries and bananas through feed tube of a food processor while machine is running and then add honey. Turn mixture into a large bowl. Mix in skim milk and vanilla.

Process mixture in an ice cream maker according to manufacturer's instructions, or place in freezer until partially frozen. Remove from freezer, beat to break down ice crystals, and then return to freezer. Repeat last procedure twice, spooning mixture into 2 1-quart containers the last time. Freeze until ready to serve.

Makes 8 servings
(82 calories per serving)

Carnation Cassata

12 Ladyfingers (page 99)
1½ cups unsweetened frozen rasp-
      berries, thawed
½ teaspoon rum extract
1 envelope unflavored gelatin
2 cups creamed cottage cheese
¼ cup honey, divided
½ cup evaporated skim milk,
      chilled
1 teaspoon vanilla extract

Line a 1½-quart casserole with plastic wrap. Arrange Ladyfingers in a single layer on top of plastic wrap.

Thoroughly drain raspberries, reserving juice in a small saucepan. Stir rum extract into reserved juice. Drizzle ¼ cup of the juice over Ladyfingers. Sprinkle gelatin over remaining juice and set aside to soften for 5 minutes.

In a large bowl, beat cottage cheese until fairly smooth. Add 3 tablespoons of the honey and beat until well blended.

Heat gelatin mixture over medium heat until gelatin dissolves. Remove from heat and beat into cheese mixture. Pour over Ladyfingers. Chill until set.

Turn dessert out onto a serving plate, carefully removing plastic wrap. Just before serving, beat evaporated skim milk in a small bowl until foamy. Drizzle in remaining honey and vanilla, and continue beating until milk is the consistency of whipped cream. Spread on cassata, top with raspberries, and serve.

Makes 10 servings
(145 calories per serving)

Strawberry Peach Pie

1 recipe for Coconut Crust
      (page 16)
3 cups fresh or unsweetened
      frozen whole strawberries
¼ cup honey
¼ cup freshly squeezed orange juice
3 tablespoons cornstarch
1 cup unsweetened frozen chunked
      peaches, thawed

Prepare Coconut Crust according to directions. Set aside to cool.

In a medium-size saucepan, combine strawberries and honey. In a jar with a tight-fitting lid, shake together orange juice and cornstarch. Add to strawberry mixture and heat, stirring constantly, until mixture thickens and becomes almost translucent. Set aside to cool.

When both piecrust and strawberries are cool, place peach chunks on bottom of piecrust. Spread strawberries on top and refrigerate until set.

Makes 10 servings
(113 calories per serving)

JUNE

Tips on Successful Dieting

FRUIT OF THE MONTH: **PEACHES**

DESSERT OF THE MONTH: **PRETTY PEACH LAYER CAKE**

DRINK OF THE MONTH: **ALMOND PEACH TREAT**

1 ENGLISH TEA CAKE	**2** FROZEN PEACH BRANDY SUPREME	**3** PUFFY APRICOT SOUFFLÉ
4 EASY GRAPE-NUTS CHERRY PUDDING	**5** CREAMY FROZEN STRAWBERRY PIE	**6** KISSEL
7 PRETTY PEACH LAYER CAKE ★	**8** PAPAYA CUSTARD	**9** FRUIT FONDUE
10 PEACHY BANANA CREPES	**11** MELON RING WITH STRAWBERRIES	**12** TWO-BERRY PIE
13 PEACH ALMOND ICE	**14** RASPBERRY CHEESE PIE	_Father's Day_ **15** BEST EVER BLUEBERRY PUFFS
16 LIGHT LEMON COOKIES	**17** POLISH BERRY SOUP	**18** PERFECT PLUM PIE
19 NECTARINE CUPS	**20** BLUEBERRY RAISIN CAKE	**21** FROZEN PEACH SOUFFLÉ
22 EASY STRAWBERRY RICE PUDDING	**23** ORIENTAL APRICOT PIE	**24** CHERRY ORANGE DELIGHT
25 ONE SUCCULENT RIPE PEACH	**26** STRAWBERRY SHELLS WITH RASPBERRY SAUCE	**27** PAPAYA MILK SHAKE
28 PINEAPPLE SURPRISE	**29** MELLOW MELON COMPOTE	**30** PEACHY ALMOND CAKE

For most of us the resolution to lose weight is like Mark Twain's declaration about giving up cigars—"It's not difficult, I've done it hundreds of times." The real problem is staying on a diet for a worthwhile period and then keeping to a sensible maintenance diet so the weight will stay off. In past years I've started on various diets with great gusto, only to lose heart rather than pounds within a week or two. The few pounds I managed to shed were soon back in place, along with the painful knowledge that I had failed myself again.

Finally the bubble of wishful thinking burst. I realized that if I were ever to lose weight and feel good about myself, I would have to do something about it now! I knew I wouldn't just wake up some morning suddenly slim, nor would I stumble onto a magic diet that effortlessly melts away pounds. I had to change my eating habits, and I had to find a way to overcome the obstacles that had kept me from doing so in the past.

With this newfound determination I began reading everything I could find on dieting. I listened to what my friends and family had to say about their successes and failures with dieting. Then I compared what I had learned with my own experiences. With hindsight it was easy to see why I had failed. I had done it all wrong. I'd concentrated on rapid weight loss programs rather than on behavior modification. I rethought my problem and came up with these ideas and bits of information that enabled me to win at the losing game.

★ A gradual weight loss is the surest way to a permanent weight loss. Avoid crash diets.

★ Keep fattening foods that might tempt you out of sight. Make a wide detour around rich food displays in shops and restaurants. Avoid all unnecessary willpower tests.

★ Eating snacks and small meals a number of times during the day can provide just as much nutrition as the larger three square meals, *and* they keep your appetite satisfied.

★ Remember that the caloric values of your snacks are part of your total daily calorie allotment (including meals), not uncounted freebies.

★ A glass of skim milk in the late evening will cut down on midnight hunger pangs.

★ Don't snack if you're not hungry. Guard against eating just to pass time.

★ Drink plenty of water before, during, and between meals to help check your appetite. Mineral water, seltzer water, and club soda can also be freely consumed. Coffee and tea, less cream or sugar, are okay in moderation, too.

★ Never stuff yourself. Stop eating as soon as you feel full. Eat some of each course at every meal to keep your diet balanced.

★ Don't concentrate on any one food at the expense of others. If a single food accounts for a quarter or more of your day's calories, your nutritional needs are probably lacking for that day.

★ If your meal includes one food high in calories, choose low-calorie foods to go with it as a way of containing your total calories.

★ Include the bulky, filling high-fiber foods in your diet. Calorie absorption from fiber is seldom complete.

★ Your main meal can be at mid-day. That way you have the rest of the day to burn off the calories.

★ Low-calorie, high-fiber diets work better than indiscriminate calorie cutting because fiber provides a full feeling. Hunger is a major cause for diet failures.

★ Salads are a wonder food for dieters, but bear in mind that a level tablespoon of commercial salad dressing contains 60 to 90 calories. Suggestion: use vinegar or a yogurt-based dressing.

★ Bread belongs on the dieter's table. It's filling and it helps provide your complex carbohydrates. Make sure it's a whole grain bread and don't use butter or other high-calorie spreads on it.

★ A diet you stay with brings the benefits of feeling better about yourself, better health, and the knowledge that you will look younger and more attractive on your next birthday than you did on your last one.

     Isn't that a dream come true?

English Tea Cake

*This light and tasty cake is frequently
served in England at tea time.*

3 eggs
⅓ cup honey
1 teaspoon vanilla extract
1 teaspoon almond extract
⅔ cup whole wheat pastry flour
⅔ cup unbleached white flour
1 teaspoon baking powder
2 tablespoons red currant jelly
2 teaspoons red grape juice

Preheat oven to 350°F. Spray bottom of an 8 × 8-inch pan with vegetable spray. Line bottom with parchment paper.

In a large bowl, beat together eggs, honey, and extracts until very thick, at least 7 minutes.

In a medium-size bowl, sift together whole wheat pastry flour, unbleached white flour, and baking powder, stirring with a wire whisk to blend. Fold into beaten eggs and turn into prepared pan, carefully smoothing top. Bake on middle shelf of oven for 20 minutes.

Cool 10 minutes in pan. Run knife around edges of pan and turn cake out onto a wire rack. Remove parchment paper and allow to cool completely.

In a small saucepan, melt jelly with grape juice. Set aside to cool until slightly thickened, about 5 minutes. Brush on top of cake.

Makes 24 tea squares
(52 calories per square)

Frozen Peach Brandy Supreme

*The small amount of half-and-half used
in this recipe gives it a deceptively creamy
texture.*

16 ounces unsweetcned frozen
     peaches, thawed
¼ cup apricot preserves
1 teaspoon brandy extract
2 teaspoons vanilla extract
2 teaspoons almond extract
1 tablespoon honey
1½ cups skim milk
½ cup half-and-half

In a food processor, puree peaches and preserves. Add extracts and process just to blend. Mix together honey, skim milk, and half-and-half in a large bowl. Add peach mixture and stir to mix.

Process mixture in an ice cream maker according to manufacturer's instructions, or turn mixture into a large, square pan and freeze until thickened but not frozen. Remove from freezer, beat to break down ice crystals, and then return to freezer. Repeat this procedure twice, packing ice milk into 2 1-quart containers the last time. Freeze until ready to serve.

Makes 8 servings
(93 calories per serving)

Puffy Apricot Soufflé

4 egg whites
¼ teaspoon cream of tartar
3 tablespoons honey
1 teaspoon vanilla extract
1 cup apricot puree (6 to 7 fresh
    apricots, peeled and pureed in
    a food processor)

Preheat oven to 300°F. Spray a 2-quart casserole with vegetable spray.

In a large bowl, beat egg whites until foamy. Add cream of tartar and continue beating, drizzling in honey and vanilla, until stiff peaks form. Fold in puree and turn into prepared casserole. Set casserole in a pan of warm water and bake on middle shelf of oven until puffy and browned, about 30 minutes. Serve immediately.

Makes 6 servings
(60 calories per serving)

Easy Grape-Nuts Cherry Pudding

2 tablespoons quick-cooking
    tapioca
2 tablespoons honey
1 egg yolk
2 cups skim milk
½ teaspoon almond extract
1 cup pitted and chopped fresh
    sweet cherries, divided
4 teaspoons grape-nuts cereal,
    divided
4 fresh sweet cherries, pitted

In a medium-size saucepan, mix together tapioca, honey, egg yolk, and skim milk. Set aside for 5 minutes for tapioca to soften.

Bring mixture to a boil and cook over medium heat for 6 to 8 minutes, stirring constantly. Remove from heat and stir in extract. Cool 20 to 30 minutes.

Divide half the pudding among 4 dessert dishes. Sprinkle ¼ cup of the chopped cherries over each serving. Divide remaining pudding among the 4 dishes, spreading over cherries. Sprinkle 1 teaspoon of the grape-nuts over each portion, top with a whole cherry, and serve.

Makes 4 servings
(134 calories per serving)

★ Pretty Peach Layer Cake

½ cup whole wheat pastry flour
½ cup unbleached white flour
1 teaspoon baking powder
2 eggs
⅓ cup plus 1 tablespoon honey
4 teaspoons freshly squeezed
   lemon juice, divided
¼ cup skim milk
4 fresh peaches
1 tablespoon honey
1 cup Delicious Diet Cream
   (page 109)

Preheat oven to 350°F.

Sift together whole wheat pastry flour, unbleached white flour, and baking powder into a small bowl. Whisk to blend.

In a large bowl, beat eggs until thick and light, about 7 minutes. Drizzle in ⅓ cup of the honey and 2 teaspoons of the lemon juice, beating for another minute.

In a small saucepan, scald skim milk.

Sift flour mixture into egg mixture gradually, folding in. Mix in hot milk quickly. Turn into 2 8-inch layer cake pans with nonstick surfaces. Bake on middle shelf of oven until cakes spring back when pressed lightly, 15 to 20 minutes.

Cool in pans inverted on wire racks.

In a small bowl, combine remaining lemon juice and remaining honey.

Peel, pit, and slice peaches. Toss with juice and honey. Put half of peaches on 1 cake layer. Top with other layer. Spread diet cream on top and arrange remaining peaches on cream.

Makes 16 servings
(87 calories per serving)

Fruit Fondue

¾ cup plain low-fat yogurt
½ cup Ruby Raspberry Sauce
   (page 127)
8 fresh strawberries
1 fresh peach
1 medium-size kiwi fruit
16 seedless green grapes

In a small bowl, combine yogurt and raspberry sauce. Chill. Before serving stir to mix.

Cut strawberries into halves. Peel, pit, and cut peach into 16 pieces. Peel and cut kiwi into eight slices, then halve slices.

Serve dip in a small bowl in the center of a plate. Surround with fruit pieces and grapes.

Makes 8 servings
(36 calories per serving)

Creamy Frozen Strawberry Pie

1 recipe for Mini Piecrust
   (page 104)
1 envelope unflavored gelatin
½ cup water
3 tablespoons honey, divided
1½ cups unsweetened frozen strawberries, thawed
¾ cup evaporated skim milk,
   chilled
1 teaspoon vanilla extract

Bake piecrust according to directions. Cool thoroughly.

In a small saucepan, sprinkle gelatin over water. Set aside for 5 minutes to soften. Heat over medium heat, stirring constantly, until gelatin dissolves. Stir in 1 tablespoon of the honey.

In a food processor, puree strawberries. Stir together gelatin mixture and pureed strawberries in a medium-size bowl. Chill until thickened but not set, about 30 minutes.

In a large bowl, beat evaporated skim milk until foamy. Add vanilla and remaining honey and beat until the consistency of whipped cream. Beat in strawberry mixture and turn into cooled pie shell. Freeze until ready to serve.

Makes 8 servings
(114 calories per serving)

Peachy Banana Crepes

1 large ripe banana
¼ cup Peach Sauce (page 120)
½ teaspoon vanilla extract
¼ teaspoon freshly squeezed lemon
   juice
4 warm Delicious Diet Crepes
   (page 30)
¼ cup plain low-fat yogurt, divided
4 fresh strawberries, optional

In a medium-size bowl, mash banana with Peach Sauce, vanilla extract, and lemon juice. Spread on crepes and roll up. Top each crepe with 1 tablespoon yogurt and a strawberry, if desired.

Makes 4 servings
(93 calories per serving)

Melon Ring with Strawberries

2 envelopes unflavored gelatin
⅔ cup boiling water
1¾ cup white grape juice
2 tablespoons freshly squeezed
   lemon juice
2 cups fresh cantaloupe balls
1 pint fresh strawberries
1 cup Mock Whipped Cream
   (page 9), **optional**

Dissolve gelatin in boiling water. Transfer to a medium-size bowl. Add grape juice and lemon juice, mixing well. Rinse a 4-cup ring mold in cold water. Distribute melon balls evenly inside mold. Pour gelatin mixture over melon balls and chill until set.

Unmold gelatin ring by running a knife around edges and then inverting it onto a plate, putting a tea towel wrung out in hot water on top of mold.

Fill center of unmolded gelatin ring with strawberries and pipe Mock Whipped Cream around bottom edge, if desired.

Makes 8 servings
(84 calories per serving)

Two-Berry Pie

This one-crust pie should be completely cooled before it's sliced or it will be runny.

2 cups fresh blueberries
2 cups fresh raspberries
½ cup water
3 tablespoons quick-cooking tapioca
⅓ cup honey
1 teaspoon almond extract
1 recipe for Mini Piecrust (page 104)

Preheat oven to 450°F. Spray a 9-inch pie plate with vegetable spray.

In a medium-size bowl, toss berries together.

In a small bowl, mix water and tapioca together and set aside for 5 minutes for tapioca to soften. Stir in honey and extract. Mix into berries well and turn into prepared pie plate, mounding slightly higher in center.

Roll out piecrust according to directions and place on top of fruit, crimping around edge with a fork. Cut generous vents in crust and bake on middle shelf of oven for 10 minutes. Reduce heat to 350°F and continue to bake until crust is lightly browned, about 30 minutes.

Makes 8 servings
(152 calories per serving)

Easy Strawberry Rice Pudding

2 cups water
1 cup brown rice
2 eggs
2 tablespoons honey
1½ cups skim milk
1 teaspoon vanilla extract
½ teaspoon strawberry extract
1 cup fresh strawberries, quartered

In a large saucepan, heat water and rice to boiling. Reduce heat, cover, and simmer until rice is soft, about 40 to 45 minutes.

In a medium-size bowl, beat eggs and honey. Stir in skim milk. Mix into rice and continue cooking, stirring constantly, until mixture thickens, about 15 minutes.

Remove from heat. Stir in extracts and strawberries.

Makes 10 servings
(115 calories per serving)

Perfect Plum Pie

This summertime favorite is easy to make, and it's delicious hot from the oven or icy cold.

3 **pounds firm fresh plums
      (16 or 17)**
3 **tablespoons quick-cooking
      tapioca**
⅔ **cup honey, warmed**
½ **teaspoon orange extract**
1 **recipe for Mini Piecrust
      (page 104)**
1 **egg white, beaten**

Preheat oven to 350°F. Spray a 1½-quart casserole with vegetable spray.

Pit and slice, but do not peel, plums into a large bowl. Toss with tapioca. Mix together honey and orange extract. Add to plums, tossing to mix. Turn into prepared casserole, and bake on baking sheet on middle shelf of oven until bubbly, about 30 minutes. Remove from oven and increase heat to 425°F.

Roll out piecrust and cut into 9-inch strips. Lay strips across plums and brush with beaten egg white. Return to oven until pastry is golden brown, about 10 minutes.

Makes 10 servings
(207 calories per serving)

Peach Sauce

2 **cups peach puree
      (about 6 medium-size
      fresh peaches)**
1 **tablespoon honey**

1 **tablespoon cornstarch**
¼ **cup water**
½ **teaspoon lemon extract**

In a medium-size saucepan, combine peach puree and honey. Dissolve cornstarch in water and then stir into puree. Bring to a boil over medium heat and cook, stirring constantly, until mixture thickens.

Remove from heat and stir in extract. Chill.

For a finer textured sauce, strain after removing from heat.

Makes about 2 cups
(11 calories per tablespoon)

Light Lemon Cookies

6 tablespoons butter, softened
¼ cup honey
1 teaspoon finely grated lemon
   peel
3 tablespoons freshly squeezed
   lemon juice
1 cup whole wheat pastry flour
1 cup unbleached white flour
1 tablespoon water, as needed

Preheat oven to 350°F. Line a 12 × 15-inch baking sheet (without sides) with foil (dull side up).

In a large bowl, beat together butter and honey. Mix in lemon peel and juice.

In a medium-size bowl, sift together whole wheat pastry flour and unbleached white flour, stirring with a wire whisk to blend. Gradually stir flour into lemon mixture. Add water if needed to form a firm but workable dough.

Shape dough into 2 rectangular pieces. Place 1 piece of dough in center of prepared baking sheet. Top with a piece of waxed paper the size of the baking sheet. Roll dough to cover baking sheet. It should be very thin. Cut into 2-inch squares, leaving them intact on the baking sheet. Bake on middle shelf of oven for 10 to 12 minutes, or until lightly browned.

Remove to wire rack to cool. Repeat rolling and baking processes with other piece of dough, using cool baking sheet.

Makes 4 dozen cookies
(37 calories per cookie)

Peach Almond Ice

2 cups water
3 cups peeled, sliced fresh peaches
½ cup honey
1½ teaspoons almond extract

In a large saucepan, bring water to a boil. Add peaches, reduce heat, and poach peaches until soft, about 10 minutes. Drain well, reserving juice, and set aside to cool.

In a food processor, puree peaches. Add reserved juice and remaining ingredients and process until blended.

Process mixture in an ice cream maker according to manufacturer's instructions or turn mixture into a large, shallow bowl or pan and place in freezer until thickened but not frozen. Remove from freezer, beat to break down ice crystals, and then return to freezer. Repeat this procedure twice, spooning mixture into a container the last time. Freeze until ready to serve.

Makes 8 servings
(89 calories per serving)

Cherry Orange Delight

1 envelope unflavored gelatin
1 cup water
3 ounces unsweetened frozen
    orange juice concentrate
1 tablespoon honey
1½ cups unsweetened frozen
    cherries

In a small saucepan, sprinkle gelatin over water. Set aside to soften for 5 minutes. Heat over medium heat, stirring constantly, until gelatin dissolves. Pour into a blender and process with remaining ingredients until liquified. Pour into dessert dishes and chill until set.

Makes 5 servings
(84 calories per serving)

Strawberry Shells
with Raspberry Sauce

1 recipe for Meringue Shells
    (page 76)
2 cups coarsely chopped fresh
    strawberries, divided
¾ cup Ruby Raspberry Sauce
    (page 127), divided

Bake Meringue Shells according to directions.
Spoon ⅓ cup of the strawberries into each Meringue Shell. Top with 2 tablespoons of the raspberry sauce and serve immediately.

Makes 6 servings
(50 calories per serving)

Blueberry Grape Sauce

A tablespoon of this sauce will add zip to a serving of ice milk, a piece of cake, a crepe, or a dish of pudding.

1½ cups unsweetened frozen
    blueberries, thawed
½ cup red grape juice

2 teaspoons cornstarch
½ cup water
1 tablespoon honey

In a medium-size saucepan, mix together blueberries and grape juice. Dissolve cornstarch in water and add to blueberries. Stir in honey. Cook over medium heat, stirring constantly, until mixture bubbles and thickens.

Remove from heat.
Serve warm.

Makes about 2 cups
(10 calories per tablespoon)

Papaya Custard

1 papaya
1 cup Slim Pastry Cream (page 246)

Peel, seed, and dice papaya.

In a medium-size bowl, mix fruit with pastry cream. Divide among 4 dessert glasses. Chill before serving.

Makes 4 servings
(95 calories per serving)

Papaya Milk Shake

2 cups skim milk
¾ cup chopped papaya pulp
2 tablespoons honey

In a food processor, blend all ingredients until very smooth. Serve immediately.

Makes 4 servings
(86 calories per serving)

Polish Berry Soup

This traditional soup is often made with either blueberries or blackberries. I prefer the combination.

1 **cup fresh blueberries**
1 **cup fresh blackberries**
2 **cups water**
¼ **cup honey**
2 **slices lemon**
1 **teaspoon ground cinnamon**
2 **cups plain nonfat yogurt**

In a medium-size saucepan, combine blueberries, blackberries, water, honey, lemon slices, and cinnamon. Bring to a boil. Reduce heat and simmer for 15 minutes.

Remove from heat and allow to cool. Remove lemon slices. Fold in yogurt and chill.

Makes 8 servings
(80 calories per serving)

Pineapple Surprise

12 **Ladyfingers** (page 99)
 1 **20-ounce can unsweetened crushed pineapple**
¼ **teaspoon brandy extract**
 1 **envelope unflavored gelatin**
 2 **cups part-skim ricotta cheese**
 3 **tablespoons honey**

Line a 2-quart casserole with plastic wrap. Arrange Ladyfingers in a single layer on the bottom and around the sides over plastic.

Drain crushed pineapple, reserving juice. Add enough water to juice to make 1½ cups. To ½ cup of the juice, add brandy extract and sprinkle mixture over Ladyfingers.

In a small saucepan, sprinkle gelatin over remaining juice. Set aside to soften for 5 minutes.

Meanwhile, beat ricotta and honey together in a large bowl.

Heat softened gelatin mixture over medium heat until gelatin dissolves. Beat into ricotta mixture. Fold in half of the drained pineapple. Turn into prepared casserole, cover with plastic wrap, and chill until set.

When ready to serve, unmold onto a serving plate. Remove plastic wrap carefully. Decorate with remaining pineapple and serve immediately.

Makes 10 servings
(146 calories per serving)

Blueberry Raisin Cake

 4 eggs
 ½ cup honey
 ¼ cup vegetable oil
 2 teaspoons vanilla extract
 ¾ cup whole wheat pastry flour
 ¾ cup unbleached white flour
 2 teaspoons baking powder
 1 teaspoon ground cinnamon
 ½ cup unsweetened frozen blueber-
      ries, thawed
 ¼ cup raisins, plumped
 ¾ cup Blueberry Grape Sauce
      (page 122), **optional**

Preheat oven to 325°F. Spray an 8 × 8-inch pan with vegetable spray.

In a large bowl, beat together eggs, honey, oil, and vanilla. Sift together whole wheat pastry flour, unbleached white flour, baking powder, and cinnamon into liquid ingredients. Mix together thoroughly.

Fold in blueberries and raisins. Turn into prepared pan and bake on middle shelf of oven until a cake tester inserted into center comes out clean, about 35 minutes.

Top each serving with a tablespoon of Blueberry Grape Sauce, if desired, and serve warm or cold.

Makes 12 servings
(178 calories per serving)

Oriental Apricot Pie

 ½ cup brown rice
 ¼ cup honey
 1 tablespoon butter
 ½ teaspoon ground cinnamon
 1 cup skim milk
 1 cup water
 2 eggs, beaten
 6 fresh apricots, pitted and cut
      into chunks
 2 teaspoons vanilla extract
 1 recipe for Skinny Piecrust
      (page 5)

Combine rice, honey, butter, cinnamon, skim milk, and water in a large saucepan. Bring to a boil, stirring constantly. Reduce heat, and simmer, covered, for 30 minutes. Remove from heat and quickly stir a little of the hot rice mixture into beaten eggs. Return to saucepan, stirring quickly. Mix in apricot chunks. Set aside to cool slightly. Stir in vanilla extract.

Preheat oven to 400°F. Spray a 9-inch pie plate with vegetable spray and line it with piecrust. Partially bake crust blind according to directions.

Fill crust with rice mixture. Lightly cover filling, but not pastry, with foil. Bake on middle shelf of oven for 30 minutes. Serve warm or cold.

Makes 8 servings
(197 calories per serving)

Best Ever Blueberry Puffs

¾ cup whole wheat pastry flour
¾ cup unbleached white flour
1¼ cups water
¼ cup butter
4 eggs, slightly beaten
2 cups Vanilla Ice Milk (page 72),
    softened, divided
2 cups Blueberry Grape Sauce
    (page 122), divided

Preheat oven to 350°F.

In a medium-size bowl, sift together whole wheat pastry flour and unbleached white flour, whisking to blend.

Put water and butter into a medium-size saucepan and bring to a rolling boil. Reduce heat and stir in flour, beating with a wooden spoon until mixture pulls away from sides of pan. Remove from heat and set aside to cool slightly.

Add eggs, one at a time, beating until smooth. Drop in mounds of about 2½ teaspoonfuls onto 2 ungreased baking sheets. Bake each batch on middle shelf of oven until lightly browned, 20 to 25 minutes.

Remove from oven and pierce sides of puffs with a sharp knife to release steam. Cool on wire racks.

When puffs are completely cool, split them crosswise and remove any soft dough.

Line a baking sheet with waxed paper. Fill each puff with about 1 tablespoon of the Vanilla Ice Milk. Place on lined baking sheet and freeze. When fro-zen, they may be removed to a plastic bag and returned to freezer for storage.

Serve each puff topped with about 1 tablespoon of the Blueberry Grape Sauce.

Makes about 30 puffs
(72 calories per puff)

Mellow Melon Compote

A pretty and cool dessert for a hot summer evening.

1½ cups fresh cantaloupe balls
1½ cups fresh watermelon balls
1½ cups fresh honeydew melon
    balls
¾ cup freshly squeezed orange
    juice
¾ cup unsweetened pineapple juice
6 mint sprigs, optional

Divide each type of melon balls among 6 parfait glasses.

In a small bowl, mix orange juice and pineapple juice together and pour over melon balls, dividing evenly. Chill until serving time. Decorate with mint, if desired.

Makes 6 servings
(69 calories per serving)

Ruby Raspberry Sauce

One of my favorite sauces, this is versatile, delicious, and low calorie.

1 cup unsweetened frozen raspberries, thawed and drained with juice reserved

2 teaspoons cornstarch

Place raspberries into a small saucepan.

In a jar with a tight-fitting lid, shake together reserved raspberry juice and cornstarch. Add enough water to make ½ cup. Stir into raspberries and bring to a boil, stirring constantly, until thickened. Strain and cool.

Makes about 1 cup
(6 calories per tablespoon)

Raspberry Cheese Pie

It's important to warm the honey for this recipe so it will mix easily with the berries.

3 cups fresh raspberries
¼ cup cornstarch
½ cup honey, warmed
16 ounces low-fat cottage cheese
2 eggs
2 tablespoons honey
1½ teaspoons vanilla extract

Preheat oven to 400°F. Lightly butter a 10-inch glass pie plate.

In a medium-size bowl, toss raspberries and cornstarch together, breaking some berries with a fork to release juice. Mix in warmed honey and turn into prepared pie plate. Bake on middle shelf of oven for 20 minutes.

While raspberries are baking, combine cottage cheese, eggs, honey, and vanilla in a blender or food processor and process until smooth. Pour over raspberries. Return to oven, reduce heat to 350°F, and bake another 40 minutes.

Allow to cool before serving.

Makes 8 servings
(192 calories per serving)

Kissel

Currants are traditional in Kissel, but the remaining fruit is optional.

1 tablespoon cornstarch
½ cup water
2 tablespoons honey
½ cup red currants
½ cup peeled, pitted, chopped fresh apricots
½ cup fresh blueberries
1 cup fresh raspberries

In a jar with a tight-fitting lid, shake together cornstarch and water. Pour into a medium-size saucepan. Stir in honey. Add currants and apricots and heat over medium heat, stirring constantly, until mixture thickens and fruit is soft. Add blueberries and cook 30 seconds. Stir in raspberries and cook an additional 30 seconds. Allow to cool before serving.

Makes 4 servings
(123 calories per serving)

Frozen Peach Soufflé

3 fresh peaches, peeled, pitted, and quartered
½ cup honey
2 eggs, separated
1 teaspoon vanilla extract
⅛ teaspoon cream of tartar

In a food processor, puree peaches and honey. Pour into top of a double boiler. Beat egg yolks in a small bowl and stir into peach mixture. Cook over simmering, but not boiling, water for 10 minutes, stirring constantly. Remove from heat and set aside to cool.

In a medium-size bowl, beat egg whites until foamy, add cream of tartar, and continue beating until stiff peaks form. Fold beaten egg whites into cooled peach mixture. Turn into a 4-cup mold. Cover and freeze.

Makes 6 servings
(132 calories per serving)

Almond Peach Treat

1 cup peeled, very ripe peach
  chunks
1 cup skim milk
1 teaspoon honey
¼ teaspoon almond extract
½ teaspoon vanilla extract

Puree peach chunks in a blender.
Add remaining ingredients. Process and
serve immediately.

Makes 3 servings
(60 calories per serving)

Peachy Almond Cake

2 eggs
½ cup honey
⅓ cup vegetable oil
1 teaspoon almond extract
¾ cup whole wheat pastry flour
¾ cup unbleached white flour
2 teaspoons baking powder
1½ teaspoons ground cinnamon
2 fresh peaches, peeled, pitted,
  and chopped

Preheat oven to 325°F. Spray an
8 × 8-inch pan with vegetable spray.

In a large bowl, beat together eggs,
honey, oil, and almond extract.

In a medium-size bowl, sift together
whole wheat pastry flour, unbleached
white flour, baking powder, and cinnamon. Add to beaten ingredients. Mix
together thoroughly. Stir peaches into
batter and turn into prepared pan. Bake
on middle shelf of oven until a cake tester inserted into center comes out clean,
about 35 minutes.

Makes 12 servings
(172 calories per serving)

Nectarine Cups

¼ cup nonfat dry milk
¼ cup cold water
1½ teaspoons freshly squeezed
      lemon juice
1 tablespoon honey
3 fresh nectarines, peeled, pitted,
      and halved
¾ cup Strawberry Sauce (page 230),
      divided

In a small bowl, mix nonfat dry milk and water together. Add lemon juice and beat until light and fluffy. Beat in honey.

Put each nectarine half in a sherbet glass and spoon whipped lemon mixture over them. Top with Strawberry Sauce. Serve immediately.

Makes 6 servings
(104 calories per serving)

JULY

Calorie-Controlled Cakes

		1	2	3
FRUIT OF THE MONTH: **RASPBERRIES** *DESSERT OF THE MONTH:* **FRESH RASPBERRY CREAM PIE** *DRINK OF THE MONTH:* **SPARKLING PUNCH**		LIGHT RHUBARB CREPES	FRENCH VANILLA CHERRY ICE MILK	PEACHY BLUEBERRY FLUFF
Independence Day 4 FOURTH OF JULY SPECTACULAR	5 MELON SOUP	6 APRICOT RAISIN PIE	7 CHEESECAKE FRAMBOISE	8 FAUX CHERRIES JUBILEE	9 PLUM ORANGE ICE	10 SUPER FRUIT KABOBS
11 ALMOND BAVARIAN CREAM WITH KIWI FRUITS	12 CHERRY TORTE	13 PEACH BARS	14 FRESH RASPBERRY CREAM PIE ★	15 LIGHT CAROB MOUSSE	16 POACHED GINGER PEACHES IN CUSTARD	17 GRAPE BANANA GELATIN LAYERS
18 MINI CAKE ROLLS	19 ORANGE LEMON FLUFF	20 HONEYDEW SHERBET	21 SHILEM TOUFU	22 ORANGE PINEAPPLE SHAKE	23 PEACH YOGURT WHIP	24 ½ CUP FRESH RASPBERRIES WITH 2 TABLESPOONS DELICIOUS DIET CREAM
25 BEAUTIFUL BLACKBERRY PIE	26 ALMOND-FLAVORED PECAN COOKIES	27 CAROB TRUFFLES	28 RASPBERRY RUM SHERBET	29 CAROB-DIPPED TANGERINES	30 THREE-MELON COMPOTE	31 RASPBERRY COCONUT PIE

$\mathcal{T}$ find pure magic in cake baking. You put a pan of loose batter into the oven and in a short time, presto, it has expanded into a beautiful golden sponge.

There are two types of cakes in this book: Butter cakes, which use butter or oil (there are only a few butter cakes because of their inherent calorie content), and foam cakes which contain neither butter nor oil.

The category called foam cakes includes both sponge cakes and angel food cakes. Although some recipes do use baking powder or baking soda as a backup, eggs always provide the major leavening power. Since foam cakes contain no oil or butter, the only fat is that in the egg yolks, if they're used. So these cakes are good diet fare.

There are three types of foam cakes—those in which whole eggs are used, those that use additional egg yolks, and those that rely totally on egg whites. All of these get their texture from the foaming eggs, hence the name foam cakes.

While I do use baking powder and baking soda in some of these cakes, for the most part they achieve their volume from air and steam. Beating in air is a critical step, and the fresher the eggs the more air they'll incorporate. In all my recipes (as in most recipes) eggs should be large eggs. This is most important in foam cakes.

Egg whites beat better when they're at room temperature or no colder than 60 degrees, but they separate more easily if they're cold. So I separate chilled eggs about 30 minutes before I start making a cake, returning only the yolks to the refrigerator.

When you beat whole or separated eggs, you make small bubbles inside the eggs. These bubbles expand in the oven. As the moisture in the batter evaporates, steam forms and gently enlarges the bubbles. Then the heat solidifies them. This is how a foam cake rises if the eggs are properly beaten—a vital step!

Sugar is sometimes used to replace the customary cream of tartar to stabilize beaten egg whites. Since I don't use sugar at all and honey doesn't have the same effect, I always use cream of tartar when I'm beating egg whites. It's added when the whites have been beaten to a foamy stage.

Beat egg whites until stiff but never until they're dry. The perfectly beaten egg white is soft, with a slight shine and soft peaks that bend over. If you overbeat whites, add a few drops of water and beat them again briefly. This often revives them.

Although foam cakes are traditionally baked in tube pans, they also can be made with great success in layers, or in jelly roll pans. Because heat comes from the middle as well as from the edges of tube pans, they allow the delicate batter to bake evenly. But layers and jelly rolls are thin enough so that the batter cooks through from the top and bottom as well as the sides and also is evenly baked. Uneven heat will make batter weep in the middle and fall.

Foam cakes are cooled completely in their pans by hanging them upside down over a counter or table top. A bottle works well for balancing a tube pan. If, however, you've baked foam layers, suspend the sides of the upside down pans.

Alas, all cakes aren't created perfect. Occasionally a layer will have a large hump in the middle. This comes from the manner in which the pan was filled and can be avoided by arranging the batter so that it's slightly higher on the edges. But if a cake has a hump, cut it off with a sharp knife.

Cake batter overflowing onto the oven makes a mess and produces a cake with burnt edges. This happens when cake pans are too full or there is too much butter in the batter—something you want to avoid because of calories, too.

A cake may fail to rise to the heights you expect for many reasons. The weather may be responsible (cakes may not rise well in humid weather), or you may have neglected to use large eggs, the eggs may have been incorrectly beaten, or they may have lost air when they were folded in. Folding does take practice. The best way to fold in any ingredient is to cut the batter down the middle with a spatula, bringing it around the bottom and side of the bowl. The more you can keep the spatula from breaking the surface of the batter the fewer bubbles will escape. Then give the bowl a quarter turn and repeat the process.

While most of the cakes in this book are diet-delicious without embellishments, there will be times you'll want to use fillings, icing, or both. To do this efficiently with little muss, place the cake on the plate on which you intend to serve it. Slip pieces of waxed paper around the edges, then frost it. The drippings will fall onto the waxed paper. Slip the paper out from under the cake and you have a perfectly clean plate under your elegantly frosted dessert.

Light Rhubarb Crepes

5 cups chopped fresh rhubarb
⅓ cup plus 1 tablespoon honey,
      divided
2 tablespoons cornstarch
½ cup water
½ cup part-skim ricotta cheese
1 teaspoon vanilla extract
12 Delicious Diet Crepes (page 30)

In a large saucepan, combine rhubarb and ⅓ cup of the honey. Dissolve cornstarch in water. Stir into rhubarb mixture. Simmer, stirring constantly, until mixture thickens. Continue cooking, stirring often, until rhubarb is tender, about 15 minutes. Chill.

In a medium-size bowl, beat together ricotta, remaining honey, and vanilla until smooth.

Divide rhubarb mixture among 12 crepes, mounding it in a row down the center from edge to edge. Top with cheese mixture and fold 2 sides over filling. Serve immediately.

Makes 6 servings
(195 calories per serving)

French Vanilla Cherry Ice Milk

2 eggs
¼ cup honey
4 cups skim milk
1½ tablespoons vanilla extract
1 cup pitted and chopped fresh
      sweet cherries with accumu-
      lated juice

In a large bowl, beat eggs and honey until light colored. Mix in skim milk and vanilla.

Process mixture in an ice cream maker according to manufacturer's instructions. When processed, stir it down with a wooden spoon and mix in cherries, along with juice from chopping them. If you're not using an ice cream maker, turn mixture into a shallow pan and freeze until mushy but not frozen. Remove from freezer, beat to break down ice crystals, and then return to freezer. Repeat this procedure twice, folding in cherries the last time. Turn into a container, cover, and freeze until ready to serve.

Makes 8 servings
(107 calories per serving)

Apricot Raisin Pie

3 eggs, separated
3 tablespoons honey
1½ cups plain nonfat yogurt
2 teaspoons vanilla extract
½ teaspoon orange extract
1 cup dried apricots
1 teaspoon whole wheat pastry flour
¼ cup raisins, plumped
⅛ teaspoon cream of tartar

Preheat oven to 325°F. Spray a 9-inch pie plate with vegetable spray.

In a large bowl, beat egg yolks and honey together until light colored. Mix in yogurt and extracts.

In a food processor, chop apricots with flour. Fold, along with raisins, into yogurt mixture.

In a medium-size bowl, beat egg whites until foamy. Sprinkle in cream of tartar and beat until stiff peaks form. Fold into yogurt mixture. Turn into prepared pie plate and bake on middle shelf of oven until puffy and lightly browned, about 30 minutes, then cover lightly with foil and bake an additional 15 to 20 minutes.

Cool before serving.

Makes 8 servings
(70 calories per serving)

Melon Soup

1 ripe cantaloupe
1 tablespoon freshly squeezed lemon juice
1 tablespoon freshly squeezed lime juice
2 tablespoons honey
¼ cup plain low-fat yogurt, divided

Cut cantaloupe in half, scooping out seeds. Peel, then cut melon into chunks. In a food processor, puree melon with lemon juice, lime juice, and honey. Chill.

Before serving, stir well. Divide among 4 dessert dishes. Top each with 1 tablespoon of the yogurt.

Makes 4 servings
(91 calories per serving)

Cheesecake Framboise

Cheesecake:
  1 tablespoon butter
  ¼ cup graham cracker crumbs
  2 envelopes unflavored gelatin
  ½ cup water
  2 eggs, separated
  1 cup skim milk
  1 pound low-fat cottage cheese
  2 teaspoons freshly squeezed
      lemon juice
  2 teaspoons vanilla extract
  ¼ cup honey
  ⅛ teaspoon cream of tartar
Topping:
  ¼ cup water
  1 tablespoon cornstarch
  2 tablespoons honey
  1 cup fresh raspberries

To prepare the cheesecake: Lightly rub butter on sides and bottom of a 9-inch springform pan. Sprinkle graham cracker crumbs evenly over bottom of pan, pressing into butter. Refrigerate.

Sprinkle gelatin over water and set aside for 5 minutes to soften.

In the top of a double boiler, beat egg yolks until fluffy and lemon colored. Stir in skim milk. Set over hot water and heat, stirring constantly, until mixture coats back of a wooden spoon, about 10 minutes. Stir in gelatin and heat, stirring constantly, until gelatin dissolves.

Blend cheese in a food processor or blender until smooth. Transfer to a large bowl. Stir egg yolk mixture into cheese along with lemon juice, vanilla, and honey. Chill until thickened but not set, about 30 minutes.

In a medium-size bowl, beat egg whites until foamy. Add cream of tartar and continue beating until stiff peaks form. Whisk cheese mixture to prevent lumps, then fold beaten whites into it. Turn into prepared springform pan and chill until set, about 1 hour.

To prepare the topping: In a jar with a tight-fitting lid, shake together water and cornstarch. Pour into a small saucepan. Add remaining ingredients and cook over medium heat, stirring constantly, until mixture thickens. Remove from heat and strain to remove raspberry seeds. When topping has cooled, spread it on top of cheesecake and return to refrigerator.

Just before serving, remove sides of springform pan.

Makes 10 servings
(140 calories per serving)

Fourth of July Spectacular

  8 egg whites
  ¼ teaspoon cream of tartar
  ¼ cup plus 2 tablespoons honey,
      divided
  2 teaspoons vanilla extract,
      divided
  ½ cup evaporated skim milk,
      chilled
  ½ cup **Ruby Raspberry Sauce**
      (page 127)
  1 cup fresh blueberries

Preheat oven to 350°F. Butter and lightly flour a baking sheet. Mark 2 8-inch circles on flour. (A pan cover does this well.)

In a large bowl, beat egg whites until foamy. Add cream of tartar and continue beating, drizzling in ¼ cup of the honey, until whites are very firm, about 6 minutes. Beat in 1 teaspoon of the vanilla and mound mixture in the circles on prepared baking sheet. Smooth surface. Place on bottom shelf of oven and reduce heat to 225°F. Bake for 3 hours.

Remove from oven and lift meringues carefully from baking sheet onto platters to cool.

When meringues have cooled, beat evaporated skim milk in a chilled bowl until foamy. Add remaining honey and vanilla. Continue beating until soft peaks form.

Frost 1 meringue with whipped milk. Place second meringue on top of it. Drizzle raspberry sauce over top. Arrange blueberries around base, cut into wedges, and serve immediately.

Makes 8 servings
(99 calories per serving)

Plum Orange Ice

1½ **pounds fresh plums (about 10 medium-size)**
¼ **cup honey**
1 **cup freshly squeezed orange juice**
2 **teaspoons vanilla extract**
1 **teaspoon orange extract**

Halve and pit, but do not peel, plums. Puree plums in a food processor.

In a medium-size saucepan, bring puree, honey, and orange juice to a boil, reduce heat, and simmer for 2 minutes. Set aside to cool. Stir in extracts.

Process mixture in an ice cream maker according to manufacturer's instructions, or turn mixture into a bowl, cover, and put in freezer until thickened but not frozen. Remove from freezer, beat to break down ice crystals, and then return to freezer. Repeat this procedure twice, turning into 2 1-quart containers before returning to freezer the last time.

Makes 12 servings
(66 calories per serving)

Peachy Blueberry Fluff

¾ cup evaporated skim milk,
     chilled
 1 tablespoon honey
½ teaspoon vanilla extract
 1 large ripe peach, peeled, pitted,
     and pureed
½ cup fresh blueberries

In a medium-size bowl, beat together skim milk, honey, and vanilla to the consistency of whipped cream. Fold in peach puree and blueberries and serve immediately.

Makes 2 servings
(161 calories per serving)

Peach Bars

These firm bars are very filling.

> 1　cup whole wheat pastry flour
> 1　cup unbleached white flour
> 1½　teaspoons baking powder
> 1½　teaspoons ground cinnamon
> ¼　teaspoon ground nutmeg
> ¼　cup butter, softened
> ¼　cup part-skim ricotta cheese
> ½　cup honey
> 2　eggs
> 1　4½-ounce jar strained peaches

Preheat oven to 350°F. Spray a 9 × 13-inch pan with vegetable spray.

Sift together whole wheat pastry flour, unbleached white flour, baking powder, cinnamon, and nutmeg into a medium-size bowl.

In a large bowl, beat butter and cheese together until smooth. Beat in honey, eggs, and peaches. Gradually mix in flour. Turn batter into prepared pan, spreading evenly. Bake on middle shelf of oven for 35 to 40 minutes.

Cool in pan, then cut into 36 bars.

Makes 36 bars
(65 calories per bar)

Cherry Torte

> 1　recipe for Pretty Peach Layer Cake (page 117)
> 1　envelope unflavored gelatin
> ½　cup water
> 1　tablespoon honey
> ½　cup freshly squeezed orange juice
> 1½　cups pitted fresh sweet cherries

Bake cake according to directions.

In a small saucepan, sprinkle gelatin over water. Set aside to soften for 5 minutes. Heat, stirring constantly, until gelatin dissolves. Stir in honey, then orange juice. Chill until quite thick but not set, 30 to 40 minutes.

Wrap and freeze 1 layer of the cake for future use. Place the second layer on a serving plate. Arrange cherries on top of cake. Spoon gelatin mixture evenly over cherries and cake, spreading to edges. It's all right for gelatin to run down sides of cake. Chill until set.

Makes 12 servings
(66 calories per serving)

Variation: To make a Strawberry Torte, substitute 1½ cups sliced fresh strawberries for the cherries and decorate center with a few whole berries. The number of calories per serving will be slightly less.

Super Fruit Kabobs

1 teaspoon freshly squeezed
    lemon juice
2 tablespoons water
8 1-inch chunks banana, divided
4 1-inch chunks avocado, divided
8 1-inch chunks fresh watermelon,
    divided
8 whole fresh strawberries, divided
8 1-inch chunks fresh cantaloupe,
    divided
¼ cup plain nonfat yogurt
2 tablespoons Ruby Raspberry
    Sauce (page 127)

Mix together lemon juice and water and brush banana and avocado pieces with mixture.

Thread 4 skewers with fruit in the following order: watermelon, banana, strawberry, cantaloupe, avocado, cantaloupe, strawberry, banana, and ending with watermelon.

In a small bowl, mix together yogurt and raspberry sauce. Serve as a dip with the kabobs.

Makes 4 servings
(86 calories per serving)

Almond Bavarian Cream with Kiwi Fruits

1¼ cups skim milk
  2 eggs, separated
  2 envelopes unflavored gelatin
  ¼ cup honey, divided
  1 teaspoon vanilla extract
  1 teaspoon almond extract
  ⅛ teaspoon cream of tartar
  1 cup evaporated skim milk,
      chilled
  2 kiwi fruits, peeled and sliced,
      optional

In the top of a double boiler, beat together skim milk and egg yolks. Sprinkle gelatin over mixture and set aside to soften for 5 minutes. Add 2 tablespoons of the honey, set over hot, not boiling, water, and cook, stirring constantly, until gelatin dissolves. Remove from heat and mix in extracts. Chill until thickened but not set, no longer than 30 minutes. Whisk briefly until smooth.

In a medium-size bowl, beat egg whites until foamy. Drizzle in remaining honey and cream of tartar. Continue beating until stiff peaks form. Fold whites into gelatin mixture.

In a chilled, medium-size bowl, beat evaporated skim milk to the consistency of whipped cream. Fold into gelatin mixture. Turn into a wet 8-cup mold and chill until set.

Unmold and decorate with kiwi slices, if desired.

Makes 12 servings
(72 calories per serving)

Light Carob Mousse

This light mousse has a simply divine texture.

- 1 **envelope unflavored gelatin**
- 1 **cup skim milk**
- 2 **tablespoons Versatile Carob Syrup** (page 148)
- 3 **tablespoons honey**
- 2 **egg yolks, beaten**
- 2 **teaspoons vanilla extract**
- 1½ **cups part-skim ricotta cheese**

In a small saucepan, sprinkle gelatin over skim milk. Set aside for 5 minutes to soften. Add carob syrup and honey, and heat to scalding. Whisk some of the hot milk mixture into beaten egg yolks. Return to pan and cook 2 minutes, stirring constantly. Remove from heat and stir in vanilla.

Turn ricotta into a blender container, and with blender running on high, pour carob-milk mixture through opening in cover, blending until well mixed. Pour into 6 dessert dishes and chill until set.

Makes 6 servings
(70 calories per serving)

 ## Fresh Raspberry Cream Pie

This elegant pie is surprisingly low in calories.

Pie:
- 1 **recipe for Skinny Piecrust** (page 5)
- 1½ **cups Slim Pastry Cream** (page 246)
- ½ **teaspoon rum extract**
- ½ **cup plain nonfat yogurt**
- 1¼ **cups fresh raspberries**

Glaze:
- 1 **teaspoon unflavored gelatin**
- ¼ **cup cold water**
- 1 **teaspoon honey**

To prepare the pie: Line a 10-inch pie plate just to the rim with pastry and bake according to directions.

While pastry cream is still warm, stir in rum extract. Chill until thick but not set. Carefully fold in yogurt and turn into prepared crust. Chill until set.

Starting at outer edge, arrange raspberries, touching, in circles to cover pastry cream.

To prepare the glaze: In a small saucepan, sprinkle gelatin over water and set aside to soften for 5 minutes. Add honey and heat until gelatin is dissolved, stirring constantly. Allow to cool but not set. Brush on berries. Chill pie well.

Makes 8 servings
(131 calories per serving)

Mini Cake Rolls

1 recipe for Jelly Roll Cake
    (page 49)
¾ cup Ruby Raspberry Sauce
    (page 127)
¾ cup Tangy Lemon Filling
    (page 222)
¼ cup Coconut Sugar (page 60)

Bake Jelly Roll Cake according to directions.

Cut cake in half crosswise. Spread half of the cake with raspberry sauce and the second half with lemon filling. Cut each piece in half crosswise. Cut pieces into thirds. Roll up, jelly roll fashion, over filling, starting from short side. Cut jelly rolls into halves, making 2 rolls from each piece. Roll in Coconut Sugar.

Makes 24 mini rolls
(60 calories per roll)

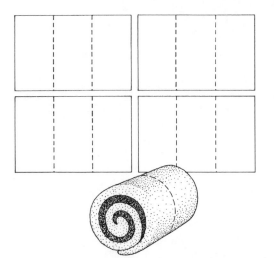

Orange Lemon Fluff

A cool treat for a hot day!

2 teaspoons unflavored gelatin
¼ cup water
2 eggs, separated
2 tablespoons honey
3 tablespoons freshly squeezed
    orange juice
1 tablespoon freshly squeezed
    lemon juice
2 egg whites
⅛ teaspoon cream of tartar
4 fresh orange sections, optional
4 mint leaves, optional

In a small saucepan, sprinkle gelatin over water. Set aside to soften for about 5 minutes, then heat over low heat, stirring constantly, until gelatin dissolves. Remove from heat.

In a small bowl, beat together egg yolks and honey. Pour a little gelatin mixture into beaten yolks, whisking constantly. Return to gelatin in saucepan, whisking well, and cook over low heat until mixture thickens slightly, about 8 minutes. Stir in orange juice and lemon juice. Pour into a small bowl and refrigerate until thickened but not set.

In a medium-size bowl, beat egg whites until foamy. Add cream of tartar and continue beating until stiff but not dry. Fold in orange-lemon mixture and divide among 4 dessert dishes. Chill until set.

If you wish, decorate each dish with an orange section and a mint leaf.

Makes 4 servings
(101 calories per serving)

Poached Ginger Peaches in Custard

4 cups water
½ cup honey
½ cup maple syrup
1 tablespoon freshly squeezed
    lemon juice
1 teaspoon ground cinnamon
1 teaspoon ground ginger
4 large, firm peaches
1½ cups Slim Pastry Cream
    (page 246)

In a medium-size saucepan, combine water, honey, maple syrup, lemon juice, cinnamon, and ginger. Bring to a boil. Reduce heat.

Halve, peel, and pit peaches. Set in poaching liquid and poach (water should be barely moving) until soft, about 10 minutes. Remove from liquid with a slotted spoon, allowing spices to cling to fruit. Place on a plate in a single layer to cool.

Whisk pastry cream briskly to loosen it. Spoon over peaches.

Makes 8 servings
(199 calories per serving)

Faux Cherries Jubilee

1 teaspoon cornstarch
¼ cup white grape juice
1 cup unsweetened frozen
    cherries, thawed
¼ teaspoon brandy extract
2 cups Vanilla Ice Milk
    (page 72)

In a small saucepan, dissolve cornstarch in grape juice. Add cherries and cook over medium heat, stirring constantly, until sauce thickens and turns red. Remove from heat and stir in brandy extract.

Divide ice milk among 4 dessert glasses. Divide sauce among glasses, spooning it over ice milk. Serve immediately.

Makes 4 servings
(186 calories per serving)

Honeydew Sherbet

1 large, ripe honeydew melon
¼ cup plus 2 tablespoons honey,
   divided
1½ cups evaporated skim milk,
   chilled

Peel, seed, and chunk melon. In a food processor, puree melon chunks. Add ¼ cup of the honey and process just to mix. Turn into a large saucepan and cook over medium heat, stirring constantly, for 5 minutes. Allow to cool.

In a large bowl, beat evaporated skim milk until soft peaks form. Drizzle in remaining honey, continuing to beat just until blended. Fold in cooled melon mixture.

Process mixture in an ice cream maker according to manufacturer's instructions, or turn mixture into a large shallow bowl or pan, cover, and freeze until mushy but not frozen. Remove from freezer, beat to break down ice crystals, and then return to freezer. Repeat this procedure twice, spooning mixture into a container the last time. Freeze until ready to serve.

Makes about 8 servings
(168 calories per serving)

Shilem Toufu (Almond Jelly)

2 envelopes unflavored gelatin
¾ cup water
3 cups skim milk
⅓ cup honey
1 teaspoon vanilla extract
1 teaspoon almond extract
1½ cups Peach Sauce (page 120),
   divided

In a medium-size saucepan, sprinkle gelatin over water. Set aside for 5 minutes to soften. Add skim milk and honey and heat over medium heat until gelatin dissolves, stirring constantly. Remove from heat and stir in extracts.

Allow to cool slightly, then divide among 6 dessert glasses. Chill until set.

At serving time spread ¼ cup of the Peach Sauce over each jelly.

Makes 6 servings
(148 calories per serving)

Versatile Carob Syrup

This wonderful syrup has many uses in making desserts.

1½ cups carob powder   1½ cups water

Sift carob powder. In a medium-size saucepan, combine carob powder and water. Cook over low heat, stirring constantly, until smooth, about 6 minutes. Cool and refrigerate in a tightly-closed container.

Stir well before each use.

Makes about 2 cups
(12 calories per tablespoon)

Orange Pineapple Shake

If you don't have an ice crusher, wrap ice cubes in a towel and pound them with a hammer.

- ½ cup crushed ice
- ½ cup unsweetened pineapple juice
- ½ cup freshly squeezed orange juice
- ½ cup skim milk
- ½ cup plain nonfat yogurt

Process all ingredients in a blender or food processor. Pour into glasses and serve immediately.

Makes 2 servings
(120 calories per serving)

Beautiful Blackberry Pie

Few people are indifferent toward blackberries. They're a love or hate food. If you love them, this low-calorie blackberry pie is certainly for you.

- 4 cups fresh blackberries
- ¾ cup honey
- 3 tablespoons quick-cooking tapioca
- 1 recipe for Mini Piecrust (page 104)
- ¾ cup Delicious Diet Cream (page 109), **divided**

In a large bowl, toss blackberries with honey and tapioca. Set aside for 15 minutes.

Preheat oven to 400°F. Line a 9-inch pie plate with Mini Piecrust according to directions. Turn blackberries into prepared crust. Cover with a foil tent and bake on bottom shelf of oven until pastry is lightly browned, about 50 minutes.

Serve warm or cold with about a tablespoon of the diet cream on each slice.

Makes 10 servings
(169 calories per serving)

Peach Yogurt Whip

 1 **envelope unflavored gelatin**
 ½ **cup freshly squeezed orange juice**
 4 **cups unsweetened frozen sliced peaches, thawed**
 2 **tablespoons honey**
 1 **teaspoon vanilla extract**
 1 **cup plain non-fat yogurt**

In a small saucepan sprinkle gelatin over orange juice. Set aside for 5 minutes to soften.

Puree peaches in a blender or food processor.

In a large bowl, stir together peach puree, honey, and vanilla.

Over low heat, heat orange juice mixture until gelatin dissolves. Cool, then add to peach mixture. Beat with an electric beater for about 2 minutes. Fold in yogurt.

Turn into 4 dessert cups and chill well.

Makes 4 servings
(150 calories per serving)

Almond-Flavored Pecan Cookies

 ½ **cup whole wheat flour**
 ½ **cup unbleached white flour**
 1 **teaspoon baking powder**
 ¼ **cup butter, cut into pieces**
 ⅓ **cup finely chopped pecans**
 1 **egg, beaten**
 2 **tablespoons honey**
 ½ **cup white grape juice**
 ½ **teaspoon vanilla extract**
 1 **teaspoon almond extract**
 ½ **teaspoon ground cinnamon**
 ¼ **teaspoon ground nutmeg**

Preheat oven to 350°F. Spray 2 baking sheets with vegetable spray.

In a medium-size bowl, whisk together whole wheat flour, unbleached white flour and baking powder. Cut butter into flour mixture with a pastry blender until mixture resembles crumbs. Mix in nuts.

In a small bowl, beat together egg and honey. Add grape juice, extracts, and spices. Mix into ingredients in medium-size bowl. Drop batter by teaspoonfuls onto prepared baking sheets. Bake each batch on middle shelf of oven for 10 minutes.

Cool on wire racks.

Makes 3 dozen cookies
(39 calories per cookie)

Grape Banana Gelatin Layers

1   envelope unflavored gelatin
1¼ cups cold water
1   6-ounce can unsweetened
     frozen grape juice concentrate
1   large, ripe banana

In a medium-size saucepan, sprinkle gelatin over water. Set aside for 5 minutes to soften. Heat until gelatin dissolves, stirring constantly. Remove from heat and stir in concentrate. Put in refrigerator until thickened but not set, 1 to 1½ hours.

Spoon a layer of gelatin mixture into each of 6 dessert glasses. Thinly slice banana. Make a banana layer on top of each gelatin layer. Continue to layer, ending with gelatin, until all ingredients are used. Chill until set.

Makes 6 servings
(78 calories per serving)

Raspberry Rum Sherbet

1   20-ounce package unsweetened
     frozen raspberries, thawed
2   eggs
½   cup honey
2   teaspoons freshly squeezed
     lemon juice
1½ cups skim milk
2   teaspoons rum extract

In a food processor, puree raspberries. Strain and discard seeds. (If you don't mind seeds, you don't have to strain puree.)

In a large bowl, beat eggs and honey until fluffy. Mix in raspberry puree, lemon juice, skim milk, and rum extract.

Process mixture in an ice cream maker according to manufacturer's directions, or turn mixture into a large shallow pan, cover, and freeze until thickened but not frozen. Remove from freezer, beat to break down ice crystals, and then return to freezer. Repeat this procedure twice, turning sherbet into 2 1-quart containers before returning to freezer the last time. Freeze until ready to serve.

Makes 8 servings
(171 calories per serving)

Carob-Dipped Tangerines

2 tablespoons carob chips
1 tablespoon butter
16 tangerine sections
¼ cup Coconut Sugar (page 60)

In the top of a double boiler set over hot water, melt together carob chips and butter. Dip both ends of tangerine sections into melted carob, then dip them in Coconut Sugar. Place onto a baking sheet lined with waxed paper and refrigerate until carob is hardened.

Serve 2 sections to each person.

Makes 8 servings
(45 calories per serving)

Three-Melon Compote

½ large cantaloupe
½ large honeydew
¼ watermelon
¼ cup unsweetened flaked coconut
½ cup freshly squeezed orange
    juice

With a melon baller, make melon balls from cantaloupe, honeydew, and watermelon, removing watermelon seeds. Toss melon balls in a glass bowl with coconut and orange juice. Cover and chill.

Toss again before serving.

Makes 8 servings
(45 calories per serving)

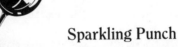

Sparkling Punch

8 cups Cran-Raspberry juice,
    chilled
4 cups unsweetened pineapple
    juice, chilled
2 cups red grape juice, chilled
2 cups club soda, chilled

Combine all ingredients and pour over ice cubes in a punch bowl.

Makes 32 servings
(53 calories per serving)

Raspberry Coconut Pie

1 recipe for Skinny Piecrust
(page 5)
2 tablespoons cornstarch, divided
2 cups skim milk, divided
2 envelopes unflavored gelatin,
divided
2 tablespoons honey, divided
1 teaspoon rum extract
½ cup unsweetened flaked coconut
1 20-ounce package unsweetened
frozen raspberries, thawed

Line a 9-inch pie plate with pastry and bake according to directions.

In a medium-size saucepan, dissolve 1 tablespoon of the cornstarch in 1 cup of the skim milk. Sprinkle 1 envelope of the gelatin over milk and set aside to soften for 5 minutes. Add 1 tablespoon of the honey and heat over medium heat, stirring constantly, until mixture thickens and gelatin dissolves. Stir in rum extract, remaining milk, and coconut. Pour into prepared pie plate and chill until set, about 2 hours.

Drain raspberries, reserving juice in small saucepan. Place raspberries into a medium-size bowl. Stir into reserved juice remaining cornstarch and remaining honey. Sprinkle remaining gelatin over top. Set aside to soften for 5 minutes. Heat over medium heat, stirring constantly, until mixture thickens and gelatin dissolves. Remove from heat and stir into raspberries. Spread on top of coconut mixture and chill until set, preferably overnight.

Makes 8 servings
(151 calories per serving)

Carob Truffles

1 cup part-skim ricotta cheese
¼ cup honey
1 teaspoon vanilla extract
¼ cup carob chips
2 tablespoons butter
¼ cup Coconut Sugar (page 60)

In a medium-size bowl, beat together ricotta, honey, and vanilla until smooth.

In the top of a double boiler set over hot water, melt together carob chips and butter. Beat into cheese mixture and chill until easy to handle. Roll into 1-inch balls between palms of hands. Roll each ball in Coconut Sugar, place on a baking sheet lined with waxed paper, and refrigerate.

Makes 3 dozen truffles
(27 calories per truffle)

AUGUST

Make Your
Diet Desserts Ahead

FRUIT OF THE MONTH: **PLUMS**

DESSERT OF THE MONTH: **VANILLA PLUM PIE**

DRINK OF THE MONTH: **MINTED LEMONADE**

1 PEACH MELBA CREPE CUPS	**2** GRAPE SNOW	**3** CINNAMON PEACH-BLUEBERRY COMPOTE
4 PIÑA COLADA CAKE	**5** FROZEN NECTARINE CUSTARD	**6** MOCHA POPCORN
7 PEACHY RHUBARB RAISIN PIE	**8** CREAMY CAROB PUDDING	**9** TANGY SUMMER COMPOTE
10 BLACKBERRY PINEAPPLE COBBLER	**11** BAKED MAPLE PEACHES	**12** CANTALOUPE POINTS
13 SNAPPY FRUIT DIP	**14** RASPBERRY NESTS	**15** VANILLA PLUM PIE ★
16 RASPBERRIES WITH STRAWBERRY SAUCE	**17** SUNSHINE LAYER CAKE	**18** PEACHY RHUBARB SAUCE
19 NO-CRUST BLUEBERRY CHIFFON PIE	**20** PLUM GOOD MERINGUE	**21** PEACH-TOPPED FROZEN ICE MOLD
22 EXOTIC COMPOTE	**23** CRUNCHY PEACH CRISP	**24** PECAN BARS
25 ALMOND-STUFFED PEACHES	**26** RASPBERRY SORBET	**27** ONE RIPE PLUM
28 CAROB COCONUT LOAVES	**29** WATERMELON BASKET	**30** CINNAMON CREAM
31 BLUEBERRY BANANA PIE		

$\mathcal{M}$ost of us look for ways to put more hours into our days and to make the hours we do have more productive. So it isn't always convenient to concoct a dessert just before it's time to serve it. That doesn't mean skipping dessert, but it does mean careful planning and knowing what foods keep and which ones do not.

You can complete some desserts well in advance, some can be partially prepared with a few last minute touches, such as whipping milk or egg whites, left until serving time, while the components of other desserts can be made ahead and then assembled at dessert time. Familiarize yourself with what can and can't be done in advance. Many fresh fruit compotes and fruit combinations not only can be prepared ahead of time but are better tasting for doing so. In fact, some of these desserts must be made up to two days ahead for maximum flavor. This gives the fruits an opportunity to mingle and take on the character of the juice in which they're marinating. Citrus fruits are especially suited for this because they don't discolor as some other fruits do.

Fruits such as apples, apricots, bananas, or pears should never be readied more than a few hours ahead if they're to be served raw. Even brushing them with lemon juice or acidulated water, which keeps fruit from darkening for an hour or so, won't prevent them from wilting for a longer period of time. (Acidulated water is water to which either vinegar or lemon juice has been added. In desserts, lemon juice is almost always the agent.) Apples, apricots, or pears cooked in a compote, a pie, or a pudding will, however, keep for several days in the refrigerator and be ready when you are.

Generally, it's not a good idea to wash fruit until it's time to use it, but it's acceptable practice to wash firm-skinned fruit, such as apples or pears, a day or so before use if you expect to be in a hurry at serving time. Be sure it's thoroughly dry.

Strawberries can be hulled a day before use, but don't wash them more than an hour or two in advance, and if they're to be sliced, do this as close to serving time as possible.

155

You can peel, cube, slice, or make melon into balls several days in advance. Store them in airtight containers in the refrigerator giving each variety of melon its own separate storage jar. If you put them together, the strongest melon—cantaloupe, for instance, with its very pungent aroma and flavor—will overpower the other melons, giving them a rancid taste and smell that will ruin your dessert.

Baked Goods for Best Keeping

Most fruit pies that aren't meant to be served warm can be prepared ahead of time as long as one fruit isn't considerably stronger than the other. Pies with fruit combinations often taste even better the second day, but you do run the risk of ending up with a soggy crust. Using a bit more thickener in the filling often eliminates this problem. Chiffon and most fruit pies need refrigeration.

When making a pie with any filling, such as pudding that is cooked separate from the crust and doesn't become quite firm, it's advisable to keep the pie shell and filling separate until you need the pie. You may need to whisk the filling to make it smooth and pourable before you add it to the pie shell. Obviously this won't work with a filling that has a gelatin base.

All the cakes in this book can be made a day or even two in advance. They should be wrapped tightly and kept in a cool place. If you're using filling or frosting, you can make it ahead (except for a few frostings made with nonfat dry milk) and then add it to the cake up to three hours before serving.

Because of their airy textures, angel food and sponge cakes (the ones best for dieters) dry out more rapidly than other, denser cakes. Don't cut them any sooner than is absolutely necessary. Once an angel food or sponge cake has been cut, wrap it so that the cut edges are completely covered with the wrap touching all surfaces, never in a loose wrap as you might an uncut cake.

Any cake that has fruit in it is best when made a day or two in advance to allow the fruit flavor to permeate the cake.

You can make jelly roll cake and assemble it as much as a day in advance of serving it without affecting the quality unless the filling is especially runny (a poor choice of filling for jelly rolls at any time). Keep the cake tightly wrapped in the refrigerator. Cake layers wrapped well in plastic and then foil will be fresh and appetizing three days later.

Pudding made with a custard or gelatin base must be made ahead of time to allow for cooling and setting. Most of these, when properly adapted, are marvelous diet desserts. Gelatin molds are super keepers, staying good as new for many days. But don't unmold one of these time savers until you're ready to serve it.

Cookies are something you can always have on hand. Store soft ones with soft ones and hard ones with hard ones or they will lose these lovely, individual characteristics.

August, with its sweltering days, is a time most people want to get cooking done ahead so that they can enjoy summer's outdoor activities and avoid being in the kitchen during the heat of afternoon or early evening. But whatever month it is, it's comforting to know that food is prepared ahead and there's time to relax.

Some desserts in this book must be served immediately after they're made. But there are enough recipes you can prepare in advance to provide you with delicious desserts whenever you have a busy schedule coming up.

For tips on storing them, see the chapter "The Proper Care, Storage, and Freezing of Desserts."

Peach Melba Crepe Cups

4 **Delicious Diet Crepes** (page 30)
4 **fresh peaches**
1 **cup Ruby Raspberry Sauce**
(page 127), **warmed, divided**
¼ **cup Delicious Diet Cream**
(page 109), **divided**

Preheat oven to 250°F.

Line 4 custard cups with crepes. Place on middle shelf of oven until warm, 5 to 10 minutes, depending on whether crepes are chilled or at room temperature.

Peel, pit, and cut peaches into chunks. Put 2 tablespoons of the raspberry sauce on bottom of each warmed crepe. Add 1 chopped peach to each crepe, then remaining raspberry sauce. Top each crepe cup with 1 tablespoon of the diet cream and serve immediately.

Makes 4 servings
(107 calories per serving)

Cinnamon Peach-Blueberry Compote

1 **cup freshly squeezed orange**
juice
1½ **tablespoons cornstarch**
¼ **cup honey**
2 **tablespoons freshly squeezed**
lemon juice
1 **teaspoon ground cinnamon**
1 **teaspoon vanilla extract**
6 **ripe peaches**
2 **cups fresh blueberries**

In a medium-size saucepan, whisk together orange juice and cornstarch. Stir in honey, lemon juice, and cinnamon. Cook over medium heat, stirring constantly, until mixture thickens. Remove from heat and stir in vanilla.

Peel, pit, and slice peaches. Add to orange juice mixture. Return to heat, and simmer until peaches are tender, about 10 minutes, stirring frequently.

Transfer peach-orange juice mixture to a large bowl, fold in blueberries, and chill.

Makes 10 servings
(118 calories per serving)

Piña Colada Cake

1 8-ounce can unsweetened
    crushed pineapple
2 teaspoons unflavored gelatin
1 tablespoon honey
1 teaspoon rum extract
½ cup ice water
⅓ cup instant nonfat dry milk
½ cup unsweetened flaked coconut
1 Heavenly Angel Food Cake
    (page 38)

Drain pineapple, reserving juice.

In a small saucepan, sprinkle gelatin over reserved pineapple juice and set aside for 5 minutes to soften. Add honey and cook over medium heat, stirring constantly, until gelatin is completely dissolved. Stir in extract. Chill until thickened but not set.

In a medium-size bowl, beat together ice water and nonfat dry milk until soft peaks form. Beat in gelatin mixture. Fold in pineapple and coconut.

Frost cake with mixture and refrigerate for at least 4 hours before serving.

Makes 8 servings
(144 calories per serving)

Grape Snow

1 envelope unflavored gelatin
1½ cups water, divided
1 tablespoon honey
1 6-ounce can unsweetened
    frozen red or white grape
    juice concentrate
3 egg whites

In a small saucepan, soften gelatin for 5 minutes in ½ cup water. Add honey and heat over low heat, stirring constantly, until gelatin dissolves.

Remove from heat. Stir in remaining water and grape juice concentrate, stirring until grape juice has melted. Chill until mixture is the consistency of unbeaten egg whites, about 1¼ hours.

Transfer grape juice mixture to a large bowl. Add egg whites and beat until mixture is fluffy and thickened. Divide among 8 dessert glasses and refrigerate until set. Keep chilled until ready to serve.

Makes 8 servings
(67 calories per serving)

Frozen Nectarine Custard

3 tablespoons honey, divided
1 egg, separated
1½ cups skim milk, divided
1 tablespoon cornstarch
1 teaspoon vanilla extract
6 ripe nectarines
1 teaspoon freshly squeezed
   lemon juice

In a small bowl, beat together 2 tablespoons of the honey and egg yolk. Mix in 1 cup of the skim milk and pour into a small saucepan. Shake together remaining skim milk and cornstarch in a jar with a tight-fitting lid. Add to egg yolk mixture, whisking to blend. Cook over low heat, stirring constantly, until mixture thickens, about 10 minutes. Stir in vanilla.

Peel, pit, and quarter nectarines. In a blender or food processor, puree nectarines, adding lemon juice and remaining honey. Mix with custard in a medium-size bowl. Place in freezer until almost firm, about 2 hours, beating every 30 to 40 minutes to avoid buildup of ice crystals.

When almost firm, add egg white and beat for about 3 minutes, scraping down sides of bowl. Cover and return to freezer until firm.

Makes 8 servings
(121 calories per serving)

Creamy Carob Pudding

2 cups skim milk, divided
3 tablespoons cornstarch
2 tablespoons honey
1 egg, beaten
1½ teaspoons vanilla extract
4 teaspoons Versatile Carob
   Syrup (page 148)

In the top of a double boiler set over boiling water, heat 1½ cups of the skim milk.

In a jar with a tight-fitting lid, shake together remaining skim milk and cornstarch. Add gradually to milk in double boiler. Stir in honey. Cook until thickened, stirring constantly. Stir a little of the hot mixture into beaten egg. Pour egg mixture into hot milk mixture gradually, stirring constantly. Cook another 2 minutes, stirring constantly. Remove from heat and mix in vanilla and carob syrup. Divide among 4 dessert dishes and chill.

Makes 4 servings
(122 calories per serving)

Blackberry Pineapple Cobbler

2½ cups fresh blackberries
½ cup unsweetened crushed
    pineapple
⅓ cup honey
1 tablespoon cornstarch
¼ cup unsweetened pineapple
    juice
½ cup whole wheat pastry flour
½ cup unbleached white flour
1½ teaspoons baking powder
2 tablespoons butter
½ cup skim milk

Preheat oven to 375°F.

In a medium-size saucepan, combine blackberries, pineapple, and honey. Dissolve cornstarch in pineapple juice and stir into blackberry mixture. Cook over medium heat, stirring constantly, until mixture thickens.

In a medium-size bowl, whisk together whole wheat pastry flour, unbleached white flour, and baking powder. Cut butter into pieces. Add to flour mixture and cut in with pastry blender or 2 knives. Stir in skim milk to form dough.

Pour fruit mixture into a 1½-quart casserole. Drop batter in 8 equal spoonfuls on top of fruit. Bake on middle shelf of oven until fruit is bubbly and batter is lightly browned, 25 to 30 minutes.

Makes 8 servings
(180 calories per serving)

Tangy Summer Compote

Always add the banana to this dessert last so it won't have time to discolor.

1 cup unsweetened canned pineapple chunks, drained with juice reserved
½ cup seedless green grapes, halved
1 cup fresh strawberries, halved
1 cup fresh cantaloupe balls
1 tablespoon freshly squeezed lemon juice
¼ cup unsweetened frozen orange juice concentrate
½ cup club soda
1 small banana

In a large glass bowl, mix together pineapple, grapes, strawberries, and cantaloupe.

In a small bowl, blend together reserved pineapple juice, lemon juice, orange juice concentrate, and club soda. Toss with fruit in large bowl. Slice banana and toss with other ingredients. Serve immediately.

Makes 8 servings
(61 calories per serving)

Mocha Popcorn

Serve this when you're going from the table to the TV.

2 **tablespoons butter**
2 **teaspoons honey**
½ **teaspoon carob powder**
¼ **teaspoon decaffeinated instant coffee**
4 **cups hot popcorn**

In a small saucepan, melt butter and honey. Add carob powder and instant coffee and stir until dissolved. Toss with popcorn and serve a cup to each person immediately.

Makes 4 servings
(86 calories per serving)

Peachy Rhubarb Raisin Pie

While this pie can be made with frozen rhubarb and frozen peaches, it's at least twice as delicious when made with the fresh fruits.

1½ **cups unsweetened frozen chopped rhubarb**
2½ **cups unsweetened frozen sliced peaches**
¼ **cup raisins, plumped**
⅓ **cup honey**
1 **tablespoon quick-cooking tapioca**
1 **recipe for Mini Piecrust**
   (page 104)

In a medium-size bowl, toss together rhubarb, peaches, raisins, honey, and tapioca. Set aside for 15 minutes.

Preheat oven to 400°F. Line a 9-inch pie plate with Mini Piecrust and partially bake according to directions.

Turn filling into prepared crust. Top with foil tent and bake on bottom shelf of oven until crust is lightly browned, 55 to 60 minutes. Serve warm or cold.

Makes 10 servings
(113 calories per serving)

Peachy Rhubarb Sauce

This sauce is tart, tangy, and delicious!

¾ **cup water**
2 **cups unsweetened frozen chopped rhubarb, thawed**
2 **cups finely chopped ripe peaches**
⅓ **cup honey**
1 **teaspoon ground cinnamon**

Combine all ingredients in a medium-size saucepan. Bring to a boil over medium-high heat. Reduce heat and simmer until fruit is tender, about 10 minutes. Serve warm or cold.

Makes 8 servings
(80 calories per serving)

Vanilla Plum Pie

1 recipe for **Skinny Piecrust**
   (page 5)
2 cups **Very Vanilla Pudding**
   (page 76)
6 ripe plums
1 teaspoon cornstarch
¼ cup water
1 tablespoon honey

Preheat oven to 425°F. Line a 9-inch pie plate with piecrust* and bake blind according to directions. Allow to cool completely.

Fill cooled pie shell with vanilla pudding. Cut plums into halves, removing pits. Place them skin sides up on pudding.

In a small saucepan, dissolve cornstarch in water. Add honey and heat, stirring constantly, until mixture thickens. Brush over plums and chill pie thoroughly before serving.

Makes 12 servings
(102 calories per serving)

*If a fluted edge is desired, simply use an 8-inch pie plate. Of course, the number of servings will be 10, and the number of calories per serving will increase slightly.

No-Crust Blueberry Chiffon Pie

2½ cups fresh blueberries, divided
½ cup honey
½ cup water
1½ envclopes unflavored gelatin
½ cup freshly squeezed orange juice
1 teaspoon freshly squeezed lemon juice
2 egg whites
⅛ teaspoon cream of tartar
½ teaspoon vanilla extract
½ cup **Delicious Diet Cream**
   (page 109)

In a large saucepan, combine 2¼ cups of the blueberries, honey, and water. Mash berries with potato masher or back of spoon, and cook over medium heat, stirring constantly, until mixture is purplish in color, 8 to 10 minutes.

In a small saucepan, sprinkle gelatin over orange juice. Set aside to soften for 5 minutes. Heat, stirring constantly, until gelatin dissolves. Stir in lemon juice and mix into cooked blueberries. Chill until the consistency of egg whites, stirring often so edges won't set.

In a medium-size bowl, beat egg whites until foamy. Add cream of tartar and vanilla, and continue to beat until stiff peaks form. Fold whites into blueberry mixture. Spoon into a 9-inch pie plate and chill until set.

Just before serving, decorate with diet cream and remaining blueberries.

Makes 8 servings
(110 calories per serving)

Sunshine Filling

3 tablespoons cornstarch
2 cups freshly squeezed
   orange juice, divided

2 tablespoons honey
½ teaspoon lemon extract

Shake together cornstarch and ½ cup of the orange juice in a jar with a tight-fitting lid.

Mix together remaining orange juice, honey, and cornstarch mixture in a medium-size saucepan. Bring to a boil over medium heat, stirring constantly, and cook, until thickened. Add lemon extract and allow to cool.

Makes about 2 cups
(15 calories per tablespoon)

Raspberry Nests

1 recipe for Meringue Shells
   (page 76)
2 cups fresh raspberries, divided
½ cup Delicious Diet Cream
   (page 109), divided

Bake Meringue Shells according to directions.

Put ⅓ cup of the raspberries into each Meringue Shell. Top with about a tablespoon of the diet cream and serve immediately.

Makes 6 servings
(42 calories per serving)

Raspberries with Strawberry Sauce

1½ cups Slim Pastry Cream
    (page 246)
1   quart fresh raspberries
¾   cup Strawberry Sauce
    (page 230), divided

Put ¼ cup of the pastry cream into each of 6 dessert dishes. Divide raspberries among the dishes. Top each with 2 tablespoons of the Strawberry Sauce and serve immediately.

Makes 6 servings
(156 calories per serving)

Sunshine Layer Cake

1 **Heavenly Angel Food Cake**
    (page 38)
1 **cup Sunshine Filling** (page 164)
2 **tablespoons unsweetened flaked
    coconut**
1 **small tangerine**

Cut cake in half crosswise, making 2 layers.

Spread ½ cup filling on bottom layer. Add top layer. Spread with remaining filling and sprinkle with coconut.

Peel and section tangerine, removing all pith. Arrange sections on top of cake.

Makes 16 servings
(100 calories per serving)

Cantaloupe Points

2 **cups Vanilla Ice Milk** (page 72),
    softened
1 **cantaloupe**
1 **cup Blueberry Grape Sauce**
    (page 122)

Line a baking sheet with waxed paper. Divide vanilla ice milk into eight scoops. Put them on prepared baking sheet and place in freezer until firm.

Cut cantaloupe in half and scoop out seeds. Peel and cut each half into 4 long pieces. Arrange on a platter. Put scoops of ice cream in the centers of cantaloupe pieces. Top with sauce and serve immediately.

Makes 8 servings
(87 calories per serving)

Baked Maple Peaches

A good busy-day dessert!

4 **large ripe peaches**
¼ **cup chopped peanuts**
½ **cup maple syrup**

Preheat oven to 350°F. Spray a 9 × 13-inch baking dish with vegetable spray.

Peel, halve, and pit peaches. Place, cut side up, in prepared baking dish and sprinkle with chopped nuts. Drizzle maple syrup over peaches. Cover and bake on middle shelf of oven until peaches are fork tender, about 20 minutes.

Makes 4 servings
(190 calories per serving)

Plum Good Meringue

Select fully ripe plums for this dessert. They're sweeter and add a lovelier flavor.

- 4 cups halved, pitted Italian prune plums
- 1 tablespoon plus 1 teaspoon honey, divided
- 2 tablespoons chopped walnuts
- 2 egg whites, at room temperature dash of cream of tartar

Preheat oven to 350°F. Spray a 1½-quart casserole with vegetable spray.

Place plums in a casserole. Drizzle with 1 tablespoon of the honey. Sprinkle with walnuts. Cover and bake on middle shelf of oven for 45 minutes.

In a medium-size bowl, beat egg whites until foamy. Add cream of tartar and remaining honey. Beat until stiff peaks form. Spread over plums, sealing edges with meringue. Return to oven until meringue is golden brown, about 10 minutes. Serve warm.

Makes 8 servings
(84 calories per serving)

Peach-Topped Frozen Ice Mold

- 1½ cups Vanilla Ice Milk (page 72), softened
- 12 Ladyfingers (page 99), halved crosswise
- 1½ cups French Carob Ice Milk (page 180), softened
- 1 cup Peach Sauce (page 120)

Line a 5 × 7-inch loaf pan with waxed paper.

Put a little Vanilla Ice Milk into bottom of pan. Stand Ladyfingers, points down, in ice milk along sides of pan. Add remaining Vanilla Ice Milk, smoothing top. Layer French Carob Ice Milk on Vanilla Ice Milk and smooth top. Cover and freeze.

At serving time, turn out onto a platter. Remove waxed paper. Top with Peach Sauce and serve immediately.

Makes 8 servings
(174 calories per serving)

Crunchy Peach Crisp

3½ cups unsweetened frozen
   sliced peaches, thawed and
   drained with juice reserved
2 tablespoons honey, warmed
2 teaspoons freshly squeezed
   lemon juice
¼ teaspoon ground ginger
¾ teaspoon ground cinnamon
½ cup quick-cooking oats
2 tablespoons ground pecans
1 tablespoon butter, softened
1 tablespoon water

Preheat oven to 350°F. Spray an
8 × 8-inch glass baking dish with vegetable spray.

In a medium-size bowl, toss peach slices with ¼ cup of the reserved juice, 1 tablespoon of the honey, lemon juice, and spices. Arrange in a layer on bottom of prepared dish.

In a small bowl, mix together oats, pecans, remaining honey, butter and water to soften oats slightly. Spread on top of peaches. Bake on middle shelf of oven until peaches are tender, about 25 minutes.

Makes 8 servings
(159 calories per serving)

Exotic Compote

1 fresh pineapple, peeled, cored,
   and cut into chunks
2 seedless oranges, peeled, sectioned, and sections quartered
3 kiwi fruits, peeled and cut into
   wedges
¼ cup freshly squeezed orange
   juice
1 tablespoon freshly squeezed
   lemon juice
1 tablespoon honey, warmed
1 banana

In a large glass bowl, toss together pineapple, oranges, and kiwis.

In a small bowl, mix together juices and honey. Toss with fruit in large bowl.

Slice banana. Toss with other ingredients, coating well.

Makes 8 servings
(87 calories per serving)

Snappy Fruit Dip

½ cup plain nonfat yogurt
½ cup sour cream
 1 tablespoon honey
 1 tablespoon minced crystallized
    ginger
 1 tangerine, peeled and sectioned,
    pith removed

¾ cup fresh blackberries
½ cup seedless white grapes

In a small bowl, combine yogurt, sour cream, honey, and ginger. Chill.

When ready to serve, arrange fruit decoratively on a plate around bowl of dip.

Makes 4 servings
(105 calories per serving)

Pecan Bars

1 egg
⅓ cup honey
1 teaspoon vanilla extract
⅓ cup whole wheat pastry flour
⅓ cup unbleached white flour
½ teaspoon baking powder
½ cup chopped pecans

Preheat oven to 350°F. Spray an 8 × 8-inch pan with vegetable spray.

In a medium-size bowl, beat together egg and honey. Stir in vanilla.

In a small bowl, sift together whole wheat pastry flour, unbleached white flour, and baking powder, whisking to blend. Stir into egg mixture and spread in prepared pan. Sprinkle with pecans and bake on middle shelf of oven for 20 minutes.

Cut into 12 bars and cool in pan.

Makes 12 bars
(94 calories per bar)

Almond-Stuffed Peaches

2 cups water
4 fresh peaches
½ cup Light Lemon Cookie crumbs
   (page 121)
1 4½-ounce jar strained pears
¼ teaspoon almond extract
1 tablespoon butter
6 tablespoons Ruby Raspberry
   Sauce (page 127), divided

In a large saucepan, bring water to a boil. Add peaches, reduce heat, and poach for 10 minutes. Remove with a slotted spoon and set aside to cool.

Preheat oven to 350°F. Spray a 9-inch pie plate with vegetable spray.

In a small bowl, mix together cookie crumbs, pears, and almond extract.

In a small saucepan, melt butter.

When peaches have cooled sufficiently to handle, peel, halve, and pit them. Place, hollow side up, in prepared pie plate. Fill indentations with pear mixture. Lightly brush fruit and filling with butter. Bake on middle shelf of oven until fruit is soft, about 10 minutes.

Top each serving with 1 tablespoon of the raspberry sauce.

Makes 6 servings
(138 calories per serving)

Blueberry Banana Pie

1 recipe for Skinny Piecrust
   (page 5)
4 cups fresh or unsweetened
   frozen blueberries
¼ cup honey
⅓ cup freshly squeezed orange
   juice
2 tablespoons cornstarch
2 medium-size ripe bananas
1 tablespoon freshly squeezed
   lemon juice

Line a 9-inch pie plate with pastry and bake blind according to directions. Set aside to cool.

In a medium-size saucepan, combine blueberries and honey. In a jar with a tight-fitting lid, shake together orange juice and cornstarch. Add to blueberry mixture and heat, stirring constantly, until mixture thickens and becomes almost translucent. Set aside to cool.

When both piecrust and blueberry sauce are cool, slice bananas into piecrust, sprinkle with lemon juice, and spread blueberry sauce on top. Refrigerate until set.

Makes 10 servings
(135 calories per serving)

Raspberry Sorbet

6   **cups fresh raspberries**
¼   **cup honey, warmed**
2   **egg whites**
⅛   **teaspoon cream of tartar**
½   **teaspoon rum extract**

In a food processor, puree raspberries. Strain to remove seeds. Stir in honey and put mixture in freezer until mushy but not frozen.

In a medium-size bowl, beat egg whites until foamy. Add cream of tartar and extract and continue beating until stiff peaks form.

Beat raspberry mixture to lighten. Fold in egg whites. Put in ice cube trays without dividers and return to freezer. Freeze until ready to serve.

Makes 8 servings
(82 calories per serving)

Carob Coconut Loaves

1¼   **cups whole whole wheat pastry flour**
1   **cup unbleached white flour**
1   **teaspoon baking powder**
1   **teaspoon baking soda**
⅓   **cup honey**
⅓   **cup vegetable oil**
1   **cup buttermilk**
2   **eggs**
1½   **teaspoons vanilla extract**
½   **cup carob chips**
¼   **cup unsweetened shredded coconut**

Preheat oven to 350°F. Lightly grease and flour a 9 × 5-inch pan.

In a large bowl, sift together whole wheat pastry flour, unbleached white flour, baking powder, and baking soda. Add honey, oil, buttermilk, eggs, and vanilla. Mix well with wooden spoon. Mix in carob chips and coconut.

Place batter into prepared pan and bake on middle shelf of oven until a cake tester inserted into center comes out clean, about 50 minutes. Allow to cool in pan for 10 minutes, then turn out onto a wire rack to cool completely.

Slice loaf crosswise into 10 slices, then halve each slice.

Makes 20 slices
(137 calories per slice)

Watermelon Basket

This favorite classic is always a crowd pleaser.

1 small watermelon basket shell
   (page 216)
1 cup fresh cantaloupe balls
1 cup halved fresh strawberries
1 cup fresh blueberries
1 cup fresh watermelon balls
1 cup fresh pineapple chunks
1 cup fresh peach chunks
1 cup seedless green grapes
1 tablespoon freshly squeezed
   lemon juice
2 tablespoons freshly squeezed
   orange juice
2 tablespoons unsweetened pineapple juice
2 teaspoons honey, warmed
½ teaspoon rum extract, optional

Chill prepared watermelon basket.
In a large bowl, combine all the fruit.
   In a small bowl, combine lemon juice, orange juice, pineapple juice, honey, and rum extract, if desired. Pour over fruit and toss.
   Just before serving, fill basket with fruit.

Makes 16 servings
(45 calories per serving)

Minted Lemonade

¼ cup honey
½ cup hot water
½ cup freshly squeezed
   lemon juice
2 cups cold water
⅛ teaspoon mint extract
4 mint leaves, optional

In a bowl, dissolve honey in hot water. Add lemon juice, cold water, and mint extract. Pour over ice in 4 glasses. Garnish with mint leaves, if desired.

Makes 4 servings
(21 calories per serving)

Cinnamon Cream

2 **cups skim milk**
1 **envelope unflavored gelatin**
2 **tablespoons honey**
1 **teaspoon ground cinnamon**
2 **eggs, separated**
6 **seedless orange sections**
  ground cinnamon for sprinkling

In the top of a double boiler set over simmering water, heat skim milk to scalding. Add gelatin and stir until dissolved. Mix in honey and cinnamon.

In a small bowl, beat egg yolks until thick. Gradually whisk about ¼ cup of the hot milk mixture into egg yolks, then whisk mixture back into remaining hot milk in top of double boiler. Continue cooking until pudding is thick and smooth, stirring constantly. Remove from heat and allow to cool.

In a medium-size bowl, beat egg whites until stiff peaks form. Fold into pudding. Divide among 6 dessert dishes. Top each with an orange section and chill.

Sprinkle with cinnamon just before serving.

Makes 6 servings
(88 calories per serving)

SEPTEMBER

Diet Ideas for Puddings and Piecrusts

FRUIT OF THE MONTH: **CANTALOUPE**

DESSERT OF THE MONTH: **CANTALOUPE SHERBET**

DRINK OF THE MONTH: **CANTALOUPE COOLER**

				1	*Labor Day* 2	3
				COLORFUL FRUIT MOLD	LAZY DAY LOAF CAKE	CANTALOUPE SHERBET ★
4	5	6	7	8	9	10
PEACH PEAR SHORTCAKES	PEACH WHIP	SURPRISE FRUIT PUDDING	PLUM EASY TARTS	PRETTY PEACHES	RAISIN SOUFFLÉ	LEMON PUDDING CAKE
11	12	13	14	15	16	17
FRENCH CAROB ICE MILK	APPLESAUCE CUSTARD	ABRACADABRA COCONUT PIE	CAROB CHIP PUDDING	FROZEN FRUITSICLES	BLUEBERRY APPLES	BANANA BITS
18	19	20	21	22	23	24
EASY ORANGE PLUM PUDDING	BLACKBERRY SHORTCAKE	VANILLA POACHED PEACHES	CRUSTLESS LEMON PUMPKIN PIE	BLINCHIKI WITH BLUEBERRY GRAPE SAUCE	BANANA FRAPPE	GINGERBREAD SQUARES
25	26	27	28	29	30	
COCONUT CAROB PUDDING	⅛ RIPE CANTALOUPE	FRESH FIGS WITH CREAMY TOPPING	EVERYDAY SUNDAES	BRANDIED PEACH TAPIOCA	TROPICAL TART	

$\mathcal{P}$uddings lend themselves well to the needs of the calorie watcher. They can be made with luscious fruits, slimming gelatin, frothy egg whites, whipped milk, and other nutritious ingredients that don't add much in the way of pounds. There are certain modifications I make to turn classic puddings into more acceptable desserts for the dieter. For example, I never use flour as a thickener. It not only has more calories, spoonful for spoonful, than cornstarch, but it takes more flour to thicken a liquid than it does to thicken the same amount of liquid with cornstarch. It takes two teaspoons of cornstarch at 18 calories or one tablespoon of flour at 28 calories to thicken a cup of milk. But even if the amount of flour and cornstarch needed had the same calorie content, I'd use cornstarch to thicken a pudding. A pudding thickened with cornstarch is translucent, showing off the colors and textures of other ingredients. And many puddings aren't cooked long enough to eliminate the raw taste of flour.

Arrowroot is an even stronger thickener than cornstarch, but it lacks the stability of cornstarch or flour so I seldom use it. One teaspoon of arrowroot replaces one tablespoon of flour.

Eggs have lots of good protein and I often use them to thicken puddings. One egg at 79 calories will thicken one cup of milk. But since they aren't diet food, I often use them in tandem with cornstarch to get the flavor of the egg and the added thickening provided by the lower calorie cornstarch.

I make puddings with skim milk instead of cream or milk. And I often use one whole egg instead of two egg yolks because most of the calories contained in the egg are in the yolk. This can be done successfully even in custards.

Bread puddings—basically custards with bread—are wonderfully versatile. You can serve them hot from the oven, or they can be made ahead and served chilled. The versions I offer in this book have less bread than those you might be used to and, of course, none of them is made with whole milk or cream—but, I can't say I miss these rich ingredients.

Puddings for Applause

Rice puddings make use of one of the world's most plentiful foods. To make diet rice puddings, I replace whole milk or cream with fruit juices or skim milk, and whole eggs with egg whites. These desserts can be cooked either on top of the stove or in the oven. Stove-top rice pudding is slightly thinner than that baked in the oven. It should be just thick enough to mound in a dish. A molded rice pudding is attractive as well as tasty. Just add gelatin, dissolved in whatever liquid you're using, to stove-top pudding and chill it in a decorative mold.

One of the most impressive puddings is a trifle. Served in a glass dish or compote, it makes dessert fit for the poshest company. Trifles are made by layering cake, fruit, and pudding in a bowl, the cake flavorfully dampened by fruit juice. Although trifles are usually made with a firm butter cake, I use a foam cake to reduce calories. Angel food cake makes a beautiful base; its pale color shows off the fruit to advantage.

There are two types of desserts that share the name "soufflé," and they have little else in common. I classify both as puddings. One is the cold soufflé with a gelatin base. Most of these fit the requirements of a diet dessert. The other is a hot, egg-based, dessert that must be served immediately upon removal from the oven. These hot soufflés are egg-rich, and most of them boast many calories. However, the showy hot soufflé can be made with egg whites instead of whole eggs or with fewer eggs than is customary to reduce calories.

Tapioca isn't just a good pudding, it's a thickener often used in pies. But on its own, it's a fluffy dessert the calorie conscious can enjoy when it's made with fruit juice or when beaten egg whites are incorporated into it.

Cobblers consist of fruits topped with pieces of dough before they're baked in the oven. Although they are a bit high in calories, they can be enjoyed if you downplay the mounds of dough, making them smaller than you may be used to.

And the gelatin puddings are a boon to the dessert-loving dieter. What in the world would those of us who have to watch calories do without gelatin!

You won't find any steamed puddings in this book. Although they're delicious, I have yet to find a diet version that can compare in texture and taste to the conventional, heavy steamed puddings I love.

Perfect Piecrusts

There's no question about it, piecrust is fattening! But it's so delicately delicious and tempting, I had to find a way to include it in my desserts. And as you'll see, there are many pies in this book that use a conventional piecrust. But there's not even one pie that needs a double crust. And the Mini Piecrust I do use is drastically calorie-reduced — it's rolled thin, and I've eliminated the large piece of crust that rims the average pie.

I make piecrust with a combination of whole wheat pastry flour and unbleached white flour. Whole wheat flour has fewer calories than its white counterpart, and it makes a dough that's easier to roll out.

I've provided recipes for meringue piecrust, coconut crust, and cookie crusts, too. They add flavor and variety to diet pies. And I think you'll agree that the wonderful juicy fruit fillings, frothy chiffons, and sumptuous pudding pies in this book make you think of anything but dieting.

Peach Pear Shortcakes

6 **Skinny Shortcakes** (page 72)
3 **ripe peaches**
1 **ripe pear**
1 **cup plain low-fat yogurt**
1 **teaspoon honey, warmed**
1 **teaspoon vanilla extract**

Split each shortcake sideways. Peel and pit peaches. Peel and core pear. Cut fruit into chunks and drop them into a bowl of cold water to which 1 teaspoon lemon juice has been added. Toss to coat fruit.

In a small bowl, combine yogurt, honey, and vanilla. Toss with peaches and pears. Divide among shortcakes, mounding mixture on bottom halves. Cover with tops of shortcakes and serve immediately.

Makes 6 servings
(189 calories per serving)

 ## Cantaloupe Sherbet

1 **envelope unflavored gelatin**
1 **cup water**
⅓ **cup honey**
1 **very ripe cantaloupe**
1 **cup skim milk**

In a medium-size saucepan, sprinkle gelatin over water. Set aside to soften for 5 minutes. Cook over medium heat, stirring constantly, until gelatin dissolves. Remove from heat and stir in honey until dissolved.

Halve cantaloupe. Scoop out seeds and discard. Peel cantaloupe and cut it into chunks. Puree cantaloupe and skim milk in a food processor. Stir into gelatin mixture.

Process mixture in an ice cream maker according to manufacturer's instructions, or turn mixture into a shallow pan, cover, and put in freezer until mushy but not frozen. Remove from freezer, beat to break down ice crystals, and then return to freezer. Repeat this procedure twice, transferring sherbet to covered containers before returning to freezer the last time. Freeze until ready to serve.

Makes 10 servings
(62 calories per serving)

Lemon Pudding Cake

2 eggs, separated
⅛ teaspoon cream of tartar
¾ cup skim milk
3 tablespoons whole wheat pastry
     flour
¼ cup freshly squeezed lemon juice
⅛ teaspoon baking soda
2 tablespoons honey
1 tablespoon butter, melted
1 teaspoon grated lemon peel
½ teaspoon lemon extract

Preheat oven to 350°F. Lightly butter a 1½-quart casserole.

In a medium-size bowl, beat egg whites until foamy. Add cream of tartar and continue beating until stiff peaks form.

In a large bowl, beat egg yolks. Shake together skim milk and flour in a jar with a tight-fitting lid. Beat into egg yolks. Add remaining ingredients and blend well.

Stir a small amount of the yolk mixture into whites to lighten, then fold whites into yolk mixture. Turn into prepared casserole and set in a pan of hot water on bottom shelf of oven. Bake for 55 to 60 minutes.

Makes 4 servings
(138 calories per serving)

Blinchiki with Blueberry Grape Sauce

1 cup skim milk
1 tablespoon freshly squeezed
     lemon juice
1 egg
1 tablespoon butter, melted and
     cooled
1 tablespoon honey
1 teaspoon vanilla extract
1¼ cups whole wheat pastry flour
1 teaspoon baking powder
1½ cups Blueberry Grape Sauce
     (page 122)

In a small bowl, mix together skim milk and lemon juice and set aside for 15 minutes.

In a medium-size bowl, beat together egg, milk mixture, butter, honey, and vanilla.

Sift together flour and baking powder into another small bowl and whisk to blend. Stir into milk mixture just until blended. Chill for 1 hour.

Spray a nonstick skillet with vegetable spray. Heat over medium heat until water dropped into skillet sizzles. Drop batter into skillet, allowing ¼ cup for each blinchiki. Cook until bubbles form, then flip over, and cook on the other side for 30 seconds.

Serve topped with Blueberry Grape Sauce.

Makes 6 servings
(178 calories per serving)

Raisin Soufflé

½ cup raisins
½ cup skim milk
½ teaspoon ground cinnamon
½ teaspoon vanilla extract
4 egg whites
⅛ teaspoon cream of tartar
1 teaspoon honey
¼ cup Peach Sauce (page 120),
    divided

Preheat oven to 350°F. Spray a 1½-quart soufflé dish with vegetable spray.

In a small saucepan, bring raisins, skim milk, and cinnamon to a boil. Reduce heat and simmer, stirring constantly, until raisins are nicely plumped. Remove from heat and stir in vanilla. Puree in a food processor.

In a medium-size bowl, beat egg whites until foamy. Add cream of tartar and honey and continue to beat until stiff peaks form. Fold raisin mixture into egg whites and turn into prepared soufflé dish. Bake on middle shelf of oven until light brown and puffy, about 30 minutes.

Top each serving with 1 tablespoon of the Peach Sauce and serve immediately.

Makes 4 servings
(92 calories per serving)

French Carob Ice Milk

2 eggs
⅔ cup honey
2 tablespoons cornstarch
1 quart skim milk, divided
1 tablespoon vanilla extract
¼ cup Versatile Carob Syrup
    (page 148)

In a small bowl, beat together eggs and honey until foamy.

In a jar with a tight-fitting lid, shake together cornstarch and 1 cup of the skim milk. Pour into the top of a double boiler set over hot water and cook over low heat, stirring constantly, until milk thickens. Whisk a small amount of hot milk into egg mixture. Return to hot milk, whisking constantly, and cook 1 minute, stirring. Turn into a large bowl and mix in remaining ingredients.

Process mixture in an ice cream maker according to manufacturer's instructions, or turn into a large pan and place in freezer until partially frozen. Remove from freezer, beat to break down ice crystals, and then return to freezer. Repeat this procedure twice, spooning mixture into 2 1-quart containers the last time. Freeze until ready to serve.

Makes 8 servings
(142 calories per serving)

Applesauce Custard

3 eggs
1 cup skim milk
½ teaspoon ground cinnamon
¼ teaspoon ground nutmeg
1½ cups Applesauce (page 81)

Preheat oven to 325°F.
In a large bowl, beat eggs slightly.
In a small saucepan, heat skim milk, cinnamon, and nutmeg to scalding. Slowly whisk into beaten eggs. Stir in applesauce and divide among 8 ½-cup, ovenproof dishes. Set dishes in a shallow pan and put on middle shelf of oven. Pour hot water into pan until it almost reaches tops of dishes. Bake until a knife inserted near centers of custards comes out clean, about 40 minutes.

Makes 8 servings
(61 calories per serving)

Coconut Carob Pudding

3 cups Creamy Carob Pudding
    (page 160), divided
½ cup unsweetened flaked coconut
8 Light Lemon Cookies (page 121),
    divided

In a medium-size bowl, mix together pudding and coconut. Put half of mixture into a 2-quart casserole. Top with cookies and remaining pudding mixture. Chill until ready to serve.

Makes 8 servings
(146 calories per serving)

Colorful Fruit Mold

1½ teaspoons unflavored gelatin
1¼ cups water
3 tablespoons honey
¼ cup freshly squeezed lemon
    juice
¾ cup sliced fresh strawberries
¾ cup fresh blueberries
1 small ripe banana

In a small saucepan, sprinkle gelatin over water. Set aside for 5 minutes to soften. Heat, stirring, until gelatin is dissolved. Remove from heat. Stir in honey and lemon juice. Chill until thickened but not set, about 30 minutes, stirring occasionally so that edges won't set.
Fold in strawberries and blueberries. Thinly slice banana and fold into gelatin mixture. Turn into a wet 1½-quart mold. Chill until set.
Turn out onto a plate before serving.

Makes 6 servings
(68 calories per serving)

Frozen Fruitsicles

⅔ cup freshly squeezed orange juice
⅔ cup unsweetened pineapple juice
⅔ cup white grape juice
1 teaspoon brandy extract, optional

In a medium-size bowl, mix together all ingredients. Pour into 8 2-ounce pop molds or into an ice cube tray and freeze.

Makes 8 fruitsicles
(35 calories per fruitsicle)

Plum Easy Tarts

1 **recipe for Mini Piecrust**
   (page 104)
4 **fresh plums**
½ **cup Slim Pastry Cream**
   (page 246), **divided**
¼ **cup Delicious Diet Cream**
   (page 109), **divided**

Preheat oven to 425°F.

Roll out dough between 2 pieces of waxed paper. Remove top piece of waxed paper and lightly flour dough. Cut into 4 4-inch circles. Fit dough, flour side down, over backs of 4 muffin cups. Bake on middle shelf of oven until lightly browned, about 10 minutes.

Carefully remove shells and place, right side up, on a wire rack. Allow to cool completely.

To serve, halve and pit plums. Place 2 plum halves in each tart shell. Add 2 tablespoons of the pastry cream and 1 tablespoon of the diet cream. Serve immediately.

Makes 4 servings
(193 calories per serving)

Banana Bits

These are lovely little cookies with just a subtle banana flavor.

½ **cup whole wheat pastry flour**
½ **cup unbleached white flour**
½ **teaspoon baking powder**
½ **teaspoon baking soda**
2 **eggs**
½ **cup honey**
1 **teaspoon vanilla extract**
1 **ripe banana**
1 **teaspoon freshly squeezed lemon**
   juice
1 **cup rolled oats**

Preheat oven to 350°F. Spray 2 baking sheets with vegetable spray.

Sift together whole wheat pastry flour, unbleached white flour, baking powder, and baking soda into a medium-size bowl.

In a large bowl, beat together eggs, honey, and vanilla until lemon colored.

In a food processor, process banana and lemon juice. Mix into egg mixture. Gradually stir in flour mixture, blending well. Stir in oats. Drop by teaspoonfuls onto prepared baking sheets. Bake, 1 sheet at a time, on middle shelf of oven until golden, 10 to 12 minutes.

Remove to wire racks to cool.

Makes 3 dozen cookies
(43 calories per cookie)

Lazy Day Loaf Cake

2 tablespoons butter
2 eggs
⅓ cup honey
½ cup whole wheat pastry flour
½ cup unbleached white flour
1½ teaspoons baking powder
¼ cup hot water
1 teaspoon almond extract

Preheat oven to 350°F. Lightly grease and flour a 4½ × 8½-inch loaf pan.

In a small saucepan, melt butter. Set aside to cool.

In a large bowl, beat eggs until thick. Beat in honey.

In a small bowl, sift together whole wheat pastry flour, unbleached white flour, and baking powder, whisking to blend well. Gradually beat into egg mixture. Beat in hot water, almond extract, and melted butter. Turn into prepared pan, and bake on middle shelf of oven until a cake tester inserted into center comes out clean, 25 to 30 minutes.

Cool for 10 minutes, then remove from pan and cool completely on a wire rack.

Makes 10 servings
(116 calories per serving)

Carob Chip Pudding

2 cups skim milk, divided
2 tablespoons cornstarch
2 tablespoons honey
1 egg, beaten
2 teaspoons vanilla extract
2 tablespoons carob chips

In the top of a double boiler set over boiling water, heat 1½ cups of the skim milk. In a jar with a tight-fitting lid, shake together remaining skim milk and cornstarch. Add gradually to hot milk and cook, stirring constantly until thickened. Stir in honey. Whisk a little of the hot mixture into beaten egg and then return to top of double boiler. Continue to cook, stirring constantly, for another 2 minutes.

Remove from heat and stir in vanilla. Allow to cool slightly, then stir in carob chips. (Pudding should still be warm.) Divide among 4 dessert dishes and chill.

Makes 4 servings
(151 calories per serving)

Vanilla Poached Peaches

Since the poaching water is discarded, you get the sweetness of the honey while avoiding most of the calories.

> 2 cups water
> ½ cup honey
> ½ vanilla bean, split lengthwise
> 4 large fresh peaches, halved, peeled, and pitted
> 1 cup Ruby Raspberry Sauce (page 127), divided
> 24 fresh raspberries

In a large saucepan, combine water, honey, and vanilla bean. Bring to a boil, stirring occasionally. Reduce heat, add peaches, cover, and cook 4 minutes. (Water should be barely simmering.) With a slotted spoon, turn peach halves over. Continue to poach until peaches are tender but not mushy, about 4 more minutes.

Carefully remove peaches to a plate. Discard poaching water. Cover peaches with plastic wrap and chill.

At serving time, spoon 1 tablespoon of the Ruby Raspberry Sauce onto each of 8 individual dessert plates. Top sauce with a peach half, spoon another tablespoon of sauce over peach, and decorate with 3 raspberries.

Makes 8 servings
(104 calories per serving)

Gingerbread Squares

> 2 tablespoons butter, softened
> 2 tablespoons honey
> 1 tablespoon molasses
> 2 eggs
> ¼ cup skim milk
> 1 cup whole wheat pastry flour
> ½ teaspoon baking powder
> 1 teaspoon ground ginger
> 1 teaspoon ground cinnamon
> ¼ teaspoon ground nutmeg
> ¼ cup raisins, plumped

Preheat oven to 350°F. Spray an 8 × 8-inch pan with vegetable spray.

In a large bowl, cream together butter, honey, and molasses. Beat in eggs and skim milk.

In a medium-size bowl, whisk together flour, baking powder, ginger, cinnamon, and nutmeg. Drain raisins and toss them with 1 tablespoon of flour mixture. Mix remaining flour mixture into moist ingredients. Fold in raisins. Spread batter in prepared pan and bake on middle shelf of oven for 15 minutes.

Cut into 9 squares. Cool on wire rack.

Makes 9 servings
(119 calories per serving)

Tropical Tart

The pineapple in this recipe must be thoroughly drained or the texture of the finished product will be watery.

- 1 8-ounce can unsweetened crushed pineapple
- 2 cups low-fat cottage cheese or part-skim ricotta cheese
- ⅓ cup honey
- 2 eggs
- ¼ cup evaporated skim milk
- 1½ teaspoons vanilla extract
- ½ cup unsweetened flaked coconut
- ½ recipe for Skinny Piecrust (page 5)

Preheat oven to 350°F. Spray a 9-inch springform pan with vegetable spray.

Drain pineapple well.

In a food processor, beat cottage cheese or ricotta until smooth. Add honey, eggs, evaporated skim milk, and vanilla and process just to mix.

Fold in pineapple and coconut and turn into prepared pan. Bake on middle shelf of oven until filling is barely firm, about 30 minutes.

While tart is baking, roll out pastry and cut it into 9 1-inch strips.

Remove tart from oven. Increase temperature to 400°F. Place strips of pastry on top of filling and return to oven until pastry is lightly browned, about 10 minutes.

Makes 10 servings
(137 calories per serving)

Cantaloupe Cooler

- 1 cup fresh cantaloupe chunks
- ½ cup freshly squeezed orange juice
- 1 teaspoon honey

Blend all ingredients in a blender. Pour over crushed ice in glasses and serve immediately.

Makes 2 servings
(63 calories per serving)

Everyday Sundaes

- 2 cups Vanilla Ice Milk (page 72), divided
- ¼ cup Creamy Carob Sauce (page 186), divided
- ¼ cup unsweetened crushed pineapple, well drained, divided
- 2 teaspoons ground walnuts, divided

Divide Vanilla Ice Milk among 4 long-stemmed dessert glasses. Top each with 1 tablespoon of the Creamy Carob Sauce, 1 tablespoon of the crushed pineapple, and ½ teaspoon of the ground walnuts, in that order. Serve immediately.

Makes 4 servings
(176 calories per serving)

Blueberry Apples

4 apples
2 tablespoons maple syrup
½ cup fresh blueberries
¼ cup Mock Whipped Cream
(page 9), **optional**

Preheat oven to 350°F.

Core apples, leaving bottoms intact. Do not peel. Place apples in a shallow baking dish.

In a small bowl, mix together maple syrup and blueberries. Stuff apples with blueberries and bake on middle shelf of oven until apples are soft, about 30 minutes.

Top with Mock Whipped Cream, if desired.

Makes 4 servings
(100 calories per serving)

Pretty Peaches

This is a delightfully tangy dessert.

1 cup plain low-fat yogurt
1 tablespoon honey
½ teaspoon freshly squeezed
lemon juice
3 tablespoons minced crystallized
ginger
2 ripe peaches

In a small bowl, gently mix together yogurt, honey, and lemon juice. Fold in ginger.

Peel, pit, and thinly slice peaches. Fold into yogurt mixture and chill, covered, until serving time.

Makes 4 servings
(71 calories per serving)

Creamy Carob Sauce

This sauce can be served either hot or cold and keeps well in the refrigerator.

1 cup Versatile Carob
Syrup (page 148)
⅓ cup honey

2 tablespoons butter
1½ teaspoons vanilla extract

In a large saucepan, bring carob syrup and honey to a boil, stirring constantly. Boil for 6 minutes, stirring constantly.

Remove from heat and stir in butter and vanilla, whisking until butter is melted. The sauce will keep, refrigerated, up to 1 month.

Makes about 1 cup
(46 calories per tablespoon)

Crustless Lemon Pumpkin Pie

3 eggs
1¼ cups pumpkin puree
¾ cup skim milk
⅓ cup plus 2 tablespoons honey
1 teaspoon ground cinnamon
¼ teaspoon ground ginger
¼ teaspoon ground nutmeg
1 cup plain nonfat yogurt
2 teaspoons grated lemon rind

Preheat oven to 350°F. Spray a 9-inch pie plate with vegetable spray.

In a large bowl, beat together eggs, pumpkin, skim milk, ⅓ cup of the honey, cinnamon, ginger, and nutmeg. Turn into prepared pie plate and bake on middle shelf of oven until a knife inserted near the center comes out clean, 50 to 55 minutes. Allow to cool.

In a small bowl, gently combine yogurt and remaining honey. Spread on top of pie. Chill.

Sprinkle with grated lemon rind, and serve immediately.

Makes 8 servings
(84 calories per serving)

Fresh Figs
with Creamy Topping

Figs should be used on the day they're purchased. They are oh, so perishable!

8 fresh figs
¾ cup evaporated skim milk, chilled
2 tablespoons honey
1 teaspoon vanilla extract
¼ teaspoon ground cinnamon
4 mint leaves, optional

Put 2 figs into each of 4 dessert dishes.

In a medium-size bowl, beat evaporated milk until foamy. Add honey, vanilla, and cinnamon and beat until the consistency of whipped cream. Divide among dessert dishes, mounding on top of figs. Decorate with mint leaves, if desired.

Makes 4 servings
(150 calories per serving)

Blackberry Shortcake

6 Skinny Shortcakes (page 72)
4 cups fresh blackberries
¾ cup Delicious Diet Cream
(page 109), divided

Cut shortcakes into halves crosswise. Divide berries among shortcakes, mounding them on bottom halves. Put tops over berries. Top each with 2 tablespoons of the diet cream.

Makes 6 servings
(193 calories per serving)

Surprise Fruit Pudding

1 20-ounce can unsweetened
   crushed pineapple
3 envelopes unflavored gelatin
2 tablespoons honey
1½ cups fresh strawberries,
   quartered
½ cup unsweetened flaked
   coconut
½ cup carob chips

Drain pineapple well, reserving juice. In a medium-size saucepan, sprinkle gelatin over reserved juice. Set aside for 5 minutes to soften. Stir in honey and heat over low heat, stirring constantly, until gelatin is dissolved.

Stir in pineapple, strawberries, and coconut. Divide among 8 dessert dishes and sprinkle each with 1 tablespoon carob chips. Chill thoroughly.

Makes 8 servings
(19 calories per serving)

Brandied Peach Tapioca

3 tablespoons quick-cooking
   tapioca
2 cups skim milk
2 tablespoons maple syrup
½ teaspoon ground cinnamon
1 egg yolk, beaten
½ teaspoon brandy extract
½ teaspoon vanilla extract
3 cups unsweetened frozen
   peaches, thawed and drained

In a medium-size saucepan, sprinkle tapioca over skim milk. Set aside for 5 minutes.

Stir in maple syrup, cinnamon, and egg yolk. Bring to a boil over medium heat, stirring constantly. Remove from heat and stir in extracts. When slightly cooled, fold in peaches. Refrigerate until ready to serve.

Makes 8 servings
(98 calories per serving)

Banana Frappe

2 ripe bananas, chunked
1 tablespoon honey
2 cups skim milk
1 teaspoon vanilla extract
½ teaspoon ground cinnamon

In a food processor, puree bananas. Add remaining ingredients and process until blended. Pour into glasses and serve immediately.

Makes 4 servings
(110 calories per serving)

Peach Whip

1   envelope unflavored gelatin
½   cup water
2   tablespoons honey
1   cup peach puree (2 to 3 medium-
       size fresh peaches, peeled and
       pureed in a food processor)
1   teaspoon freshly squeezed
       lemon juice
2   egg whites, at room temperature
⅛   teaspoon cream of tartar

In a small saucepan, sprinkle gelatin over water. Set aside for 5 minutes to soften. Heat over medium heat, stirring constantly, until gelatin dissolves. Remove from heat. Stir in honey, peach puree, and lemon juice. Chill until thickened but not set, stirring occasionally, about 30 minutes.

In a medium-size bowl, beat egg whites until foamy. Add cream of tartar and continue beating until stiff peaks form. Fold into gelatin mixture and chill until set.

Makes 6 servings
(60 calories per serving)

Abracadabra Coconut Pie

It's magic! This tasty treat forms a crust as it bakes.

2   cups skim milk
4   eggs
¼   cup honey
2   tablespoons maple syrup
½   cup whole wheat pastry flour
3   tablespoons butter, cut into pieces
1   teaspoon vanilla extract
¾   cup unsweetened flaked coconut

Preheat oven to 350°F. Spray a 9-inch pie plate with vegetable spray.

In a blender, combine skim milk, eggs, honey, maple syrup, flour, butter, and vanilla. Process until smooth. Stir in coconut. Turn into prepared pie plate and bake on middle shelf of oven until a knife inserted near center comes out clean, about 50 minutes. Serve chilled.

Makes 10 servings
(155 calories per serving)

Easy Orange Plum Pudding

3 **tablespoons cornstarch**
2 **cups freshly squeezed orange**
    juice
3 **tablespoons honey**
4 **fresh plums**

In a medium-size saucepan, dissolve cornstarch in orange juice. Mix in honey and cook over medium heat, stirring constantly, until thickened, about 15 minutes.

Pit plums and cut into eighths. Stir into orange juice mixture. Turn into a medium-size bowl and chill.

Makes 6 servings
(111 calories per serving)

OCTOBER

The Proper Care, Storage, and Freezing of Desserts

FRUIT OF THE MONTH: **PINEAPPLE**

DESSERT OF THE MONTH: **TROPICAL PINEAPPLE DELIGHT**

DRINK OF THE MONTH: **ORANGE PINEAPPLE PUNCH**

				1	2	3
				FAUX CAFE WHIP	ONE SLICE FRESH PINEAPPLE	SPICY PUMPKIN CUSTARD
4	5	6	*Rosh Hashanah* 7	8	9	10
PEPPERMINT ALASKA	PRETTY STRAWBERRY BAVARIAN	LEMON CHIFFON PIE	ROSH HASHANAH CARROT CAKE	VANILLA CREAM WITH RASPBERRY SAUCE	APPLE RAISIN TART	FRESH PINEAPPLE SORBET
11	*Columbus Day* 12	13	14	15	*Yom Kippur* 16	17
RAISIN RICE CHEWS	DISCOVERY CAKE	LEMELON	CRAN-PINEAPPLE PIE	SNOW PUDDING WITH CUSTARD SAUCE	YOM KIPPUR DATE NUT CAKE	TROPICAL PINEAPPLE DELIGHT ★
18	19	20	21	22	23	24
STUFFED DATES	CRANBERRY PINEAPPLE FLUFF	CAMOCHA PIE	GRAPEFRUIT GRANITA	BAKED PRUNE WHIP	LIME-GLAZED BAKED PINEAPPLE	UPPER CRUST LEMON CUSTARD PIE
25	26	27	28	29	30	*Halloween* 31
ORANGE CAROB WHIP	OCTOBER CAKE	AUTUMN SUNDAE	ORANGE WHIP	COOL PINEAPPLE CREPES	COMPANY APPLES	PUMPKIN CUPCAKES

It's a shame to spend time baking and cooking only to have your efforts ruined because of improper storage. All desserts need proper care to stay at their fresh best.

Puddings, for instance, should be delicate, but many of them form an unattractive tough skin on top as they cool. There are two methods for preventing this. You can pour a very thin layer of skim milk over the top of the pudding, then stir it in at serving time. Or you can cover the pudding with a piece of plastic wrap, arranging it so it just touches the pudding. The milk adds an extra touch, but it also adds calories! So for a diet pudding, unless it's particularly low cal, the latter makes more sense.

Store each kind of cookie in its own airtight container. Never keep different varieties together. Crisp cookies absorb the moisture from moist cookies leaving the moist cookies dry and the crisp cookies rubbery. And the flavors quickly mingle, robbing the cookies of their identities. For example, the spices in ginger cookies will permeate delicate vanilla or lemon wafers, and the raisins in Hermits will muddy the taste of carob crisps. To keep moist cookies moist, store them away from the crisps and add a slice of bread to the container.

Nothing dries out more rapidly than cake. (Although the cakes in this book stay fresh longer than most because they're made with honey.) All cakes should be completely cool before they're stored or frosted. Tightly wrap unfrosted cake in plastic wrap to insure freshness or store a frosted cake in a cake keeper. If you don't have one, invert a large bowl over the cake. A slice of lemon kept with a cake imparts moistness. The cut edges of cake dry out fast. To avoid this, place a piece of waxed paper against the edge before you store the cake.

Fruit pies keep well at room temperature, but pies with custard, chiffon pies, or those with cream fillings should be refrigerated after being lightly covered.

Freezing Desserts

The freezer is a marvel for keeping desserts. It's particularly helpful for the dieter. When I have leftover cake, I cut it into serving-size pieces, wrap each individually, and put them in the freezer. I only defrost enough for one meal. This little system makes it difficult to go back for seconds. The time it would take to defrost the cake is enough for me to resist the impulse to overeat.

Not all desserts freeze well. Anything with a milk sauce tends to curdle, cream pies become lumpy, and gelatin desserts weep and fall apart when they're thawed. (However, frozen desserts, made with gelatin bases, such as sherbets, work out very well.)

Wrapping desserts properly before freezing them is important. There are many good materials for this purpose. You have your choice of plastic freezer wrap, heavy duty plastic bags, or aluminum foil (which I use over plastic freezer wrap for extra protection). For cookies, doughs, or sauces there's an assortment of rigid frostproof containers. I prefer square ones because they're easy to stack in the freezer.

I color code every package I freeze so I'll know at a glance whether it contains pie, cake, or cookies, and whether the pie or cookies are baked or unbaked. I use brightly colored stickers for this and mark the contents and date of freezing on them. And I rotate the desserts so that the last ones frozen are at the bottom of the freezer. There's a master list next to my freezer, and I write down what goes in, checking it off when I remove it. I know this sounds like a big job, but it really isn't, and it takes the guesswork out of freezer storage.

Everyone likes to have cookies on hand for unexpected guests, lunches, or after-school treats. And they are favorite choices for the freezer—they keep well and thaw fast. Cookies can be frozen baked or unbaked. Baked cookies defrost in about 15 minutes, except for bar cookies which take about one hour. If you freeze a large piece of dough instead of individual cookies, allow several hours at room temperature for it to thaw.

Package crisp cookies carefully in layers, with cardboard between, before freezing them. Or you may prefer to freeze the batter to avoid any possible breakage. Rolled cookies are at their best frozen raw, in a roll. To bake them, slice off as many as you need at the thickness you prefer, pop them in the oven, and return the rest of the roll to the freezer. This method provides the convenience of freezing while still retaining the flavor of fresh-baked cookies.

Freeze unbaked drop cookies individually on a baking sheet, then store them in a rigid container. When you bake these or any other frozen cookies, add a few minutes to the cooking time to allow for thawing in the oven.

Cakes

I seldom freeze a frosted cake. To begin with, unfrosted cakes last four to five months in the freezer, while frosted ones are past their prime in two or three months. And the types of frostings that freeze best are those made with confectioners' sugar (something I never use), or butter (which because of its calories, I use sparingly). Most of the few frostings I use are made with whipped egg whites, the very worst candidates for the freezer.

Cake batter is so easy to make and takes so long to defrost, it isn't worth the trouble of freezing and defrosting it. And spices become strong and acquire an off taste when they're frozen. This is especially true of cloves which get so bitter a cake becomes almost inedible. So spice cakes are better eaten fresh.

To freeze a whole, unfrosted cake, wrap it first in plastic wrap, then in foil. But if you're freezing a frosted cake, freeze it unwrapped on a baking sheet. Then wrap it carefully in plastic freezer wrap, and store it in a stiff cardboard box, sealed airtight with freezer tape. To defrost this type of cake, you can either let it stand at room temperature for about three hours without unwrapping it, or unwrap the cake and cover it with a large bowl or cake keeper.

A cake should be completely thawed before it's frosted because the surface condensation that accumulates during defrosting prevents icing from sticking. And if you do get the frosting on while the middle of the cake is still frozen, the moisture will make the cake soggy.

Pastry

Pastry freezes extremely well either baked or unbaked. You can roll it out without chilling it if it's going to be frozen, or you can freeze it in a ball and roll it out later. It can be frozen in flat pieces that are easily made into a crust, or the crust can be made before freezing. There are choices aplenty!

If you're going to bake piecrusts before freezing them, allow them to cool thoroughly, freeze them without wrapping, then wrap them individually and stack them together in the freezer.

You also can freeze filled pies either baked or oven-ready. When freezing an unbaked top-crust pie, don't cut perforations in the crust until you're ready to bake it. Freeze the unbaked pie unwrapped. Then wrap it in plastic wrap and foil, label it, and return it to the freezer.

Baked pies must be thoroughly cooled before they're frozen. And the top of the pie must be protected during the initial freezing. Another pie plate inverted over the top does this nicely. When the pie is frozen, remove it from the freezer and wrap it as you would an unbaked pie.

Pastry and pies frozen before baking are always better tasting than those baked before freezing. The pastry has a flakier texture and that just-baked flavor. But baked pies keep in the freezer about twice as long as the unbaked ones. So if I know I'm going to want long-term storage, I do bake pies first.

You can thaw pies, still wrapped, at room temperature for six to eight hours; unwrapped, in a 325°F oven for 30 to 40 minutes; or in a microwave oven, following the manufacturer's instructions (they differ according to the oven's power).

Bake unbaked frozen pies in a preheated, 400°F oven until the pastry is golden brown, about one hour. Check the progress at the end of 45 minutes. A glass pie plate is helpful for monitoring a pie with only a bottom crust. Place the pie on the bottom shelf of the oven where it should brown beautifully, keeping pace with the bubbly hot filling. For top-crust pies, choose the middle shelf.

Peppermint Alaska

1 recipe for Mini Piecrust
   (page 104)
4 cups French Peppermint Ice Milk
   (page 227)
½ cup Creamy Carob Sauce
   (page 186)
3 egg whites
¼ teaspoon cream of tartar
2 tablespoons honey
½ teaspoon vanilla extract

Line an 8-inch pie plate with pie crust and bake blind according to directions. Cool thoroughly.

Fill cooled piecrust with scoops of ice milk, packing them down. Spoon carob sauce over ice milk and freeze. When well frozen, wrap pie in plastic wrap.

At serving time, preheat oven to 500°F.

In a medium-size bowl, beat egg whites until foamy. Add cream of tartar and continue beating, drizzling in honey and vanilla, until stiff peaks form.

Remove pie from freezer and pile meringue on top, sealing edges well. Make peaks with back of spoon. Bake on middle shelf of oven until meringue is lightly browned, about 4 minutes. Serve immediately.

Makes 10 servings
(170 calories per serving)

Spicy Pumpkin Custard

1½ cups pureed cooked pumpkin
2 eggs
1½ cups skim milk
¼ cup honey
1 tablespoon whole wheat pastry flour
1 tablespoon unbleached white flour
1 teaspoon ground cinnamon
½ teaspoon ground ginger
½ teaspoon ground nutmeg
1½ teaspoons vanilla extract

Preheat oven to 350°F.

In a large bowl, beat together pumpkin, eggs, skim milk, and honey. Combine whole wheat pastry flour, unbleached white flour, and spices in a small bowl and beat into moist ingredients just until mixed. Stir in vanilla.

Turn into 6 custard cups and place in a large shallow pan. Pour hot water into pan to the depth of the ingredients in custard cups. Bake on middle shelf of oven for 45 to 50 minutes, or until a knife inserted near centers of custards comes out clean.

Set custard cups on a heatproof surface to cool. Chill before serving.

Makes 6 servings
(122 calories per serving)

Fresh Pineapple Sorbet

1 ripe pineapple
2 tablespoons honey
½ cup water
2 tablespoons unsweetened flaked
     coconut, optional

Peel, core, and chunk pineapple. Puree pineapple, honey, and water in a food processor.

Process mixture in an ice cream maker according to manufacturer's instructions, or turn mixture into a large pan and freeze until thickened but not solid. Remove from freezer, beat to break down ice crystals, and then return to freezer. Repeat this procedure twice, spooning mixture into a container the last time. Freeze until ready to serve.

Serve sprinkled with coconut, if desired.

Makes 4 servings
(102 calories per serving)

Pretty Strawberry Bavarian

1 envelope unflavored gelatin
¼ cup skim milk
½ 20-ounce package unsweetened
     frozen strawberries, thawed
2 tablespoons freshly squeezed
     lemon juice
2 tablespoons honey
2 egg yolks
1 cup evaporated skim milk
1 cup ice water

Sprinkle gelatin over skim milk. Set aside to soften for 5 minutes.

Drain berries, reserving juice. In a small saucepan, bring strawberry juice, lemon juice, and honey to a boil. Add gelatin mixture and stir until gelatin has dissolved. Remove from heat and allow to cool.

Poor into blender or food processor, whirling briefly. Add strawberries and egg yolks, blending until smooth. Add evaporated skim milk and ice water and blend until just mixed.

Wet the inside of a 6-cup decorative mold with cold water. Pour mixture into mold and chill until set.

When ready to serve, turn out onto attractive plate.

Makes 6 servings
(123 calories per serving)

Apple Raisin Tart

1 recipe for Mini Piecrust
    (page 104)
4 medium-size apples
1 tablespoon freshly squeezed
    lemon juice
2 tablespoons cornstarch
1 4½-ounce jar strained peaches
¼ cup raisins
¼ cup honey
1½ teaspoons ground cinnamon

Preheat oven to 400°F. Line a 9-inch pie plate with piecrust according to directions and set aside.

Peel, core, and thinly slice apples into a large bowl. Mix in lemon juice.

In a small bowl, dissolve cornstarch in strained peaches. Add to apple mixture. Add raisins, honey, and cinnamon, tossing to blend well. Turn into pie shell and bake on bottom shelf of oven for 15 minutes. Turn oven down to 375°F and bake until apples are soft and lightly browned, about 30 minutes more.

Makes 10 servings
(120 calories per serving)

Faux Cafe Whip

A summertime treat for coffee lovers.

1 envelope unflavored gelatin
2½ teaspoons decaffeinated instant
    coffee
⅓ cup honey
1¾ cups boiling water
1½ teaspoons vanilla extract

In a medium-size bowl, dissolve gelatin, coffee, and honey together in boiling water. Add vanilla extract and chill until thick but not set.

Beat until volume doubles. Divide among 4 dessert dishes and chill until set.

Makes 4 servings
(91 calories per serving)

Stuffed Dates

12 pitted dates
¼ cup Reduced Calorie Peanut
    Butter (page 54), **divided**
¼ cup Coconut Sugar (page 60)

Stuff each date with 1 teaspoon of the peanut butter. Roll in Coconut Sugar.

Makes 6 servings
(156 calories per serving)

Vanilla Cream
with Raspberry Sauce

A decorative mold turns this into an elegant dessert.

2 envelopes unflavored gelatin
1 cup water
2½ cups skim milk
⅓ cup honey
3 eggs, separated
1 teaspoon vanilla extract
⅛ teaspoon cream of tartar
2 cups Ruby Raspberry Sauce
   (page 127), **divided**

Sprinkle gelatin over water in the top of a double boiler. Set aside to soften for 5 minutes. Set over hot water and heat, stirring constantly, until gelatin dissolves. Stir in skim milk and honey. Beat egg yolks and whisk into milk. Heat, stirring constantly, until mixture thickens enough to coat the back of a spoon. Remove from heat immediately. Stir in vanilla. Chill until thick but not set.

In a medium-size bowl, beat egg whites until foamy. Add cream of tartar and continue beating until stiff peaks form. Fold into custard. Pour into a 6-cup mold and chill until set, about 2½ hours.

Unmold and spoon 1 cup of the sauce over top. Pass remaining sauce at the table.

Makes 10 servings
(104 calories per serving)

Rosh Hashanah Carrot Cake

3 eggs, separated
⅛ teaspoon cream of tartar
½ cup honey, divided
2 cups shredded carrots
1 teaspoon orange extract
½ cup whole wheat pastry flour
¼ cup unbleached white flour
1 teaspoon baking powder
2 tablespoons raisins, plumped
¼ cup unsweetened grated coconut

Preheat oven to 325°F. Spray a 9-inch springform pan with vegetable spray.

In a medium-size bowl, beat egg whites until foamy. Add cream of tartar and continue beating, drizzling in ¼ cup of the honey, until stiff peaks form.

In a large bowl, with same beaters, beat egg yolks and remaining honey until thick and lemon colored. Stir in carrots and orange extract.

Sift together whole wheat pastry flour, unbleached white flour, and baking powder into another medium-size bowl. Toss with raisins and coconut, and stir into carrot mixture. Fold in beaten egg whites and turn into prepared pan. Bake on middle shelf of oven until cake springs back when lightly pressed, 40 to 45 minutes. Remove sides of pan and cool.

Makes 10 servings
(126 calories per serving)

Cool Pineapple Crepes

1 cup Orange Pineapple Sherbet
(page 70), **softened, divided**
4 Delicious Diet Crepes (page 30)
½ cup Perfect Pineapple Sauce
(page 55), **divided**

Place ¼ cup of the sherbet along center of each crepe, from top edge to bottom edge. Roll 1 side, then the other side over sherbet. Top each crepe with 2 tablespoons of the Perfect Pineapple Sauce.

Makes 4 servings
(164 calories per serving)

Discovery Cake

Because cakes don't always turn out exactly the same size every time, there may be some pudding left over from the filling.

1 recipe for Heavenly Angel Food Cake (page 38)
1 recipe for Very Vanilla Pudding (page 76)
1 recipe for Creamy Carob Pudding (page 160)

Bake cake according to directions.

While puddings are still soft, swirl them together in a large bowl to achieve a marbled effect.

With a sharp knife, cut a 1-inch slice from top of cake. Set aside. Make a cut around cake 1 inch from outer edge to a depth of about 1 inch from bottom of cake. Make a cut around cake about ½ inch from inner edge (where tube was) to about 1 inch from bottom. Carefully scoop out cake, being sure to leave a ¾-to-1-inch layer of cake on bottom. (Reserve scooped-out cake for Mock Doughnut Holes, page 18.) Fill cavity in cake with pudding combination, packing firmly to avoid air holes. Place top of cake over pudding, cover with plastic wrap, and chill well before serving.

Makes 16 servings
(149 calories per serving)

Lemon Chiffon Pie

The lion's share of calories is eliminated by using a partial crust, but the wonderful pastry flavor remains.

½ recipe for 1 Skinny Piecrust
     (page 5)
2 tablespoons cornstarch
¾ cup freshly squeezed lemon
     juice, strained
1 envelope unflavored gelatin
1 cup water
⅓ cup plus 1 tablespoon honey,
     divided
1 egg yolk, beaten
3 egg whites, at room temperature
⅛ teaspoon cream of tartar

Line bottom and slightly up sides of a 9-inch pie plate with pastry and bake blind according to directions.

In a jar with a tight-fitting lid, shake together cornstarch and lemon juice.

In a small saucepan, sprinkle gelatin over water. Set aside to soften for 5 minutes. Add cornstarch mixture and ⅓ cup of the honey, and cook over medium heat, stirring constantly, until mixture clears and starts to thicken. Whisk a little of the hot lemon mixture into egg yolk. Return to saucepan, and continue cooking, stirring constantly, for 2 minutes. Remove from heat. Turn into a bowl and chill until thickened but not set.

In a medium-size bowl, beat egg whites until foamy. Add cream of tartar and remaining honey and continue beating until stiff peaks form. Fold into lemon mixture. Turn into prepared pie shell and chill until set.

Makes 8 servings
(107 calories per serving)

Lemelon

Save any leftover gelatin mixture for a snack.

½ cup freshly squeezed lemon
     juice, strained
1½ cups water, divided
1½ envelopes unflavored gelatin
¼ cup honey
¼ teaspoon lemon extract
     natural yellow food coloring
1 ripe cantaloupe
½ cup unsweetened crushed
     pineapple, well drained

In a medium-size bowl, combine lemon juice and 1 cup of the water.

In a small saucepan, sprinkle gelatin over remaining water. Set aside to soften for 5 minutes. Add honey and heat over medium heat, stirring until gelatin dissolves. Remove from heat and stir in lemon extract and food coloring. Chill until quite thick, but not set.

Cut melon in half. Scoop out seeds. Fill each melon half with water, then pour the water into a measuring cup from the melon halves. Subtract ½ cup. What's left is the amount of gelatin mixture you will need to fill the cantaloupe. Measure that amount of thickened gelatin. Fold in drained pineapple and fill each melon half with mixture, smoothing tops. Return to refrigerator until set.

With a sharp knife dipped in hot water, slice each melon half into quarters. Serve immediately.

Makes 8 servings
(161 calories per serving)

Cran-Pineapple Pie

1½ cups fresh cranberries
1 20-ounce can unsweetened
crushed pineapple
1 tablespoon cornstarch
1 tablespoon honey
½ teaspoon ground cinnamon
¼ teaspoon ground nutmeg
1 teaspoon vanilla extract
1 recipe for Mini Piecrust
(page 104)

Wash cranberries and put into a medium-size saucepan. Drain pineapple, reserving juice. Add pineapple to cranberries. Dissolve cornstarch in reserved juice and add to saucepan. Stir in honey, cinnamon, and nutmeg. Bring to a boil, stirring constantly, until mixture thickens. Reduce heat and boil, stirring often, until cranberries pop, about 15 minutes. (Mixture should be red.) Remove from heat and stir in vanilla.

Preheat oven to 350°F. Spray a 9-inch pie plate with vegetable spray. Line bottom with Mini Piecrust and bake blind according to directions.

Carefully spoon in filling. Cover filling with a tent of foil. Bake on middle shelf of oven for 20 minutes. Chill before serving.

Makes 8 servings
(130 calories per serving)

Raisin Rice Chews

A light and wholesome snack!

3 egg whites
⅛ teaspoon cream of tartar
1 teaspoon vanilla extract
1 teaspoon honey
2 cups Puffed Rice cereal
¼ cup raisins, plumped
¼ cup unsweetened flaked coconut

Preheat oven to 325°F. Line a baking sheet with parchment paper.

In a large bowl, beat egg whites until foamy. Add cream of tartar, vanilla, and honey. Continue beating until stiff peaks form. Fold in remaining ingredients. Divide into 12 portions and mound them on prepared baking sheet. Bake on middle shelf of oven until lightly browned, 12 to 15 minutes.

Carefully remove to wire rack to cool completely.

Makes 1 dozen cookies
(30 calories per cookie)

Tropical Pineapple Delight

1 20-ounce can unsweetened
    crushed pineapple
1 envelope unflavored gelatin
½ teaspoon vanilla extract
⅔ cup instant nonfat dry milk
⅔ cup ice water
1 tablespoon freshly squeezed
    lemon juice
2 tablespoons honey
1 cup unsweetened flaked coconut

Drain pineapple, reserving juice. Pour 1 cup of reserved juice into a medium-size saucepan, adding enough water to make 1 cup if necessary. Sprinkle gelatin over juice. Set aside for 5 minutes to soften. Stir over low heat until gelatin dissolves. Remove from heat and stir in crushed pineapple and vanilla extract. Chill until thick but not set, about 1 hour.

In a large bowl, beat together nonfat dry milk and ice water until soft peaks form, about 4 minutes. Drizzle in lemon juice and honey while beating and continue to beat until stiff peaks form. Fold in coconut and pineapple mixture. Divide among 8 dessert glasses and chill until set.

Makes 8 servings
(115 calories per serving)

Snow Pudding with Custard Sauce

1 envelope unflavored gelatin
1¼ cups water
½ cup honey
3 tablespoons freshly squeezed
    lemon juice
3 egg whites
⅛ teaspoon cream of tartar
1 cup Slim Pastry Cream
    (page 246), **divided**

In a small saucepan, sprinkle gelatin over water. Set aside for 5 minutes to soften. Heat over medium heat, stirring constantly, until gelatin dissolves. Remove from heat and turn into a medium-size bowl. Mix in honey and lemon juice and chill until thickened but not set.

In a large bowl, beat egg whites until foamy. Add cream of tartar and continue beating until stiff peaks form. Fold in gelatin mixture and turn into a 2-quart mold that has been rinsed in cold water. Chill until set.

Unmold and top each serving with 2 tablespoons of the pastry cream.

Makes 8 servings
(113 calories per serving)

Carob Cookie Crust

1 cup Carob Thin cookie
    crumbs (page 50)

1 tablespoon butter, melted

Stir crumbs and butter together. Press onto bottom of a 9-inch pie plate. Chill for 30 minutes, or bake for 10 minutes at 350°F.

Makes 1 crust
(10   71-calorie servings)

Cranberry Pineapple Fluff

2 cups cranberry juice
2 tablespoons honey
1 envelope unflavored gelatin
½ cup unsweetened crushed pine-
    apple, drained
6 purple grapes, optional

Mix cranberry juice and honey together in a small saucepan. Sprinkle gelatin over juice and set aside to soften for 5 minutes. Heat over low heat, stirring constantly, until gelatin is dissolved.

Turn into a medium-size bowl and chill until thickened but not quite set. Then beat until fluffy. Fold in pineapple, divide among 6 dessert dishes, and chill until set.

Decorate each dish with a grape before serving, if desired.

Makes 6 servings
(76 calories per serving)

Baked Prune Whip

2 cups pitted prunes
2 tablespoons honey
¼ cup white grape juice
1 teaspoon ground cinnamon
4 egg whites
⅛ teaspoon cream of tartar

Preheat oven to 350°F. Spray a 2-quart casserole with vegetable spray.

In a food processor, puree prunes with honey, grape juice, and cinnamon.

In a large bowl, beat egg whites until foamy. Add cream of tartar and continue beating until stiff peaks form. Fold prune puree into beaten egg whites. Turn into prepared casserole and bake on middle shelf of oven until puffy, 20 to 25 minutes. Serve immediately.

Makes 8 servings
(116 calories per serving)

Yom Kippur Date Nut Cake

3 eggs
⅓ cup honey
1 teaspoon vanilla extract
⅓ cup whole wheat pastry flour
⅓ cup unbleached white flour
1 teaspoon baking powder
½ cup chopped dates
¼ cup chopped pecans

Preheat oven to 350°F. Spray an 8 × 8-inch pan with vegetable spray.

In a large bowl, beat together eggs and honey for 5 minutes. Beat in vanilla.

Sift together whole wheat pastry flour, unbleached white flour, and baking powder into a small bowl. In another small bowl, toss dates and nuts with 2 tablespoons of the flour mixture. Fold the rest of the flour into egg mixture. Fold in dates and nuts.

Turn into prepared pan and bake on middle shelf of oven for 25 minutes.

Cool in pan. Cut into 9 squares.

Makes 9 servings
(148 calories per serving)

Camocha Pie

To make this dessert even lower in calories, spray pie plate with vegetable spray and eliminate the crust.

1 recipe for Carob Cookie Crust (page 205)
2 eggs
1½ cups low-fat cottage cheese
¾ cup evaporated skim milk
2 teaspoons cornstarch
½ cup honey
1 teaspoon decaffeinated instant coffee
1 tablespoon vanilla extract

Preheat oven to 350°F.

Prepare piecrust according to directions.

In a food processor, blend remaining ingredients until smooth. Pour over piecrust and bake on middle shelf of oven until firm, about 40 minutes.

Makes 12 servings
(86 calories per serving)

Lime-Glazed Baked Pineapple

1 fresh pineapple
¼ cup honey, warmed
2 teaspoons freshly squeezed lime
   juice
4 orange slices, halved

Preheat oven to 325°F.

Peel, core, and cut pineapple into 8 slices. Arrange in a large shallow pan.

In a small bowl, combine honey and lime juice. Drizzle over pineapple and bake on middle shelf of oven for 12 minutes.

Serve warm decorated with orange slices.

Makes 8 servings
(67 calories per serving)

Orange Pineapple Punch

2 cups freshly squeezed orange
   juice
1 cup pineapple juice
2 teaspoons freshly squeezed
   lemon juice
1 teaspoon freshly squeezed
   lime juice
2 teaspoons honey

Combine all ingredients and serve over cracked ice.

Makes 4 servings
(102 calories per serving)

Grapefruit Granita

This ice is tart and refreshing.

1 cup honey
2 cups water
4 cups grapefruit juice
2 tablespoons freshly squeezed
   lemon juice

In a medium-size saucepan, boil together honey and water for 2 minutes, stirring constantly. Set aside to cool.

Combine honey mixture with remaining ingredients.

Process mixture in 2 batches in an ice cream maker according to manufacturer's instructions (if watery, place in freezer overnight), or turn mixture into a large pan and freeze until mushy but not solid. Remove from freezer, beat to break down ice crystals, and then return to freezer. Repeat this procedure twice, spooning mixture into 2 1-quart containers the last time. Freeze until ready to serve.

Makes 10 servings
(144 calories per serving)

Orange Carob Whip

1 envelope unflavored gelatin
1 cup skim milk
2 tablespoons Versatile Carob
    Syrup (page 148)
2 eggs, separated
3 tablespoons honey
2 tablespoons unsweetened
    frozen orange juice
    concentrate
1½ cups part-skim ricotta cheese

In a small saucepan, sprinkle gelatin over skim milk. Set aside for 5 minutes to soften. Add carob syrup and heat to scalding.

In a small bowl, beat egg yolks. Add a little of the hot carob mixture to egg yolks, whisking constantly. Add mixture to saucepan and continue cooking, stirring constantly, for 2 minutes. Stir in honey and orange juice concentrate.

Put ricotta into blender container and blend at high speed. Pour carob-orange mixture through opening in cover, blending until well mixed. Pour into a large bowl and chill until thickened but not set.

In a medium-size bowl, beat egg whites until stiff peaks form. Fold into thickened pudding and return to refrigerator to chill until set.

Makes 8 servings
(129 calories per serving)

Upper Crust Lemon Custard Pie

Most of the cookie crumbs in this pie rise to the top during cooking.

½ cup Carob Thin cookie crumbs
    (page 50)
3 eggs
¼ cup honey
1½ cups skim milk
1 teaspoon vanilla extract
3 tablespoons freshly squeezed
    lemon juice
1 teaspoon grated lemon peel,
    optional

Preheat oven to 325°F. Spray a 9-inch pie plate with vegetable spray.

Spread cookie crumbs on bottom of pie plate.

In a large bowl, beat eggs slightly. Beat in remaining ingredients until just blended. Carefully pour over crumbs in pie plate. Bake on middle shelf of oven for 1 hour. Allow to cool before serving.

Makes 8 servings
(118 calories per serving)

October Cake

1 recipe for Jelly Roll Cake
    (page 49)
1 cup low-fat cottage cheese
¼ cup maple syrup
⅓ cup pureed cooked pumpkin
2 teaspoons vanilla extract
½ teaspoon ground cinnamon

Bake cake according to directions.
In a food processor, blend remaining ingredients. Refrigerate until thickened.
Cut cake in half, crosswise. Spread half of pumpkin frosting on 1 half. Top with second half of cake and spread with remaining frosting. Refrigerate until ready to serve.

Makes 12 servings
(171 calories per serving)

Autumn Sundae

2 cups Vanilla Ice Milk (page 72),
    divided
1 cup Cranberry Applesauce
    (page 244), **divided**
¼ cup Mock Whipped Cream
    (page 9), **divided, optional**

Divide ice milk among 4, long-stemmed dessert glasses. Top each with ¼ cup of the Cranberry Applesauce and 1 tablespoon of the Mock Whipped Cream, if desired. Serve immediately.

Makes 4 servings
(149 calories per serving)

Pumpkin Cupcakes

½ cup whole wheat pastry flour
½ cup unbleached white flour
½ teaspoon baking soda
½ teaspoon baking powder
1½ teaspoons ground cinnamon
½ teaspoon ground allspice
2 eggs
⅓ cup honey
2 teaspoons molasses
2 tablespoons vegetable oil
¼ cup skim milk
½ cup pureed cooked pumpkin
1 teaspoon vanilla extract
72 raisins, optional
12 small Orange Fans (page 214),
    optional

Preheat oven to 350°F. Spray a 12-cup muffin tin with vegetable spray.
Sift together whole wheat pastry flour, unbleached white flour, baking soda, baking powder, cinnamon, and allspice into a medium-size bowl.
In a large bowl, beat eggs until light colored. Beat in remaining ingredients. Mix in dry ingredients and divide among prepared muffin cups. Bake on middle shelf of oven for 15 to 20 minutes.
Decorate, if desired, and cool on wire racks.

Makes 12 servings
(116 calories per serving)

Company Apples

5 McIntosh apples
   ground cinnamon for sprinkling
4 egg whites
¼ teaspoon cream of tartar
1 teaspoon vanilla extract

Preheat oven to 350°F. Spray a large shallow baking dish with vegetable spray.

Core, but do not peel, apples, cutting them into halves from top to bottom. Place, cut side up, in prepared dish. Sprinkle with cinnamon and bake on middle shelf of oven until fork tender, 25 to 30 minutes.

In a medium-size bowl, beat egg whites until foamy. Add cream of tartar and continue beating until stiff peaks form. Beat in vanilla.

Spoon meringue on tops of baked apples. Increase heat to 400°F and return apples to oven until meringue is golden brown, about 5 minutes. Serve warm.

Makes 10 servings
(55 calories per serving)

Orange Whip

2 eggs, separated
2 cups skim milk
1 envelop unflavored gelatin
¼ cup honey
2 teaspoons orange extract
6 mint leaves, optional

In a small bowl, beat egg yolks until fluffy.

In the top of a double boiler, mix together egg yolks and skim milk. Sprinkle gelatin over top and set aside for 5 minutes to soften. Stir in honey and cook over low heat, stirring constantly, until gelatin has dissolved and mixture has thickened slightly. Remove from heat and stir in orange extract. Chill until thickened but not set.

In a medium-size bowl, beat egg whites until stiff. Fold into orange gelatin. Divide among 6 long-stemmed dessert glasses and chill until set.

Just before serving, decorate with mint leaves, if desired.

Makes 6 servings
(102 calories per serving)

NOVEMBER

Decorating Desserts
with Diet in Mind

FRUIT OF THE MONTH: **PRUNES**

DESSERT OF THE MONTH: **PRUNE BARS**

DRINK OF THE MONTH: **CRANBERRY DELIGHT**

				1	2	3
				FROZEN PUMPKIN DESSERT	CHINESE MANDARIN ALMOND CUSTARD	AUTUMN FRUIT MEDLEY
4	**5**	**6**	**7**	**8**	**9**	**10**
PRUNE BARS ★	MANDARIN KABOBS	PERSIMMON PUDDING	TOPLESS APPLE CRANBERRY PIE	LEMON CAKE ROLL	CAROB COFFEE TREAT SUPREME	SAUCY CREPES
11	**12**	**13**	**14**	**15**	**16**	**17**
PEPPERMINT MERINGUE PIE	TWO-GRAPEFRUIT TREAT	HONEY CHEESE PIE	CRANBERRY NUT CAKES	COCONUT SOUFFLÉ	FRENCH PEPPERMINT ICE MILK	BANANA TAPIOCA
18	**19**	**20**	**21**	**22**	**23**	**24**
SURPRISE PEANUTTY VANILLA PIE	FRESH ORANGE GELATIN	THREE COOKED PRUNES	MOLASSES GINGER JOYS	INDIVIDUAL BRANDY SOUFFLÉS WITH STRAWBERRY SAUCE	ORANGE BANANA POPS	APPLE PEAR SCALLOP
25	*Thanksgiving* **26**	**27**	**28**	**29**	**30**	
INDIAN PUDDING	PUMPKIN PINEAPPLE PIE	HAYSTACKS	CREAMY / CAROB CHIP CHEESECAKE	FLUFFY GRAPE DESSERT	GREEK YOGURT PRUNE PIE	

$\mathcal{D}$esserts always should offer a feast for the eyes as well as the palate. But never is this more important than when you're watching calories and trying to make the food you eat special. You don't need sugar-sweetened ornaments to have delicious-looking desserts.

Fruit, with all its nutritional pluses, can be made into beautiful garnishes and containers from which to serve desserts. Choose fruits that are compatible in texture, shape, and size with the desserts they're intended to adorn. When fruit is one of the recipe ingredients, show it off as attractively as possible. A single, perfect slice or chunk of fruit is also an attractive decoration for an individual serving of pudding or for the top of a cupcake.

Frozen grapes add an easy-to-do but impressive flourish. Place seedless grapes on a baking sheet and pop them into the freezer. When they're frozen, put them into a plastic bag and store them in the freezer.

Pineapple is a great diet food, and fresh pineapple spears are a pretty, low-calorie addition to cakes, pies, or puddings. To make them, cut the top and bottom off a fresh pineapple. With a sharp knife, cut the shell off—from top to bottom—a strip at a time. To remove the eyes, cut around the peeled pineapple, diagonally. Then cut the pineapple into spears. The spears may be used whole or cut into shorter pieces.

I often make an attractive little decoration for cupcakes, individual puddings, or other small desserts by pitting cherries and cutting them into four or five petals joined at the bottom. I then place a blueberry in the center of each cherry, and presto there are tiny flowers. Two or more mint leaves around each one adds a realistic touch.

Finely grated lemon peel, made by using the fine side of a grater, gives a finishing touch to plain-looking desserts when sprinkled over them. Try it to dress up carob or vanilla pudding, pumpkin pie, or cupcakes. Aside from appearance, it also adds a subtle zip to the taste of a dessert.

Citrus Decorates in Every Season

Citrus fruits star as helpers in making desserts pretty. The peels keep well, and the fruits don't brown when exposed to air.

Lemon or orange shells are splendid serving vessels for puddings, mixed fruit desserts, sherbets, or ices. To make them, cut the fruit in half with a sharp knife. Scrape out the pulp, reserving it for future use. For an added ornamental touch, scallop the edges with a sharp knife. If the shell is tippy, slice a very small piece off the bottom to level it. After you've filled the shell you may want to add an orange or lemon fan. These colorful decorations are used to add interest to puddings or compotes.

To make a long strip of orange or lemon peel, run a citrus peeler from the stem end of the fruit all around the peel in one continuous piece. This versatile ornament can be used to make bows, or arranged in other shapes on top of puddings, pies, cakes, or anything else your fancy dictates.

A design I'm partial to is the orange star. To make it, use five orange fans. Arrange them, skin sides together, and points turning out, in the center of a cake or chiffon pie. This design can be made from halved strawberries, also.

Halved citrus slices add interesting designs and borders to cakes.

Pineapple chunks also make attractive borders for almost any cake or pie. They can be arranged in flower formations, using cherries or grapes as centers.

Peach slices overlapped in a ring resemble a lovely bloom when a strawberry or raspberry is positioned in the center.

Strawberries can turn a dessert into a showpiece! If you need something spectacular for the center of a pie, cake, or a strawberry dessert, try a strawberry rose. First, slice several large strawberries lengthwise. Place some of the slices, points out, in a circle in the center of the dessert. Make another smaller circle overlapping and inside the first one. Place a whole berry, hull side down, in the center.

For a strawberry fan, a simpler decoration, slice a large strawberry, with the green cap on, from the point down to, but not through, the stem end. Push the slices apart into a fan.

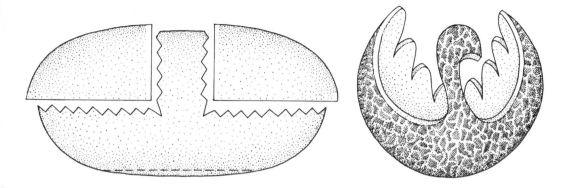

The peels and shells of many fruits make attractive containers for individual servings or magnificent serving bowls for special desserts. A watermelon basket is an example of this. To prepare the basket, cut off the bottom of the melon so the melon won't tip. Make the next four cuts through the melon as shown in the illustration, and remove the top two sections.

Scoop the melon out of the shell and handle, leaving the skin and white rind. Remove the seeds from the melon and cut the fruit pulp into balls with a melon baller.

With a sharp knife, cut the exposed edges of the basket into a saw-tooth pattern.

For a really spectacular presentation, cut a grapefruit, a honeydew, or a cantaloupe into a dove. First sketch the head, neck and tail onto the melon. With a sharp knife, cut along the lines through the skin. Carefully cut away the top part of the shell. Scoop out the fruit, leaving the dove as a serving piece for melon balls or a fruit compote.

Experiment with fruit decorations, and come up with your own favorite designs. It's easy and fun—and you can always eat the mistakes!

Not by Fruits Alone

Fruit is a delightful and versatile dessert decoration, but it isn't the only way to adorn diet desserts. Natural food colors perk up puddings, frostings, molded desserts, and frozen treats. Dollops of meringue, either colored or white, in an ornamental pattern on cakes or pies, add interest and few calories.

Ricotta cheese flavored with vanilla and a touch of honey to taste prettifies an otherwise unadorned cake or pie when it's piped around the rim.

Coconut Sugar (page 60) is another useful ornament for low-calorie desserts. It's used either snowy white or tinted with natural food dyes to a rainbow of colors. Sprinkle a few drops of coloring over the coconut sugar, and work it in with the back of a spoon. It takes longer to get the color even than it does with frosting.

Beautiful Cakes

Although frosted cakes look lovely, and they aren't necessarily off-limits to the calorie watcher, you can decorate unfrosted cakes, too. Or, as a compromise, frost just the top with a light icing that provides a background for further embellishment.

The bottom of a cake is more level than the top, so it's best to turn cakes (except those baked in a tube pan) upside down before decorating them. This may leave a slightly rocky cake if it has risen higher in the middle than on the edges. To solve this problem, level off the hump using a serrated knife.

To make sure that a filled cake will look its best, follow this rule: Unless you're using a solid, heavy-textured filling, only spread it to within about ¼ inch of the edges of the bottom layer. The weight of the top layer will squish the filling out to the edges.

Any sauce that's smooth, such as Ruby Raspberry Sauce (page 127) is helpful for decorating unfrosted or frosted cakes. Either dribble it in patterns over the top of the cake or use a cake decorator with a writing tip.

Versatile Carob Syrup (page 148) will dress up a cake, too. Spread it in parallel lines, then with the tip of a knife or spoon, draw through the lines, making a wavy design. This is particularly effective on a cake that's lightly iced with white or pink frosting.

Nuts or seeds can be arranged in simple designs on top of cakes. I often make a circle of nuts with a cherry or perhaps a citrus fan (page 214) in the middle to add interest.

I love coconut sugar. It has so many uses. One of the easiest ways to decorate a cake with coconut sugar is to use a paper doily or to make a stencil by folding a piece of waxed paper in fourths and cutting it into a design. You don't have to be an artist for this! Just use sharp scissors. Place the stencil on top of the cake and sprinkle white or colored coconut sugar on it. (Sometimes I mix several colors of coconut sugar together for this.) Carefully remove the waxed paper or doily and you'll have a colorful design.

It's fun to bake cakes in a variety of shapes — a heart for Valentine's Day, a tree for Christmas, a pumpkin for Thanksgiving, a bunny for Easter. Many of these ornamental cake pans are available in stores, but specially shaped cakes can also be made from cakes baked in square or rectangular pans. Cut a pattern from waxed paper. Place it on the cooled cake, and cut around it with a sharp knife. If you choose this method, let the crumbs on the cut edges become quite firm before attempting to frost the cake.

Before I started making caloriewise desserts, I thought of decorated cakes as frosted cakes. Even now, some of the cakes I decorate are frosted, but frosting isn't essential. A cake that's lightly sprinkled with coconut sugar can then be decorated with colored Decorator Frosting (page 34), using a cake decorating kit. Or the same decorations can be placed on an undecorated cake and still look lovely.

A cake roll often becomes flat or the filling may squish out when it's cut with a knife. One way to avoid this is to wrap a heavy piece of thread around the roll at the point where you want to cut it. Pull both ends down, just as if you were tying them together. The thread will slice cleanly through the roll.

Pretty Pies

I like to decorate pies, too. Instead of using a top crust, I sometimes cut shapes from the pastry and lay them on top of the pie filling just before baking it. This works best with a fairly firm pie. If you try this on an egg-based pie filling, the tiny pastries will sink to the bottom before the filling is strong enough to support them.

There are several ways to decorate with strips of pastry. You can make the conventional lattice top, or arrange strips in a spoke pattern. A long strip of pastry, stood on edge and arranged in a spiral over the top of a pie is unusual. To do this, piece the strips together with cold water.

What is apple pie without cheese? To add this conventional accompaniment without upping the calories too much, cut an apple shape from a slice of cheese and place it in the center of the pie just before serving it.

Frozen Pumpkin Dessert

1   16-ounce can pumpkin puree
½ cup honey
1   egg
1   tablespoon unsweetened frozen
      orange juice concentrate
½ teaspoon ground cinnamon
⅛ teaspoon ground nutmeg
1½ teaspoons vanilla extract
1   cup half-and-half
2   cups skim milk

In a large bowl, beat together pumpkin, honey, and egg. Add orange juice concentrate, spices, and vanilla and beat in. Mix in half-and-half and skim milk.

Process mixture in an ice cream maker according to manufacturer's instructions, or freeze in an 8 × 8-inch pan until thickened but not solid, about 1 hour. Remove from freezer, beat to break down ice crystals, and then return to freezer. Repeat this procedure twice, putting dessert into 2 1-quart containers before returning to freezer the last time. Freeze until ready to serve.

Makes about 16 servings
(80 calories per serving)

Chinese Mandarin Almond Custard

The Orientals serve few desserts. Those they do serve are elegant but simple like this one.

1   envelope unflavored gelatin
1   cup water
¼ cup honey
1   cup skim milk
1   teaspoon almond extract
1   11-ounce can mandarin oranges

In a small saucepan, sprinkle gelatin over water. Set aside to soften for 5 minutes. Heat over low heat, stirring constantly, until gelatin dissolves. Stir in honey. Mix in skim milk and almond extract. Pour into 4 ½-cup molds and chill until set.

Unmold on dessert plates. Decorate with mandarin oranges.

Makes 4 servings
(101 calories per serving)

Autumn Fruit Medley

1 tablespoon honey
1 teaspoon freshly squeezed
   lemon juice
1 tablespoon water
1 seedless orange
1 large apple
1 ripe banana
1 Bosc pear
16 seedless green or red grapes,
   halved

In a small bowl, mix together honey, lemon juice, and water.

Peel and section orange. Quarter sections and place them into a glass bowl. Core, but do not peel, apple. Cut it into chunks and add to bowl, tossing with orange pieces. Cut banana into rounds. Halve rounds and add to other fruit, tossing. Peel and core pear. Cut into chunks and toss with other fruit. Add grapes and honey mixture, tossing to coat well. Chill until serving time.

Makes 8 servings
(60 calories per serving)

Prune Bars

1 cup pitted prunes
1 cup plus 1 tablespoon whole
   wheat pastry flour, divided
¾ cup apple juice
2 tablespoons butter
1 tablespoon honey
1 teaspoon baking powder
½ teaspoon baking soda
1 teaspoon ground cinnamon
¼ teaspoon ground nutmeg
1 egg
2 tablespoons chopped pecans,
   optional

Preheat oven to 350°F. Spray an 8 × 8-inch pan with vegetable spray.

In a food processor, chop prunes with 1 tablespoon of the flour. Put into a small saucepan with apple juice and butter. Bring to a boil, stirring constantly, until butter melts. Mix in honey. Pour into a large bowl and allow to cool slightly.

Sift flour, baking powder, baking soda, cinnamon, and nutmeg into a medium-size bowl. Whisk to blend. Stir into prune mixture.

Beat egg and stir into batter. Fold in nuts, if desired, and turn into prepared pan. Bake on middle shelf of oven for 25 to 35 minutes.

Allow to cool in pan. Cut into 16 pieces.

Makes 16 bars
(80 calories per bar)

Tangy Lemon Filling

3 tablespoons cornstarch
⅓ cup freshly squeezed
    lemon juice
1 cup water

¼ cup honey
1 egg yolk
1 teaspoon butter

In a jar with a tight-fitting lid, shake together cornstarch and lemon juice, or whisk in a small bowl until thoroughly blended. Pour into a small saucepan. Add water and honey and cook over medium heat, stirring constantly, until mixture thickens.

In a small bowl, whisk egg yolk. Pour some of the hot lemon mixture into egg yolk, whisking constantly. Return to saucepan and continue cooking, stirring constantly, for 2 minutes. Remove from heat and stir in butter. Cool before using. (Filling will thicken as it cools.)

Makes about 1½ cups
(19 calories per tablespoon)

Carob Coffee Treat Supreme

¾ cup decaffeinated coffee, cooled
¼ cup water
3 tablespoons honey
1 envelope unflavored gelatin
8 Carob Thins (page 50)
3 egg whites
¼ teaspoon cream of tartar
1½ teaspoons vanilla extract

In a small saucepan, combine coffee, water, and honey. Sprinkle gelatin over mixture and set aside to soften for 5 minutes. Heat, stirring constantly, over medium heat until gelatin dissolves. Pour into a medium-size bowl and chill, stirring occasionally, until mixture is thick but not set.

Break cookies into small pieces and fold into gelatin.

In another medium-size bowl, beat egg whites until foamy. Sprinkle in cream of tartar and vanilla and continue beating until stiff peaks form. Fold into gelatin and chill until set.

Makes 6 servings
(85 calories per serving)

Saucy Crepes

1 cup Applesauce (page 81)
½ teaspoon ground cinnamon
8 warm Delicious Diet Crepes
  (page 30)
½ cup plain low-fat yogurt
1 tablespoon honey
½ teaspoon vanilla extract
  ground cinnamon for sprinkling

In a small saucepan, heat together applesauce and cinnamon. Spread 2 tablespoons of the mixture on each crepe and roll up.

In a small bowl, gently whisk together yogurt, honey, and vanilla. Top each crepe with 1 tablespoon of the mixture. Sprinkle with cinnamon and serve immediately.

Makes 8 servings
(71 calories per serving)

Persimmon Pudding

This delicate pudding has a custard base.

3 eggs
1 cup evaporated skim milk
½ teaspoon ground cinnamon
2 cups unsweetened persimmon
  pulp*

In a large bowl, beat eggs slightly.

Heat evaporated skim milk in a small saucepan to scalding. Stir in cinnamon. Slowly whisk into beaten eggs. Stir in persimmon pulp and divide among 9 ovenproof 8-ounce dessert dishes. Set dishes in a large shallow pan and put pan on middle shelf of oven. Pour enough hot water into pan to almost reach the tops of the dishes. Bake for about 40 minutes, or until knife inserted near centers comes out clean.

Makes 9 servings
(75 calories per serving)

*Found in specialty foods stores.

Peppermint Meringue Pie

1 recipe for Meringue Pie Shell
  (page 107)
4 cups French Peppermint Ice Milk
  (page 227)
1 cup seedless red grapes

Bake pie shell according to directions. Allow to cool.

At serving time, fill cooled meringue shell with scoops of ice milk. Decorate with grapes and slice. Serve at once.

Makes 10 servings
(86 calories per serving)

Banana Tapioca

1 recipe for Fluffy Almond Tapioca
  (page 80)
1 ripe banana, coarsely chopped
¼ cup raisins, plumped
¼ teaspoon ground cinnamon

In a medium-size bowl, gently combine all ingredients and serve.

Makes 6 servings
(135 calories per serving)

Cranberry Nut Cakes

These loaves freeze nicely and are handy to have for those times when unexpected visitors arrive.

1¼ cups whole wheat pastry flour
1 cup unbleached white flour
1 teaspoon baking powder
1 teaspoon baking soda
⅔ cup honey
⅓ cup vegetable oil
1 cup buttermilk
2 eggs
1 teaspoon orange extract
1½ cups chopped fresh cranberries
¼ cup chopped walnuts

Preheat oven to 350°F. Lightly butter and flour 2 9 × 5-inch loaf pans.

In a large bowl, sift together whole wheat pastry flour, unbleached white flour, baking powder, and baking soda. Add honey, oil, buttermilk, eggs, and orange extract and mix well with a wooden spoon. Mix in cranberries and nuts.

Divide between prepared pans and bake on middle shelf of oven for 40 to 45 minutes, or until a cake tester inserted in centers comes out clean.

Allow to cool in pans for 10 minutes, then turn out onto wire racks to cool completely. Slice each loaf into 10 slices, then halve each slice.

Makes 20 servings per loaf
(138 calories per serving)

Topless Apple Cranberry Pie

1 recipe for Skinny Piecrust
    (page 5)
6 apples
8 cups water
1 tablespoon freshly squeezed
    lemon juice
1½ cups fresh cranberries
3 tablespoons honey
1 tablespoon cornstarch
2 teaspoons ground cinnamon

Preheat oven to 400°F. Line bottom and sides of a 10-inch pie plate with pastry, crimping edges, and bake according to directions.

Peel, core, and thinly slice apples, dropping them into water mixed with lemon juice to prevent discoloration.

Drain apples and toss with remaining ingredients. Turn into prepared piecrust. Loosely cover pie with foil and bake on lowest shelf of oven for 30 minutes. Pull foil away from edge of piecrust (keep filling covered) and continue to bake until apples are fork tender, about 20 more minutes. Serve warm or cold.

Makes 10 servings
(127 calories per serving)

Lemon Cake Roll

This slightly tart dessert is a wonderfully satisfying finale to a light dinner.

    5 eggs
    ⅓ cup honey
    1 tablespoon freshly squeezed
        lemon juice
    2 teaspoons vanilla extract
    ½ cup whole wheat pastry flour
    ½ cup unbleached white flour
    1½ cups Tangy Lemon Filling
        (page 222)

Preheat oven to 275°F. Line bottom of a 15½ × 10½-inch jelly roll pan with parchment paper.

In a large bowl, beat eggs. Add honey, lemon juice, and vanilla and continue beating until eggs thicken, about 10 minutes.

Into a medium-size bowl, sift together whole wheat pastry flour, and unbleached white flour, whisking to blend. Remeasure 1 cup and gradually sift into egg mixture, beating constantly. Pour batter into prepared pan, spreading evenly to sides and smoothing top with spatula. Bake on middle shelf of oven until top springs back when lightly pressed with finger, about 20 minutes.

While cake is baking, spread a tea towel on a flat surface. Put waxed paper on top of it. Turn baked cake out onto lined towel. Remove parchment paper. Trim off edges of cake and roll cake up in lined towel until cool.

Unroll cake, remove towel and waxed paper, spread with Tangy Lemon Filling, and then roll cake up without towel.

Makes 10 servings
(166 calories per serving)

Two-Grapefruit Treat

    1 seedless pink grapefruit
    1 seedless white grapefruit
    ½ cup freshly squeezed orange
        juice
    ½ cup white grape juice
    ¼ cup unsweetened flaked coconut,
        divided

Peel and section grapefruits. Cut sections into halves, reserving juice in a medium-size bowl. Mix orange juice, grape juice, and reserved grapefruit juice together. Toss with grapefruit sections and chill to mingle flavors.

To serve, divide among 4 dessert dishes and sprinkle each with 1 tablespoon of the coconut.

Makes 4 servings
(98 calories per serving)

Fresh Orange Gelatin

    1 cup freshly squeezed orange juice
    1 cup water, divided
    1 envelope unflavored gelatin
    1 tablespoon honey
    ¼ teaspoon orange extract

In a medium-size bowl, combine orange juice and ½ cup water.

In a small saucepan, sprinkle gelatin over remaining water. Set aside for 5 minutes to soften. Add honey and heat over medium heat stirring constantly, until gelatin dissolves. Add to juice. Mix in orange extract and chill until set.

Makes 4 servings
(50 calories per serving)

Surprise Peanutty Vanilla Pie

The surprise is the luscious layer of Reduced Calorie peanut butter on the bottom of this dessert.

1 recipe for Skinny Piecrust
    (page 5)
2 tablespoons Reduced Calorie
    Peanut Butter (page 54),
    thinned with water if necessary
2 cups Very Vanilla Pudding
    (page 76)

Line a 9-inch pie plate with pastry and bake according to directions. Set aside to cool.

Spread peanut butter on bottom of cooled crust. Fill with vanilla pudding which has cooled but isn't set. Chill until serving time.

Makes 8 servings
(135 calories per serving)

Orange Banana Pops

1 cup freshly squeezed orange
    juice
1 medium-size ripe banana, cut
    into chunks
1 tablespoon freshly squeezed
    lemon juice

In a food processor, puree together all ingredients. Measure puree and add enough water to make 2 cups, mixing in well. Pour into 8 2-ounce pop molds and freeze.

Makes 8 pops
(28 calories per pop)

Coconut Soufflé

2 eggs
½ cup evaporated skim milk
¼ cup maple syrup
1½ cups low-fat cottage cheese
2 teaspoons vanilla extract
½ cup unsweetened flaked
    coconut
4 egg whites
¼ teaspoon cream of tartar
1 tablespoon honey

Preheat oven to 350°F. Spray a 1½-quart casserole with vegetable spray.

In a blender, blend together eggs, evaporated skim milk, and maple syrup. Add cottage cheese, vanilla, and coconut and blend for about 1 minute.

In a large bowl, beat egg whites until foamy. Add cream of tartar and, while beating, drizzle in honey. Continue beating until stiff peaks form. Fold in cheese mixture and turn into prepared casserole. Set casserole in a large shallow pan and place on middle shelf of oven. Fill pan with enough hot water to reach a depth of 1 inch. Bake for about 30 minutes, or until top of casserole is golden and puffy. Place foil lightly over top and continue baking another 20 minutes. Serve immediately.

Makes 10 servings
(102 calories per serving)

French Peppermint Ice Milk

The addition of an egg is what makes this a French-type ice milk.

    1 egg
    ¼ cup honey
    ½ teaspoon peppermint extract
    4 cups skim milk
       natural red food coloring

In a large bowl, beat together egg and honey until fluffy. Mix in peppermint extract and skim milk. Add a few drops of food coloring to obtain a light pink color.

Process mixture in an ice cream maker according to manufacturer's instructions, or turn mixture into a shallow pan and freeze until thickened but not solid. Remove from freezer, beat to break down ice crystals, and then return to freezer. Repeat this procedure twice, turning mixture into a covered container the last time. Freeze until ready to serve.

Makes 8 servings
(85 calories per serving)

Molasses Ginger Joys

Allow baking sheet to cool between batches!

    ⅓ cup butter, softened
    ⅓ cup molasses
    ⅓ cup honey
    1 egg, slightly beaten
    1¼ cups whole wheat pastry flour
    1¼ cups unbleached white flour
    1 teaspoon baking powder
    1 teaspoon ground cinnamon
    ½ teaspoon ground ginger

Preheat oven to 350°F. Spray a baking sheet with vegetable spray.

In a large bowl, beat together butter, molasses, and honey. Beat in egg.

In a medium-size bowl, whisk together whole wheat pastry flour, unbleached white flour, baking powder, cinnamon, and ginger. Stir into moist ingredients. Cover and chill for 1 hour.

Divide dough into fourths. Roll out 1 section between lightly floured pieces of waxed paper to an oblong about ⅛-inch thick. Cut into 2-inch circles with a cookie cutter or a juice glass. Roll out and cut second piece of dough. Place on prepared baking sheet and bake on middle shelf of oven until cookies are brown on the bottom, 5 to 8 minutes.

Cool on wire racks.

Repeat with remaining dough. Reroll scraps and make more cookies.

Makes 4 dozen cookies
(50 calories per cookie)

Apple Pear Scallop

2 apples
2 pears
⅓ cup water
2 tablespoons honey
½ teaspoon brandy extract
1 teaspoon ground cinnamon

Preheat oven to 350°F.

Peel, core, and thinly slice apples and pears. Toss with other ingredients in a 1½-quart casserole, and bake on middle shelf of oven until fruit is fork tender, about 25 minutes. Serve warm.

Makes 4 servings
(121 calories per serving)

Individual Brandy Soufflés with Strawberry Sauce

3 egg whites
¼ teaspoon cream of tartar
3 tablespoons honey, divided
1 teaspoon vanilla extract
½ cup evaporated skim milk, chilled
½ teaspoon brandy extract
1 cup Strawberry Sauce (page 230)

Preheat oven to 350°F. Spray 8 8-ounce ovenproof dishes with vegetable spray.

In a medium-size bowl, beat egg whites until foamy. Add cream of tartar, 2 tablespoons of the honey, and vanilla and continue beating until stiff peaks form.

In a large bowl, beat chilled evaporated skim milk until foamy. Add remaining honey and brandy extract and continue beating until soft peaks form.

Fold beaten whites into beaten milk mixture. Turn into prepared dishes and bake on bottom shelf of oven until soufflés have risen and are lightly browned, about 15 minutes. Remove from oven. Serve immediately with 2 tablespoons of Strawberry Sauce on each soufflé.

Makes 8 servings
(77 calories per serving)

Indian Pudding

This classic dessert is traditionally baked in the oven, but I find it easier to make in an electric slow cooker.

2¼ cups skim milk
3 tablespoons honey
3 tablespoons dark molasses
⅓ cup yellow cornmeal
¼ teaspoon ground ginger
½ teaspoon ground cinnamon
¼ teaspoon ground nutmeg
⅛ teaspoon baking soda
1 egg, beaten

Lightly butter inside of electric slow cooker.

In a medium-size saucepan, scald skim milk. Stir in honey and molasses.

In a small bowl, combine cornmeal, ginger, cinnamon, nutmeg, and baking soda. Mix slowly into scalding milk, stirring constantly. Stir a little of the hot mixture into beaten egg. Return to saucepan, stirring constantly. Bring to a boil. Remove from heat and turn into prepared slow cooker. Cover and cook on low for 3 hours.

Makes 5 servings
(153 calories per serving)

Mandarin Kabobs

This is one of the few authentic Japanese desserts. But I use a honey sauce instead of the traditional Sake for dipping the orange sections.

　2　tablespoons honey
　2　tablespoons water
24　mandarin orange sections
　¼　cup sesame seeds
20　mint leaves

In a small bowl, mix together honey and water. Coat orange sections with mixture then roll them in sesame seeds. Put 6 sections on each of 4 skewers, alternating with mint leaves. (Begin and end with an orange section.) Chill for several hours before serving.

Makes 4 servings
(104 calories per serving)

Strawberry Sauce

A tablespoon of this sauce dresses up plain desserts while adding only a few calories.

1　cup unsweetened frozen strawberries, thawed and drained with juice reserved

2　teaspoons cornstarch
¼　cup strawberry jelly

Place strawberries into a small saucepan.

Dissolve cornstarch in ¼ cup of the reserved juice. Mix into strawberries along with jelly. Bring to a boil and cook, stirring constantly, until thickened. Remove from heat, strain, and cool.

Makes about 1 cup
(10 calories per tablespoon)

Greek Yogurt Prune Pie

1 recipe for Mini Piecrust
    (page 104)
2 eggs, separated
2 tablespoons honey
1½ cups plain nonfat yogurt
1½ teaspoons vanilla extract
1½ teaspoons ground cinnamon
¼ teaspoon ground nutmeg
1 cup pitted prunes
2 tablespoons whole wheat flour
⅛ teaspoon cream of tartar

Preheat oven to 425°F.

Line a 9-inch pie plate with piecrust according to directions.

In a large bowl, beat egg yolks and honey together until light colored. Stir in yogurt, vanilla, cinnamon, and nutmeg.

In a food processor, chop prunes, adding flour to keep prune pieces separated. Stir into yogurt mixture.

In a medium-size bowl, beat egg whites until foamy. Add cream of tartar and continue beating until stiff peaks form. Fold into yogurt mixture and turn into pie shell. Bake on middle shelf of oven for 10 minutes. Reduce heat to 325°F and continue baking until filling is puffy and lightly browned, about 30 minutes. Serve warm or cold.

Makes 10 servings
(136 calories per serving)

Honey Cheese Pie

1 recipe for Mini Piecrust
    (page 104)
1 cup part-skim ricotta cheese
3 eggs
⅓ cup honey
1 cup skim milk
1½ teaspoons vanilla extract

Preheat oven to 425°F. Line a 9-inch pie plate with pastry according to directions.

In a large bowl, beat together ricotta cheese and eggs until fluffy. Beat in honey, skim milk, and vanilla. Pour into piecrust, and bake on bottom shelf of oven until a knife inserted near center comes out clean, about 30 to 35 minutes.

Makes 10 servings
(132 calories per serving)

Fluffy Grape Dessert

1 envelope unflavored gelatin
1 cup cold water
1 cup grape juice
10 seedless red grapes, quartered

In a small saucepan, sprinkle gelatin over water. Set aside for 5 minutes to soften. Heat over medium heat, stirring constantly, until gelatin dissolves. Mix in grape juice. Pour into a medium-size bowl and chill until thickened but not set, stirring occasionally so edges won't set.

Beat until about doubled in volume. Fold in grapes. Divide among 6 dessert dishes and chill until set.

Makes 6 servings
(35 calories per serving)

Creamy Carob Chip Cheesecake

32 ounces low-fat cottage cheese
⅓ cup honey
2 tablespoons unbleached white flour
2 tablespoons freshly squeezed lemon juice
2 teaspoons vanilla extract
4 eggs
½ cup carob chips, chopped

Preheat oven to 325°F. Lightly butter bottom and sides of a 9-inch springform pan.

In a food processor, blend cheese until smooth. Add remaining ingredients except carob chips through feed tube while processor is running. (If work bowl of processor is small, mix ingredients in 2 batches.) Mix in chips and pour into prepared pan. Bake on middle shelf of oven for 1 hour. Turn off heat and leave cheesecake in oven for 1 hour more. Allow to cool thoroughly.

Chill until serving time.

Makes 12 servings
(153 calories per serving)

Cranberry Delight

1½ cups cranberry juice
1 cup unsweetened pineapple
    juice
½ cup grapefruit juice
1 cup club soda

Combine all ingredients. Chill. Stir and serve.

Makes 6 servings
(72 calories per serving)

Pumpkin Pineapple Pie

1 recipe for Mini Piecrust
    (page 104)
½ cup unsweetened crushed
    pineapple, well drained
1½ cups pumpkin puree
⅓ cup skim milk
3 eggs, beaten
3 tablespoons honey
1 teaspoon ground cinnamon
½ teaspoon ground ginger
½ teaspoon ground nutmeg

Bake Mini Piecrust blind according to directions.

Puree pineapple in a food processor or blender. Turn into a medium-size bowl and beat with remaining ingredients until smooth. Pour into baked pie shell. Place on middle shelf of preheated 350°F oven and bake until a knife inserted near center comes out clean, 45 to 50 minutes.

Makes 10 servings
(109 calories per serving)

Haystacks

2 **eggs**
⅓ **cup honey**
1 **teaspoon vanilla extract**
¾ **cup whole wheat pastry flour**
1 **cup unsweetened flaked coconut**

Preheat oven to 325°F. Spray 2 baking sheets with vegetable spray.

In a medium-size bowl, beat together eggs and honey for 6 minutes. Beat in vanilla.

With a wooden spoon, gradually mix in flour. Fold in coconut and drop by teaspoonfuls about 1-inch apart on prepared baking sheets. Bake on middle shelf of oven, one batch at a time, until lightly browned, 15 to 18 minutes.

Remove to wire racks to cool.

Makes 3 dozen cookies
(29 calories per cookie)

DECEMBER

Dessert Parties—How to Show Off Your Low-Calorie Specialties

FRUIT OF THE MONTH: **GRAPES**

DESSERT OF THE MONTH: **LIGHT SPONGE CAKE**

DRINK OF THE MONTH: **EASY EGGNOG**

				1	2	3
				SMOOTH ALMOND MOUSSE	FROZEN PEPPERMINT ROLL	DEEP DISH BLUEBERRY PEAR PIE
4	5	6	7	8	9	10
EASY CHEESY DESSERT	DARLING CLEMENTINES	SPICY OATMEAL COOKIES	LIGHT SPONGE CAKE ★	FRUIT AND SHERBET PARFAITS	MARVELOUS MAPLE CREPES	FRUITED CHEESE DESSERT
11	12	13	14	15	16	17
CRAN-APPLE LOAF	PINEAPPLE GRAPE TAPIOCA	ALMOND STRAWBERRY RICE PUDDING	APRICOT RAISIN CONFECTIONS	ALMOND POTS DE CRÈME	CRANBERRY APPLESAUCE	SPECTACULAR SQUASH PIE
18	19	20	21	22	23	Christmas Eve 24
FROZEN FRUIT CUSTARD	GINGER PEARS	APPLESAUCE DROPS	BAKED BLUEBERRY WHIP	FRUITY SUNDAES	EGGNOG SOUFFLÉ	SPARKLING FRUIT TART
Christmas 25	26	27	28	29	30	New Year's Eve 31
CHRISTMAS TRIFLE	APPLE CIDER SORBET	TWENTY GRAPES	APPLE BANANA CUPCAKES	CAROB COCONUT PIE	SMOOTH STRAWBERRY PUDDING	PRETTY PARTY PUFFS

236

$\mathcal{D}$ecember is a festive month and a good time to discuss parties. Of course, the party suggestions in this chapter apply to other months, too.

I really enjoy a party and, if I'm to be the hostess, my favorite type is a dessert party. Just about everything can be made in advance. I bake cakes well ahead, freezing them until the day of the party, and I make pies, cookies, and confections the day before. A few hours before guests are expected, I make the punch and set the table. This leaves me free to enjoy my guests.

For this type of party, I suggest preparing a variety of desserts. Then there's no need to worry about guests' likes and dislikes. There will be something for everyone.

The success or failure of any party depends largely on the planning that goes into it. One of the cardinal rules is that your party fit the size of your home. Don't try to entertain 30 guests at a time in a tiny apartment. If there are 30 people you want to invite, have two parties, planning each group carefully.

Whether it's a sit-down affair or buffet style (the way I prefer to have dessert parties), be sure you have enough chairs for all the guests and enough small tables so that no one has to balance a plate and a glass while eating.

Plan a Perfect Setting

Although your table should look lovely, remember the desserts are the actual stars of your party. Everything else should work to show them off. A white cloth is always a safe choice, setting off both dishes and food handsomely.

Cloth napkins are much more elegant than paper ones and more substantial, too. If your party is to take place any time before dinner, choose a luncheon-size napkin of about 13 × 13 inches. But for an evening party, put out large, luxurious 22 × 22-inch napkins.

A table is more festive if it has a centerpiece. You can use one of the desserts, but I don't like to do this because as soon as the dessert is cut into, the centerpiece disappears. And some guests hesitate to help themselves to what was obviously meant to be decorative. Flowers and candles are traditional and still acceptable ornaments.

A Buffet That Works Well

A buffet party needs a planned traffic pattern that works! If the flow leads your guests to a blank wall where they must turn around, encountering other guests going in the opposite direction, you're bound to have bumps and spills. A table positioned so that guests move around it is best. Act as a guide, moving everyone in the same direction. If you do have to place the table against a wall, put candles or flowers at the back, arranging the food well toward the front where it can be easily reached.

Set your serving table so that guests come to plates, napkins, and utensils before the food. Be sure there are enough serving pieces. Every dessert should have its own.

Because your desserts will be cut into small pieces, set your table with small plates. You don't want a piece of cake to look lost on a huge plate. I use small, four-ounce beverage glasses too. Guests return for further helpings if they desire.

Don't crowd your table with more desserts and drinks than it can accommodate without looking crowded. Not only is it unattractive, it is difficult for guests to help themselves to the food. Set up another table if necessary. I usually have the beverage in a separate place.

Serve a wide variety of different, yet compatible desserts. For instance, if you're serving two cakes and one's a carob tube cake, make the other one a lemon cake roll, or a pumpkin cake. And a chiffon pie would go well with a pastry of a different texture, like fruit. For a party of this type, I select desserts without gooey fillings or runny sauces. To top it off, I include a punch that won't overpower the dessert flavors. I always serve punch at parties. This eliminates the need to find out the beverage preference of each guest and then prepare it. (You'll find several of my favorite punch recipes throughout the book.) And, of course, I make sure to have a large supply of ice on hand.

If one of the desserts you're serving is chilled, place it over a bowl of ice to keep it fresh. But be sure it's securely set and not precariously balanced on the ice. Set out pads for hot desserts.

I always plan at least three pieces of dessert for each person. It isn't my job as hostess to police the calorie intake of my guests. I provide low calorie desserts; how much they eat is up to them. And, yes, I usually do have leftovers, but I wrap them up and tuck them into the freezer for future use.

I slice all the desserts for a buffet into small pieces before I put them on the table. And I put the first piece (the most difficult to remove) on a plate beside the rest of the dessert.

An open house presents food problems. If guests will be dropping in at different times, don't put all the desserts out at once. Save a surprise or two for the middle of the party. You don't want your desserts to look wilted or picked over when the last of your guests arrive.

With delicious diet desserts, a carefully planned table setting, and congenial guests, your party is bound to be a success.

Smooth Almond Mousse

2 cups part-skim ricotta cheese
¼ cup skim milk
2 tablespoons honey
2 teaspoons vanilla extract
1½ teaspoons almond extract
½ teaspoon ground cinnamon

In a food processor, combine all ingredients. Divide among 4 dessert dishes and chill for several hours before serving.

Makes 4 servings
(129 calories per serving)

Frozen Peppermint Roll

1 recipe for Jelly Roll Cake
   (page 49)
1 recipe for French Peppermint Ice
   Milk (page 227), softened
¼ cup Coconut Sugar (page 60)

Bake Jelly Roll Cake according to directions.

Quickly spread softened ice milk over cake. Sprinkle with Coconut Sugar. Roll up from narrow end and place, seam side down, on plastic wrap. Wrap roll. Wrap again in foil and freeze.

Take out of freezer 10 minutes before serving and remove outer wrap.

Makes 10 servings
(151 calories per serving)

Deep Dish Blueberry Pear Pie

This pie will be easier to slice cold than hot.

6 fresh pears
8 cups water
1 tablespoon freshly squeezed
   lemon juice
2 cups unsweetened frozen blueberries, thawed
¼ cup honey
1 tablespoon cornstarch
1 teaspoon ground ginger
1 recipe for Skinny Piecrust
   (page 5)

Preheat oven to 400°F. Spray bottom of a 10-inch pie plate with vegetable spray.

Peel, core, and thinly slice pears, dropping them into water mixed with lemon juice to prevent discoloration.

Drain pear slices. In a large bowl, toss them with remaining ingredients except piecrust. Turn into prepared pie plate.

Roll out piecrust and place it over filling, crimping edges over rim of pie plate. Cut vents in piecrust and bake on middle shelf of oven for 50 minutes. If crust is browning too fast, cover it with foil and continue baking.

Makes 10 servings
(149 calories per serving)

Darling Clementines

*If the clementines are difficult to find,
you may use seedless oranges instead.*

1 envelope unflavored gelatin
1 cup water, divided
3 tablespoons honey, divided
1 cup freshly squeezed orange juice
1 teaspoon orange extract
½ cup evaporated skim milk, chilled
½ teaspoon ground cinnamon
1 teaspoon vanilla extract
3 clementines

In a small saucepan, sprinkle gelatin over ½ cup of the water. Set aside to soften for 5 minutes. Heat, stirring constantly, until gelatin dissolves. Stir in 2 tablespoons of the honey, remaining water, orange juice, and orange extract. Chill until very thick but not set.

In a medium-size bowl, beat evaporated skim milk until foamy. Add cinnamon, vanilla, and remaining honey. Continue beating until soft peaks form. Beat in gelatin mixture.

Peel clementines and separate into sections. Cut sections into halves and divide among 6 dessert glasses. Top each with gelatin mixture and chill until set.

Makes 6 servings
(105 calories per serving)

Spicy Oatmeal Cookies

¼ cup butter, softened
⅓ cup honey
1 egg
1 teaspoon vanilla extract
½ cup whole wheat pastry flour
½ cup unbleached white flour
⅔ cup rolled oats
¼ teaspoon baking powder
¼ teaspoon baking soda
2 teaspoons ground cinnamon
½ teaspoon ground nutmeg
¼ cup raisins, plumped

Preheat oven to 350°F.

In a medium-size bowl, beat butter until fluffy. Beat in honey, then egg and vanilla.

In a medium-size bowl, whisk together dry ingredients. Stir in raisins and mix into moist ingredients.

Drop by rounded teaspoonfuls onto 2 ungreased baking sheets. Bake each batch on middle shelf of oven until golden, 8 to 10 minutes.

Makes 30 cookies
(57 calories per cookie)

Light Sponge Cake

This versatile cake lends itself to any number of toppings.

- ½ cup whole wheat pastry flour
- ½ cup unbleached white flour
- 6 eggs, separated
- ¼ teaspoon cream of tartar
- 1½ tablespoons water
- ⅔ cup honey
- 2 teaspoons vanilla extract
- 1 cup Mock Whipped Cream (page 9), **divided**
- 12 seedless green or red grapes

Preheat oven to 350°F. Line bottom of an 11½ × 7½-inch pan with parchment paper.

Sift together whole wheat pastry flour and unbleached white flour.

In a large bowl, beat egg whites until foamy. Add cream of tartar and continue beating until stiff peaks form.

In a small bowl, beat egg yolks and water until lemon colored. Drizzle in honey and beat until mixture doubles in volume. Mix in vanilla. Fold flour into egg yolks. Fold batter into egg whites. Spoon into prepared pan and bake until cake springs back when lightly pressed, 20 to 25 minutes.

Invert, placing edges of cake pan on 2 glass bowls. When cool remove from pan and carefully strip off paper.

Just before serving, put a dollop of Mock Whipped Cream and a grape on each piece of cake.

Makes 12 servings
(146 calories per serving)

Fruited Cheese Dessert

- 1⅓ cups part-skim ricotta cheese
- ¼ cup honey
- 1 teaspoon vanilla extract
- 1 cup sliced unsweetened frozen strawberries
- ½ cup quartered seedless green grapes
- 4 teaspoons ground pecans

Thoroughly blend together ricotta cheese, honey, and vanilla. Fold in strawberries and grapes. Divide among 4 dessert dishes. Sprinkle pecans on top.

Makes 4 servings
(98 calories per serving)

Cran-Apple Loaf

- 1 **Lazy Day Loaf Cake** (page 183)
- 1 cup **Cranberry Applesauce** (page 244)
- ¼ **cup Coconut Sugar** (page 60)

Split cake in half, lengthwise. Spread sauce on lower half and put upper half on top of sauce. Sprinkle with Coconut Sugar.

Makes 12 servings
(114 calories per serving)

Fruit and Sherbet Parfaits

This lovely blending of flavors makes an elegant company dessert.

1 pint Raspberry Rum Sherbet
   (page 150)
1 ripe honeydew melon
1 pint fresh blueberries
   mint leaves, optional

With a melon baller, make small balls of Raspberry Rum Sherbet, placing them on a baking sheet lined with waxed paper. Cover with waxed paper and place in freezer.

Halve melon and scoop out seeds. Make melon balls with melon baller. Chill.

Just before serving, divide ingredients among 8 parfait glasses, alternating melon and blueberries with sherbet in several layers. Decorate with mint leaves, if desired. Serve immediately.

Makes 8 servings
(179 calories per serving)

Marvelous Maple Crepes

¾ cup part-skim ricotta cheese
1 cup low-fat cottage cheese
1 tablespoon honey
3 tablespoons maple syrup, divided
1½ teaspoons vanilla extract
8 Delicious Diet Crepes (page 30)
½ cup plain low-fat yogurt
   ground cinnamon for sprinkling

In a medium-size bowl, beat together ricotta cheese, cottage cheese, honey, 1 tablespoon of the maple syrup, and vanilla. If mixture is runny, chill it until it thickens.

Divide mixture among crepes, spreading it on tops, and fold each in half.

In a small bowl, stir remaining maple syrup into yogurt. Spoon over crepes, sprinkle with cinnamon, and serve immediately.

Makes 8 servings
(126 calories per serving)

Cranberry Applesauce

1 tablespoon cornstarch
¾ cup water
¾ cup fresh cranberries
2 tablespoons honey
1 teaspoon freshly squeezed lemon
   juice
1 teaspoon ground cinnamon
2 apples
1 teaspoon vanilla extract

Dissolve cornstarch in water. Pour into medium-size saucepan. Add cranberries, honey, lemon juice, and cinnamon.

Peel, core, and chop apples, stirring them into cranberry mixture as you chop them. Bring to a boil, stirring constantly. Reduce heat and simmer, stirring often, until cranberries burst and mixture thickens, about 15 minutes. Stir in vanilla.

Makes 2 cups
(64 calories per cup)

Pineapple Grape Tapioca

¾ cup unsweetened pineapple juice
2 teaspoons honey
¼ cup quick-cooking tapioca
1 teaspoon vanilla extract
1 egg yolk
1¼ cups skim milk
2 egg whites
⅛ teaspoon cream of tartar
20 seedless green grapes,
   quartered

Pour pineapple juice into a medium-size saucepan. Mix in honey. Sprinkle tapioca over top and set aside to soften for 5 minutes. Bring to a boil over medium heat stirring constantly. Stir in vanilla. Remove from heat.

In a small bowl, beat egg yolk and skim milk together. Put a little of the hot mixture into beaten yolk. Return to pan, whisking to blend. Cook over low heat, whisking constantly, until mixture thickens, about 10 minutes. Remove from heat and let cool.

In a medium-size bowl, beat egg whites until foamy. Add cream of tartar and continue beating until stiff peaks form. Fold into cooled tapioca. Chill.

When ready to serve, fold in grapes.

Makes 8 servings
(62 calories per serving)

Apricot Raisin Confections

1 cup unsweetened flaked coconut,
   divided
1 cup dried apricots
¼ cup raisins
1 tablespoon honey
2 teaspoons freshly squeezed
   orange juice

In a food processor, process ½ cup of the coconut until it is coconut sugar. Set aside on a plate.

Process remaining ingredients in food processor. Roll mixture into balls of about 1 tablespoon each between palms of hands. Roll balls in coconut sugar.

Makes 32 cookies
(25 calories per cookie)

Easy Cheesy Dessert

2 cups low-fat cottage cheese
¼ cup honey
¼ teaspoon ground cinnamon
1 teaspoon vanilla extract
½ cup Perfect Pineapple Sauce
(page 55), **divided**

In a food processor or an electric mixer, beat together cottage cheese, honey, cinnamon, and vanilla until smooth. Divide among 4 sherbet glasses. Cover with plastic wrap and chill well.

Serve each portion topped with 2 tablespoons of the sauce.

Makes 4 servings
(175 calories per serving)

Slim Pastry Cream

½ envelope unflavored gelatin
½ cup cold water
1 cup skim milk, divided
1 tablespoon cornstarch

2 egg yolks
3 tablespoons honey
1 teaspoon vanilla extract

In a small saucepan, sprinkle gelatin over cold water. Set aside to soften for 5 minutes.

In a medium-size saucepan, heat ¾ cup of the skim milk. Shake remaining skim milk and cornstarch together in a jar with a tight-fitting lid, or whisk together until well blended.

In a small bowl, beat egg yolks and honey together until lemon colored. Beat in cornstarch mixture.

Pour hot skim milk into the top of a double boiler and set over hot water. Slowly whisk in egg yolk mixture and cook, stirring constantly, until custard coats the back of a wooden spoon. Remove from heat and pour into a medium-size bowl.

Heat softened gelatin until dissolved. Stir into pastry cream. Mix in vanilla. Allow to cool before using.

Makes about 1½ cups
(19 calories per tablespoon)

Almond Pots de Crème

½ cup instant nonfat dry milk
2 cups boiling water
2 tablespoons honey
1 teaspoon almond extract
1 teaspoon vanilla extract
3 eggs, beaten

Preheat oven to 350°F.

In a medium-size bowl, dissolve nonfat dry milk in water. Add honey and extracts, stirring to blend. Pour a little of the mixture into beaten eggs, whisking well. Return to bowl, whisking constantly. Pour into 6 ovenproof cups and put in shallow pan on middle shelf of oven. Pour water into pan until it reaches halfway up the sides of cups. Bake until just set, about 30 minutes.

Chill before serving.

Makes 6 servings
(94 calories per serving)

Spectacular Squash Pie

1 recipe for Skinny Piecrust
   (page 5)
2 eggs
1 10-ounce package frozen squash,
   thawed
⅓ cup honey
½ teaspoon vanilla extract
1 cup skim milk, divided
2 tablespoons cornstarch
2 teaspoons ground cinnamon
¾ teaspoon ground nutmeg

Preheat oven to 350°F. Line a 9-inch pie plate with pastry and set aside.

In a large bowl, beat eggs. Add squash, honey, and vanilla and beat to mix well.

In a jar with a tight-fitting lid, shake together ½ cup of the skim milk, cornstarch, and spices. Mix into squash. Stir in remaining milk. Turn into piecrust and bake on bottom shelf of oven until filling is set and crust is browned, 55 to 60 minutes.

Cool before serving.

Makes 10 servings
(118 calories per serving)

Almond Strawberry Rice Pudding

1¼ cups skim milk
2 tablespoons honey
2 eggs, beaten
1 teaspoon vanilla extract
¼ teaspoon almond extract
2 cups cooked rice
1 cup fresh or unsweetened frozen strawberries, quartered

Preheat oven to 325°F. Spray a 1½-quart casserole with vegetable spray.

In a large bowl, beat together skim milk, honey, eggs, and extracts. Stir in rice and fold in berries. Bake on middle shelf of oven until set near, but not in, the center, about 45 minutes.

Allow to cool before serving.

Makes 8 servings
(95 calories per serving)

Applesauce Drops

¼ cup butter, softened
¼ cup cream cheese, softened
⅓ cup honey
1 egg
1½ teaspoons vanilla extract
1 cup whole wheat pastry flour
1 cup unbleached white flour
1 teaspoon baking powder
1 tablespoon ground cinnamon
½ teaspoon ground nutmeg
1½ cups Applesauce (page 81)
1 cup rolled oats

Preheat oven to 350°F. Spray a baking sheet with vegetable spray.

In a large bowl, beat together butter, cream cheese, and honey. Beat in egg and vanilla.

Into a medium-size bowl, sift together whole wheat pastry flour, unbleached white flour, baking powder, cinnamon, and nutmeg. Whisk to blend.

In another medium-size bowl, mix together Applesauce and rolled oats. Mix into moist ingredients. Stir in flour mixture and drop batter by heaping teaspoonfuls onto prepared baking sheet. Bake, one batch at a time, on middle shelf of oven until browned on the bottoms, 15 to 18 minutes.

Cool on wire racks. Bake second batch on cooled baking sheet.

Makes 5 dozen cookies
(37 calories per cookie)

Frozen Fruit Custard

2 cups evaporated skim milk, chilled
2 tablespoons honey
1 teaspoon vanilla extract
1½ teaspoons rum extract
2 cups Slim Pastry Cream (page 246)
¼ cup chopped dates
¼ cup raisins, plumped
¼ cup unsweetened flaked coconut

Lightly oil a 12-cup ring mold or bundt pan.

In a large bowl, beat evaporated skim milk until soft peaks form. Continue beating, drizzling in honey and extracts. Fold in pastry cream, dates, raisins, and coconut. Turn into prepared mold or pan, cover, and freeze.

To unmold, dip bottom of mold in warm water for 60 seconds. Unmold on a plate and slice with a warm, sharp knife.

Makes 10 servings
(142 calories per serving)

Fruity Sundaes

1 large banana
1 cup unsweetened frozen melon balls, thawed
8 seedless green or red grapes, halved
1½ cups unsweetened frozen raspberries, thawed, divided
2 cups Vanilla Ice Milk (page 72), divided

Slice banana into a medium-size bowl. Mix in melon balls, grapes, and 1 cup of the raspberries. Divide mixture among 4 dessert dishes. Top each with ½ cup of the Vanilla Ice Milk. Divide remaining raspberries among dishes, spooning them over ice milk. Serve immediately.

Makes 4 servings
(192 calories per serving)

Baked Blueberry Whip

This dish is reminiscent of a soufflé in texture, but this meringue-based dessert doesn't rise as high or collapse as low as a classic soufflé.

1½ cups fresh or unsweetened frozen blueberries, thawed
½ cup grape juice
1½ tablespoons cornstarch
½ cup water
2 tablespoons honey, divided
4 egg whites
¼ teaspoon cream of tartar

In a medium-size saucepan, combine blueberries and grape juice. Dissolve cornstarch in water and mix into blueberry mixture. Stir in 1 tablespoon of the honey and cook over medium heat, stirring constantly, until mixture bubbles and thickens. Remove from heat and set aside to cool.

Preheat oven to 325°F. Spray a 2-quart casserole with vegetable spray.

In a large bowl, beat egg whites until foamy. Add cream of tartar and remaining honey and continue beating until stiff peaks form. Fold into cooled blueberry mixture. Turn into prepared casserole and bake on middle shelf of oven for 30 minutes. Serve warm.

Makes 10 servings
(46 calories per serving)

Eggnog Soufflé

1 envelope unflavored gelatin
1 cup skim milk
¼ cup honey
4 eggs, separated
1 teaspoon vanilla extract
½ teaspoon rum extract
¼ teaspoon cream of tartar
½ teaspoon ground nutmeg

Lightly oil a 4-cup soufflé dish and fit it with a soufflé collar.*

In a medium-size saucepan, sprinkle gelatin over skim milk. Set aside to soften for 5 minutes. Add honey and heat over medium heat just until gelatin dissolves.

In a small bowl, beat egg yolks. Add a little of the hot milk mixture, stirring constantly. Gradually return to hot milk and cook, stirring constantly, until mixture thickens enough to coat the back of a metal spoon. Remove from heat. Stir in vanilla and rum extracts and chill until thickened but not set.

In a medium-size bowl, beat egg whites until foamy. Add cream of tartar and continue beating until stiff peaks form. Fold into gelatin mixture and turn into soufflé dish. Chill until set.

Before serving, remove soufflé collar and sprinkle top of soufflé with nutmeg.

Makes 8 servings
(87 calories per serving)

*To make a soufflé collar, cut a piece of foil 10 inches wide and long enough to encircle soufflé dish plus 2 inches. Fold lengthwise. Tie collar around dish with string, allowing foil to extend 3 inches above rim. Tape seam together. Butter or oil inside of collar.

Christmas Trifle

This is a happy ending for a Christmas gathering.

20 Ladyfingers (page 99)
½ cup Strawberry Sauce (page 230)
3 cups Very Vanilla Pudding (page 76), divided
¾ cup seedless green grapes, halved
½ cup unsweetened frozen raspberries, thawed
¾ cup mandarin orange sections, halved
½ cup evaporated skim milk, chilled
1 tablespoon honey

Line bottom of a 2-quart glass bowl with half of the Ladyfingers. Drizzle Strawberry Sauce over them. Make a layer of 1½ cups vanilla pudding.

In a medium-size bowl, toss fruit together. Arrange half of it on top of the pudding. Repeat layers. Refrigerate for at least 2 hours.

At serving time, beat evaporated skim milk in a small bowl until foamy. Add honey and beat until soft peaks form. Spread on top of trifle and serve immediately.

Makes 12 servings
(174 calories per serving)

Sparkling Fruit Tart

1 recipe for **Skinny Piecrust**
   (page 5)
1 cup creamed cottage cheese
1 cup **Slim Pastry Cream**
   (page 246)
½ teaspoon almond extract
1 medium-size banana
2 kiwi fruits
2 fresh peaches
1 tablespoon freshly squeezed
   lemon juice
¼ cup red currant jelly

Bake piecrust according to directions. Cool.

In a medium-size bowl, beat together cottage cheese, pastry cream, and almond extract. Spread on bottom of prepared piecrust.

Peel and thinly slice all fruit. Halve kiwi slices. Arrange fruit decoratively on top of cheese mixture. Brush bananas and peaches lightly with lemon juice to prevent discoloration.

In a small saucepan, melt currant jelly. Brush on all fruit. Serve immediately.

Makes 12 servings
(129 calories per serving)

Pretty Party Puffs

A crowd-pleasing dessert!

¾ cup whole wheat pastry flour
¾ cup unbleached white flour
1¼ cups water
¼ cup butter
4 eggs, slightly beaten
2 cups **Sunshine Filling** (page 164),
   divided

Preheat oven to 400°F.

In a medium-size bowl, sift together whole wheat pastry flour and unbleached white flour, whisking to blend.

Put water and butter into a medium-size saucepan and bring to a rolling boil. Reduce heat and stir in flour, beating with a wooden spoon until mixture pulls away from sides of pan. Remove from heat and set aside to cool slightly.

Add eggs, 1 at a time, beating until smooth. Drop batter by slightly mounded teaspoonfuls onto an ungreased baking sheet. Bake on middle shelf of oven for about 20 minutes, or until lightly browned.

Pierce sides of each puff with tip of a sharp knife to release steam and place puffs on wire racks to cool.

When cool, split each puff crosswise with a sharp knife, removing any soft or uncooked dough. Fill each puff with 2 teaspoons of filling and replace tops. To serve, pile in a pyramid on a large plate.

Makes about 4 dozen puffs
(40 calories per puff)

Carob Coconut Pie

2¼ cups skim milk, divided
1½ envelopes unflavored gelatin, divided
1 cup part-skim ricotta cheese
¼ cup plus 1 tablespoon honey, divided
2 teaspoons vanilla extract, divided
¼ cup carob chips
2 tablespoons butter
1 tablespoon cornstarch
½ cup unsweetened flaked coconut

Spray a 9-inch deep-dish pie plate with vegetable spray.

In a small saucepan, sprinkle ½ envelope of the gelatin over ¼ cup of the skim milk. Set aside to soften for 5 minutes.

In a medium-size bowl, beat together ricotta, ¼ cup of the honey, and 1 teaspoon of the vanilla until smooth.

In the top of a double boiler set over hot water, melt together carob chips and butter.

Heat softened gelatin mixture over medium heat stirring constantly, until gelatin dissolves. Beat gelatin mixture, along with carob mixture, into cheese mixture and spread on bottom of prepared pie plate. Chill until set.

In a medium-size saucepan, dissolve cornstarch in 1 cup of the skim milk. Sprinkle remaining gelatin over top and set aside to soften for 5 minutes. Add remaining honey and cook over medium heat, stirring constantly, until mixture thickens slightly and gelatin dissolves. Stir in remaining vanilla, remaining skim milk, and coconut. Gently pour over top of carob mixture and chill until set.

Makes 10 servings
(166 calories per serving)

Apple Cider Sorbet

3 cups apple cider
1½ teaspoons ground cinnamon
2 tablespoons honey
1 cup hot water

Pour cider into a large bowl. Dissolve cinnamon and honey in hot water. Add to cider.

Process mixture in an ice cream maker according to manufacturer's instructions, or turn mixture into a large shallow pan and freeze until mushy. Remove from freezer, beat to break down ice crystals, and then return to freezer. Repeat this procedure twice, putting sorbet in a covered container the last time. Freeze until ready to serve.

Makes 8 servings
(60 calories per serving)

Apple Banana Cupcakes

1 6-ounce can unsweetened frozen
  apple juice concentrate, thawed
2 ripe bananas, chunked
2 eggs
2 tablespoons honey
1 teaspoon vanilla extract
1 cup whole wheat pastry flour
1 cup unbleached white flour
2 teaspoons baking powder
1 teaspoon ground cinnamon

Preheat oven to 350°F. Line a 12-cup muffin tin with paper liners.

In a food processor, blend apple juice, bananas, eggs, honey, and vanilla until smooth.

Into a medium-size bowl, sift together remaining ingredients. Stir with a wire whisk to blend well.

In a large bowl, stir together both mixtures until well blended. Turn into prepared muffin cups, filling to tops, and bake on middle shelf of oven for 20 minutes.

Makes 12 servings
(146 calories per serving)

Smooth Strawberry Pudding

2 envelopes unflavored gelatin
½ cup cold water
1 cup skim milk
3 tablespoons honey
1½ teaspoons vanilla extract
4 cups unsweetened frozen strawberries, thawed
8 mint leaves, optional

In a medium-size saucepan, sprinkle gelatin over water. Set aside for 5 minutes to soften. Add skim milk and honey and heat over medium heat, stirring constantly, until gelatin dissolves. Remove from heat and stir in vanilla.

In a food processor, puree strawberries. Add gelatin mixture and process until just blended. Divide among 8 dessert glasses and chill until set.

Decorate with mint leaves before serving, if desired.

Makes 8 servings
(68 calories per serving)

Easy Eggnog

2 egg whites
1 cup skim milk
2 teaspoons honey
2 teaspoons vanilla extract

Combine all ingredients in a blender and process for 30 seconds on high setting.

Makes 2 servings
(82 calories per serving)

Ginger Pears

6 firm ripe pears
¼ cup honey
⅓ cup hot water
¼ teaspoon ground ginger
1 tablespoon butter

Preheat oven to 350°F.

Peel, halve, and core pears. Arrange in a large casserole.

In a small bowl, mix together honey, hot water, and ginger. Pour over pears and dot with butter. Cover and bake on middle shelf of oven for 30 minutes.

Makes 6 servings
(160 calories per serving)

Index

Allspice, 25
Almond(s), 25
    in Bavarian cream with kiwi fruits, 143
    beverages, 129
    coconut chiffon pie, 57
    flavored pecan cookies, 149
    jelly, 147
    mandarin orange custard, 220
    mousse, 240
    peach cake, 129
    peach ice, 121
    pots de creme, 247
    pudding, 247
    strawberry rice pudding, 247
    stuffed in peaches, 169
    tapioca, 80
    yogurt, 79
Ambrosia
    grape, 29
    strawberry, 29
Angel food cake, 6, 38, 106, 159, 165
Anise seeds, 25
Appetite. controlling, 113-114
Apple(s), 87-88. *See also* Apple
  juice; Applesauce
    American baked, 35
    baked, 12
    baked with meringue topping, 210

    banana cupcakes, 253
    beverage, 18
    with blueberries, 186
    cake, 11
    carob crumb, 78
    cranberry loaf, 242
    cranberry pie, 224
    German pancakes, 8
    grading of, 87-88
    in mixed fruit, 221
    peanut butter, 55
    pear scallop, 228
    pie, 20
    prepared in advance, 155
    raisin tart, 199
    sorbet, 252
    types of, 887-88
Apple cider sorbet, 252
Apple juice, 46
Applesauce, 8, 81
    cranberry, 244
    cranberry sundae, 209
    crepes, 223
    custard, 181
    drop cookies, 248
    fluff, 77
    meringue, 108
Apricot(s), 88-89. *See also* Apricot juice

brandy ice, 75
    in cooked mixed fruit, 128
    in frozen peach brandy supreme, 115
    pie, 125
    prepared in advance, 155
    puffy souffle, 116
    raisin confections, 244
    raisin pie, 138
    ripeness of, 88-89
Apricot juice, 46
Auto suggestion, 3
Avocados, 89
    in fruit kabobs, 143

Baked Alaska
    beautiful, 16-17
    peppermint, 197
Baked goods, preparing in advance, 156-57.
    See also Pastry; *specific types of
    baked goods*
Banana(s)
    apple cupcakes, 253
    baked, 64
    blueberry pie, 169-70
    cookies, 182
    cream pie, 51
    in exotic compote, 167
    frozen, 84
        pudding, 59
        squares, 32
    in fruit kabobs, 143
    in fruit mold, 181
    in fruit sundae, 249
    in fruit tart, 251
    gelatin, 42
    grape gelatin layers, 150
    ice milk, 13
    milk shake, 188
    mint treat 71
    in mixed fruit, 221
    orange pops, 226
    peachy crepes, 118
    pudding layers, 35
    ripeness of, 89
    smoothies, 101
    strawberry cream pudding, 71
    strawberry freeze, 6, 110
    in summer compote, 161
    tangy fluff, 7

tapioca, 223
    torte, 28
Bars
    peach, 142
    pecan, 169
    prune, 221
Baskets (fruit)
    dessert, 75
    papaya, 108
    watermelon, 171, 216
Bavarian cream
    almond, with kiwi fruits, 143
    coffee, 69
    peach nut, 13
    strawberry, 198
Beverages. *See also* Milk Shakes;
    Punches; Shakes: *under specific fruits*
    almond peach, 129
    apple-grape drink, 18
    cantaloupe, 185
    cranberry, 233
    fruited dessert shake, 29
    fruit juices, 45-46
    grape fizz, 64
    minted lemonade, 171
    orange pineapple punch, 207
    punch, 108, 151
    strawberry fizz, 83
    teas, 46-47
    tomato zip, 39
    water, 43
Blackberry (Blackberries)
    in blueberry soup, 124
    in fruit dip, 168
    pie, 148-49
    in pineapple cobbler, 161
    shortcake, 187
Blinchiki with blueberry grape sauce, 179
Blueberry (Blueberries), 4
    with apples, 186
    baked whip, 249
    banana pie, 169-70
    blackberry soup, 124
    chiffon pie, 163
    cobbler, vi, 4
    in cooked mixed fruit, 128
    crustless cheesecake, 100
    fluffy omelet, 41
    in fruit mold, 181
    ice milk, 100

maple yogurt, 98
in mixed fruit, 103
peach compote, 158
peach fluff, 141
pear pie, 240
puffs, 126
raisin cake, 125
raspberry parfait, 37
raspberry pie, 119
rice pudding, 8
ripeness of, 89-90
in sherbet parfaits, 243
tangerine pie, 101-102
in watermelon basket, 171
Blueberry-grape sauce, 122
with blinchiki, 178
with cantaloupe points, 165
Blueberry-raspberry meringue, 139-40
Bombe, holiday ice cream, 6
Brandy
apricot ice, 75
extract, 25
peach supreme, 115
with peach tapioca, 188
souffles with strawberry sauce, 229
zabaglione, 61
Bread puddings, 175
pear, 38
raisin pear, 53
strawberry, 80
tangerine, 63
Breads, 114
carob coconut, 170
cran-apple, 242
gingerbread squares, 184
Buffet, 238-39
Butter, x, xiv
Buttermilk, xiii

Cake batter, 195
Cake rolls
decorative, 219
frozen peppermint, 240
jelly, 48, 49, 157
lemon, 225
molasses ginger, 229
prepared in advance, 156
prune, 48
pumpkin frosted, 209

raspberry-lemon filled, 145
Cakes. See also Cake rolls; Cheesecake;
Cupcakes; Gingerbread; Shortcakes
angel food, 6, 38, 106, 157, 165
apple and spice, 11
baking, 133-36
be my Valentine, 31
blueberry raisin, 125
carob, 18
carrot, 52, 200
cranberry nut, 224
date nut, 206
decoration of, 217-219
decorative shapes of, 218
discovery, 201
English tea, 115
foam, 133-34
freezing of, 195
frosted, 195
frostings for, 136
gingerbread, 184
yogurt-topped, 71
jelly roll, 48, 49, 157
ladyfingers, 48, 50, 111, 124, 250
lazy day loaf, 183
orange filling layer, 165
papaya layer, 106
peach layer, 117, 142
peachy almond, 129
pina colada, 159
pineapple fromage, 82
prepared in advance, 156
pretty peach layer, 117
pruneau roll, 48
prune cupcakes, 98
pumpkin frosted, 209
raspberry gelatin, 111
skinny shortcakes, 72
spice, 60
sponge, 242
storage of, 192, 194
vanilla-carob pudding, 201
Calories of some fruit juices, 46
Candy
apricot raisin, 244
carob, 74
prune confections, 106
Cantaloupe(s), 90
beverages, 185
in fruit kabobs, 143

and lemon gelatin, 202
in melon compote, 126, 151
in mixed fruit, 103
points, 165
sherbet, 178
soup, 138
storage of, 156
and strawberries, 118
in summer compote, 161
in watermelon basket, 171
Cantaloupe dove, 216
Carbohydrates, complex, 114
Carob, xiii, xvi. *See also* Carob sauce;
  Carob syrup
  apple crumb, 78
  cake, 18
  chip cookies, 52
  chip pie, 64
  chip pudding, 18, 64, 183
  coconut loaves, 170
  coconut pie, 252
  coconut pudding, 181
  coffee gelatin, 222
  confections, 74
  cookie crust, 205
  cookies, 18, 50, 52
  creamy pudding, 160
  ice milk, 75, 180
  mousse, 144
  orange whip, 208
  tangerines, 151
  thins, 18, 50
  truffles, 152
Carob chip(s)
  cheesecake, 232
  cookies, 52
  in meringue cookies, 82
  pie, 64
  pudding, 18, 64, 183
Carob sauce, 58, 71, 183
  on sundaes, 185
Carob syrup, 35, 148
  as decoration, 218
Carrot
  cake, 52, 200
  juice, 46
Cheese. *See also* Cheesecake; Cottage cheese;
  Cream cheese; Ricotta cheese
  cookies, 4
  honey pie, 231

  pineapple cake, 82
  strawberry pudding, 53
Cheesecake
  creamy carob chip, 232
  crustless blueberry, 100
  lemon, 56
  pineapple, 82
  with raspberry topping, 139
Cherry (Cherries)
  faux jubilee, 146
  in French vanilla ice milk, 137
  as garnish, 214
  grapefruit meringue, 33
  grape-nuts pudding, 16
  orange gelatin, 56, 122
  pie, 37
  storage of, 90
  torte, 142
  unsweetened frozen, 10
  varieties of, 91
Chinese gooseberries. *See* Kiwi fruit
Chocolate, xi
Cinnamon, 23, 25
  cream pudding, 172
Citrus fruit. *See also* specific citrus fruits
  as decoration, 214-216
  pie, 50
Citrus slices, as decoration, 215
Clementines, 241
Cloves, 23, 25
Club soda, 45
Cobblers, 176
  blackberry-pineapple, 161
  blueberry, 4
Coconut. *See also* Coconut sugar
  carob loaves, 170
  carob pie, 252
  carob pudding, 181
  chiffon pie, 57
  ice milk, 13
  pastries, 234
  pie, 189
  piecrust 16,
  raspberry pie, 152
  snow balls, 55
  souffle, 226
  thumb print cookies, 15
Coconut sugar, 15, 36, 55, 60, 64, 84, 145
  with dates, 199
  as decoration, 215, 216

Coffee, 45
 Bavarian cream, 69
 carob gelatin, 222
 crustless pie, 27
 granita with cream, 9
 souffle, 97
 whipped gelatin, 199
Compote(s)
 cinnamon peach-blueberry, 158
 decorative shells for, 216
 exotic fruit, 167
 melon, 126, 151
 prepared in advance, 153, 156
 tangy summer, 161
Cookies
 almond-flavored pecan, 149
 applesauce drops, 248
 apricot raisin confections, 244
 banana, 182
 carob chippers, 52
 carob thins, 18, 50
 cheese, 4
 coconut thumb prints, 15
 crisp, 203
 date orange, 63
 freezing of, 193, 194
 friendly hermits, 27
 light lemon, 35, 121
 mellow meringues, 82
 molasses ginger joys, 227
 oatmeal, 27, 241
 orange date, 63
 peanut butter drop, 74
 pecan, 149
 Pfeffernusse, 39
 prepared in advance, 156
 raisin rice chews, 203
 spicy oatmeal, 241
 storage of, 196
 unbaked drop, 196
Cornstarch, xi, 175
Cottage cheese, x, xiv
 cheesecake, 189
 mocha pie, 206
 pie, 83
 with pineapple sauce, 245
 in raspberry pie, 121
Cranberry (Cranberries), 91. *See also*
 Cranberry juice
 apple loaf, 242

apple pie, 224
in applesauce, 244
applesauce sundae, 209
beverages, 233
nut cakes, 224
pineapple fluff, 205
pineapple pie, 203
Cranberry juice, 46
Cream, x, xiii. *See also* Bavarian cream
 delicious diet, 109
 pastry, 246
Cream cheese, x, xiv
Crepes
 applesauce, 223
 delicious diet, 30, 31, 62, 84
 light rhubarb, 137
 mango strawberry, 84
 maple, 243
 peach melba, 158
 peachy banana, 118
 perfect pear, 31
 pineapple, 201
 strawberry pecan, 107
 tangerine, 62
Crisp, peach, 167
Cupcakes
 apple banana, 253
 prune, 98
 pumpkin, 209
Currants, in cooked mixed fruit, 128
Custard, 175
 applesauce, 77, 181
 frozen fruit, 248
 frozen nectarine, 160
 mandarin orange almond, 220
 old-fashioned, 73
 papaya, 123
 poached ginger peaches in, 146
 sauce with snow pudding, 204
 spicy pumpkin, 197
 splash, 57
 vanilla with raspberry sauce, 240
Custard pie. *See under* Pies.

Dairy products, xiii
Date(s)
 in fruit custard, 249
 nut cake, 206
 orange cookies, 63

in prune confections, 106
stuffed, 199
Decorations
for cakes, 217-19
coconut sugar as, 60, 217
food colors as, 212
fruit as, 209-212
meringue as, 110
for pies, 219
ricotta cheese as, 216
Dessert baskets, 75
Desserts. *See also* specific types of
buffet, 238-39
decoration of, 213-19
freezing of, 194-95
preparing of in advance, 155-57
serving, 239
setting for, 237-38
storage of, 193-95
Diet foods, xii-xiii
Dieting, sticking to, 113-14
Dips, fruit, 168
Doughnut holes, mock, 16

Easter baskets, meringue, 75
Eggnog, 254
Eggnog souffle, 250
Eggs
beating of, 133
blueberry omelet, 41
in puddings, 176
whites of in souffles, 177
Exercise, 67
benefits of, 68
mental advantages of, 3
with music, 68
Extracts, 25

Fiber, xi, 114
Figs, xi
with creamy topping, 187
Fillings
freezing of, 194
orange-honey, 164, 165
preparing of in advance, 156
tangy lemon, 222
Fizz. *See* Beverages
Flavorings, 25

Flour, xi, 175
unbleached white, 177
whole wheat pastry, 177
Fluff(s)
applesauce, 77
banana, 7
cranberry pineapple, 205
grape, 232
orange lemon, 145
papaya, 110
peach blueberry, 141
strawberry, 40
Fondue, fruit, 117
Food colors, 218
French toast, strawberry, 15
Frosting, xi, 136, 217. *See also* Toppings
decorator, 31, 34
easy vanilla, 11
Frozen desserts. *See also* Ice cream; Ice milk;
Sherbet(s); Sorbet(s); *specific types of
desserts*
baked Alaska, 16-17
banana mint treats, 71
bananas, 84
banana squares, 32
banana strawberry, 110
blueberry ice milk, 100
coffee granita with cream, 9
creamy strawberry pie, 117-18
extracts in, 25
fruit custard, 248
fruit pudding, 59
fruitsicles, 181
grapefruit granita, 207
grape pops, 97
holiday ice cream bombe, 6
mock mocha pops, 35
nectarine custard, 160
orange banana pops, 226
orange sorbet, 41
peach almond ice, 121
peach brandy supreme, 115
peach souffle, 128
peach-topped ice mold, 167
peppermint Alaska, 197
pineapple snow, 98
plum orange ice, 140
pumpkin, 220
ruby red granita, 103
snow balls, 55

strawberry fluff, 40
Fruits, xi-xii. *See also specific fruits*
  baked
    apple, 35
    apple and pear, 228
    apple pear bake, 12
    carob crumb apples, 78
    ginger pears, 254
    jungle treat, 64
    pears, 21, 54, 59, 69
  basket. 171
  cinnamon peach-blueberry compote, 158
  citrus pie, 50
  as diet food, 87, 96
  dried. xii
  exotic compote, 167
  fondue, 117
  frozen, xi-xii
  as garnishes, 213
  kabobs, 143
  mixed, 14, 103, 108, 151, 161, 221
    cooked, 128
    melons, 126
    nectarine cups, 130
    pears a la creme, 20
    peels, 216
    pie, 81
    preparing of in advance, 155-56
    puddings, 176
    punch, 151
    shells, 216
    and sherbet parfaits, 243
    shopping for, 87
    strawberry ambrosia, 29
    tart, 251
    three-melon compote, 151
    washing, 155
    yogurt pie, 40
Fruit cup. *See also* Fruits, mixed
    nectarine, 130
    orange, 10
Fruit dip, 168
Fruit juices, 45-46. *See also* Beverages
    calorie count of, 46
Fruit mold, 181. *See also* Gelatin(s)
Fruitsicles, 181

Garnishes, 213, 214
Gelatins, xi

banana royal, 42
Bavarian cream with kiwi fruits, 143
carob coffee treat supreme, 222
cherry orange delight, 122
clementine, 241
coffee whip, 199
fruit mold, 181
grape banana, 150
jelly shakes, 12
lemon and melon, 202
lemon razzmatazz, 36
light lemon, 7
lime chiffon pie, 105
mint, 58
molds, 157
orange, 225
orange-cherry, 56
peach nut Bavarian, 13
pineapple Charlotte, 48
pineapple snow, 98
puddings, 176
raspberry, 111
tangy banana fluff, 7
Ginger, 23, 35
  molasses joys, 227
Gingerbread
  squares, 184
  yogurt-topped, 71
Granita
  coffee with cream, 9
  grapefruit, 207
  ruby red, 103
Grape(s). *See also* Grape blueberry sauce;
  Grape juice; Grape-nuts (cereal)
  in ambrosia, 29
  banana gelatin, 42
  banana gelatin layers, 150
  beverage, 18, 64. *See also* Grape juice
  in Christmas trifle, 250
  fluffy dessert, 232
  frozen pudding, 59
  in fruit dip, 168
  in fruit fondue, 117
  in fruit pie, 40, 81
  in fruit sundae, 249
  as garnish, 213
  in mixed fruit, 11, 221
  orange meringue cups, 58
  pineapple tapioca, 244
  with ricotta cheese, 242

seedless green, 10, 14
snow, 159
strawberry pie, 78
in summer compote, 161
varieties of, 91-92
in watermelon basket, 171
Grape blueberry sauce, 122, 126
with blinchiki, 179
Grapefruit(s). *See also* Grapefruit juice;
Grapefruit-orange juice
in ambrosia, 29
dove, 216
granita, 207
meringue, 23
pie, 19
treat, 225
vitamins in, 91
Grapefruit juice, 46
Grapefruit-orange juice, 46
Grape juice, 46
frozen granita, 103
gelatin, 12
Grape-nuts (cereal)
cherry pudding, 116
pudding, 28

Herbal teas, 46-47
Honey, ix-x
and cheese pie, 231
shopping for, xii
Honeydew dove, 216
Honeydew melon(s), 92
in melon compote, 126, 151
sherbet, 147
in sherbet parfaits, 243

Ice cream, xi
holiday bombe, 6
Ice milk, xi. *See also* Frozen desserts;
Milk shakes; Sundaes
banana coconut, 13
blueberry, 100
with cantaloupe points, 165
French carob, 6, 75, 166, 180
French peppermint, 227, 240
French vanilla cherry, 137
fruit shake, 29
in fruit sundae, 249

peach-topped mold, 166
pumpkin, 220
in sundaes, 185, 249
vanilla, 55, 71, 72, 75, 137
Ices
apricot brandy, 75
peach almond, 121
plum orange, 140
Icing. *See* Frosting

Jelly. *See also* Cake rolls, jelly
almond, 147
shakes, 12
Jubilee, faux cherries, 146

Kabobs
fruit, 143
mandarin orange, 230
Key limes, 93. *See also* Lime(s)
Kiwi fruit, 92
almond Bavarian cream with, 143
in exotic compote, 167
in fruit fondue, 117
in fruit tart, 251

Ladyfingers, 99
in carnation cassata, 111
in Christmas trifle, 250
in citrus pie, 50
in peach-topped frozen ice mold, 166
in pineapple Charlotte, 48
in pineapple surprise, 124
Lemon(s). *See also* Lemonade; Lemon filling;
Lemon juice; Lemon peel decoration;
Lemon shells; Lemon teas
cake roll, 225
cheesecake, 56
chiffon pie, 202
cookies, 35, 121
custard pie, 208
extract, 25, 26
filling, 222
gelatin, 7, 202
and melon gelatin, 202
orange fluff, 145
pudding cake, 179
pumpkin pie, 187

raspberry, gelatin, 36
razzmatazz, 36
ripeness and storage of, 92
sorbet, 62
squares, 101
torte, 28
Lemonade, 45
minted, 171
Lemon filling
in cake roll, 145
in pie, 12
Lemon juice, 45
Lemon peel decoration, 214-15
Lemon shells, 214
Lemon teas
balm tea, 46-47
verbena tea, 46-47
Lime(s), 92-93. *See also* Key limes
baked pineapple glazed with, 207
chiffon pie, 105
Loaf cake, 16-17, 183
carob coconut, 170
cran-apple, 247
Loaves. *See* Breads; Cakes

Mandarin orange(s). *See also* Orange(s)
almond custard, 220
in Christmas trifle, 250
in coffee Bavarian cream, 69
fruit pie, 40
kabobs, 229
sections, 7
Mango(es), 93
strawberry crepe stacks, 84
yogurt pudding, 107
Maple syrup
with baked peaches, 165
in blueberry yogurt, 98
crepes, 243
meringue kisses, 100
in pear torte, 5
pudding, 28
Margarine, xiv
Melons. *See also specific types of*
compote, 126, 151
in fruit sundae, 249
mixed, 126
peeling and slicing of, 156
rings, with strawberries, 118

shells, 216
soup, 138
Meringue. *See also* Pies
applesauce, 108
cookies, 82
as decoration, 216
grapefruit, 33
lite kisses, 100
orange, 58
plum, 166
raspberry-blueberry, 139-40
Meringue shells, 75, 76, 107, 122
Milk. *See also* Ice milk; Milk shakes
low-fat, xiii
nonfat dry, x, xiii
sauces, freezing of, 194
skim, x, 46, 175
whole, x
Milk shakes. *See also* Shakes
banana, 188
orange pineapple, 148
papaya, 123
Mint, 25
banana treat, 71
gelatin, 58
Mocha
cheese pie, 206
mock pops, 35
popcorn, 162
Molasses
ginger cake rolls, 227
ginger joys, 227
pudding, 229
Molds. *See* Gelatin(s)
Mousse
almond, 240
carob, 144
Muskmelons. *See* Cantaloupe(s)

Nectarine(s)
cups, 130
frozen custard, 160
Nutmeg, 23, 25
Nuts. *See also specific types of*
and cranberry cake, 224
and date cake, 206
as decoration, 218

Oatmeal cookies, 241
Omelets, fluffy blueberry, 41
Orange(s). *See also* Mandarin orange(s);
    Orange filling; Orange juice; Orange peel
    decoration; Orange star
        in ambrosia, 29
        banana pops, 226
        carob whip, 208
        cherry gelatin, 122
        in cinnamon cream pudding, 172
        citrus pie, 50
        date cookies, 63
        in exotic compote, 167
        extract, 25, 26
        in fruited cups, 10
        gelatin, 56, 225
        lemon fluff, 145
        meringue cups, 58
        in mixed fruit, 10, 221
        pie, 19
        pineapple punch, 207
        pineapple shake, 148
        pineapple sherbet, 70
        plum ice, 140
        plum pudding, 190
        pudding, 106
        ripeness of, 93
        shells, 214
        shopping for, 93-94
        sorbet, 41
        storage of, 94
        whip, 210
Orange filling, 164
    in layer cake, 165
    in party puffs, 251
Orange juice, 46
Orange peel decoration, 215
Orange star, 215

Pancakes, apple-filled German, 8
Papaya(s), 94
    baskets, 108
    custard, 123
    fluff, 110
    layer cake, 106
    milk shake, 123
Papaya juice, 46
Parfaits
    fruit and sherbet, 243

Presidents' Day patriotic, 37
    tapioca, 103
Parties, dessert, 237-39
    setting, 237-38
Pastry. *See also* Baked goods; *specific types of*
    coconut, 234
    cream, 246
    freezing of, 195-96
    strips as decoration, 219
Peach(es), xi-xii. *See also* Peach brandy;
    Peach sauce
        almond cake, 129
        almond ice, 121
        almond-stuffed, 169
        baked maple, 165
        in banana crepes, 118
        bars, 142
        beverages, 129
        blueberry compote, 158
        blueberry fluff, 141
        crunchy crisp, 167
        as decoration, 215
        frozen souffle, 128
        in fruit fondue, 117
        in fruit tart, 251
        gelatin, 13
        layer cake, 117
        melba crepe cups, 158
        in mixed fruit, 14
        pear shortcakes, 178
        poached ginger in custard, 146
        pudding, 97
        raspberry torte, 105
        rhubarb raisin pie, 162
        rhubarb sauce, 162
        scallop, 10
        souffle, 77
        strawberry pie, 111
        vanilla poached, 184
        varieties of, 94
        in watermelon basket, 171
        whip, 189
        with yogurt sauce, 186
        yogurt whip, 149
Peach brandy
    frozen, 6
    supreme, 115
    tapioca, 188
Peach sauce, 63, 118, 120
    with almond jelly, 147

with frozen ice mold, 166
Peanut butter
    apples, 55
    cookies, 74
    with dates, 199
    low-calorie, 54
    vanilla pie, 226
Peanut pie, 10
Pear(s)
    a la creme, 20
    apple scallop, 228
    baked, 12, 21, 54, 59
    blueberry pie, 240
    bread pudding, 38
    crepes, 31
    easy baked rings, 21
    ginger, 254
    in mixed fruit, 14, 221
    peach shortcakes, 178
    pie, 10
    prepared in advance, 155
    raisin bread pudding, 53
    with raspberry sauce, 19
    sauce, 19
    spicy baked, 54
    stuffed baked, 59
    surprise, 69
    torte, 6
    varieties of, 94
Pecan(s)
    almond flavored cookies, 149
    bars, 169
    and date cake, 206
    with ricotta cheese and fruit, 242
    in strawberry crepe rolls, 107
Peppermint
    extract, 26
    frozen cake roll, 240
    ice milk, 227
    meringue pie, 223
Peppermint Alaska, 197
Persimmon(s), 94
    pudding, 223
Piecrusts. *See also* Shells
    carob cookie, 205
    coconut, 16, 19
    decorative, 219
    freezing of, 196
    making perfect, 177
    meringue, 51, 64, 107, 110, 177

mini, 37, 104
skinny, 5, 20, 33, 40, 57, 81
Pies. *See also* Shells
    almond coconut chiffon, 57
    apple raisin, 20
    apricot, 125
    apricot raisin, 138
    banana cream, 51
    black and white pudding, 33
    blackberry, 148-49
    blueberry banana, 169-70
    blueberry raspberry, 119
    blueberry tangerine, 101-102
    carob chip, 64
    carob coconut, 252
    cherry, 37
    citrus, 50
    coconut, 189
    cottage cheese, 83
    cottage cheese mocha, 206
    cran-pineapple, 203
    creamy frozen strawberry, 117-18
    crustless blueberry chiffon, 163
    crustless coffee, 27
    crustless lemon pumpkin, 187
    custard, 193
    decoration of, 219
    deep dish blueberry pear, 240
    dream, 12
    freezing of, 196
    fruit, 81, 193
    fruity yogurt, 40
    grapefruit orange, 19
    grape strawberry, 78
    honey cheese, 231
    lemon chiffon, 202
    lemon custard, 208
    lime chiffon, 105
    oriental apricot, 125
    peach rhubarb raisin, 162
    peach strawberry, 111
    peanut pear, 10
    peanut vanilla, 226
    peppermint Alaska, 197
    peppermint meringue, 223
    pina colada, 79
    pineapple upside-down, 32
    plum, 120, 163
    prepared in advance, 155, 156
    prune yogurt, 231

pumpkin pineapple 233,
raspberry cheese, 127
raspberry coconut, 152
raspberry cream, 144
rhubarb peach raisin, 162
squash, 247
storage of, 193
strawberry grape, 81
strawberry peach, 111
strawberry rhubarb, with meringue
    crust, 110
topless apple cranberry, 224
upside-down pineapple, 32
vanilla plum, 163
yogurt prune, 231
Pina colada
    cake, 159
    pie, 79
Pineapple(s). *See also* Pineapple juice;
    Pineapple sauce
    blackberry cobbler, 161
    canned, xii
    in compote, 161
    cranberry fluff, 203
    cranberry pie, 203
    crepes, 201
    crushed, 10
    as decoration, 215
    in exotic compote, 167
    fromage cake, 82
    in fruit pie, 81
    in fruit pudding, 188
    in fruit shake, 29
    as garnish, 213
    gelatin, 48
    grape tapioca, 244
    in lemon and melon gelatin, 202
    lime-glazed baked, 207
    orange punch, 207
    orange shake, 148
    orange sherbet, 70
    pie, 40
    pudding, 204
    pumpkin pie, 233
    ripeness of, 95
    snow, 98
    sorbet, 198
    storage of, 95
    in summer compote, 161
    surprise, 124

in tropical tart, 185
upside-down pie, 22
in watermelon basket, 171
Pineapple juice, 48
Pineapple sauce, 55
    with blended cottage cheese, 245
    with snow balls, 55
Plum(s), 95
    meringue, 167
    orange ice, 140
    orange pudding, 190
    pie, 120, 163
    tarts, 182
Popcorn
    mocha, 162
    spice, 64
Popsicles
    fruitsicles, 181
    mock mocha, 35
    orange banana, 226
Prune(s)
    bars, 221
    confections, 106
    cupcakes, 98
    whipped, 205
    yogurt pie, 231
Pudding cake, lemon, 179
Puddings. *See also* Bread puddings; Custard;
    Meringue; Pudding cake, lemon; Rice
    pudding; Tapioca
    almond pots de creme, 247
    almond strawberry rice, 247
    with angel food cake, 201
    banana layers, 35
    banana smoothies, 101
    black and white pudding pie, 33
    blueberry rice, 8
    bread, 175
    carob chip, 183
    cinnamon cream, 172
    coconut carob, 181
    coffee Bavarian cream, 69
    cooking, 175
    creamy carob, 33, 160
    fluffy almond tapioca, 80
    frozen fruit, 59
    gelatin, 176
    grape-nuts cherry, 116
    ideas for, 176
    Indian, 229

ingredients in, 175
lite surprise, 18
mango yogurt, 107
maple, 28
orange, 106
orange plum, 190
peach, 97
peach blueberry fluff, 141
pear bread, 38
persimmon, 223
pineapple delight, 204
prepared in advance, 155, 157
raisin pear bread, 53
rice, 176
royal red tapioca, 29
snow with custard sauce, 204
storage of, 193
strawberry, 253
strawberry banana cream, 71
strawberry Bavarian, 198
strawberry bread, 80
strawberry cheese, 53
strawberry rice, 119
surprise, 188
sweet potato, 86
tangerine bread, 63
vanilla, 250
vanilla cream with raspberry sauce, 200
Vermont, 28
very vanilla, 33, 35, 59, 76, 163
Puffs
blueberry, 126
orange filled, 251
Pumpkin(s)
cupcakes, 209
frosted cake, 209
frozen dessert, 220
and lemon pie, 187
orange pineapple, 207
pineapple pie, 233
spicy custard, 197
Punches, 151

Raisin(s), 10
apple tart, 199
apricot confections, 244
apricot pie, 138
blueberry cake, 125
cookies, 27

frozen pudding, 59
in fruit custard, 248
nut cookies, 39
peach rhubarb pie, 162
pear bread pudding, 53
pie, 20
rice chews, 203
souffle, 130
Raspberry (Raspberries). *See also* Raspberry-
blueberry meringue; Raspberry sauce
blueberry parfait, 37
blueberry pie, 119
with cheesecake, 139
cheese pie, 127
coconut pie, 152
in cooked mixed fruit, 128
cream pie, 144
in fruit fondue, 117
in fruit sundae, 249
and ladyfingers, 111
lemon gelatin, 36
peach torte, 105
ripeness of, 95
rum sauce, 14
rum sherbet, 17-18, 75, 150, 243
shells, 164
sorbet, 170
with strawberry sauce, 164
Raspberry-blueberry meringue, 139-40
Raspberry sauce, 19, 61, 103, 127
on almond-stuffed peaches, 169
in cake roll, 145
on fruit kabobs, 143
in peach melba crepe cups, 158
rum, 14
strawberry shells with, 122
vanilla cream with, 200
Reward system, 3
Rhubarb
crepes, 137
peach raisin pie, 162
peach sauce, 1626
strawberry pie, 110
Rice
in apricot pie, 125
pudding, 176
almond strawberry, 247
blueberry, 8
strawberry, 119
raisin chews, 203

Ricotta cheese, xiv
    as decoration, 216
    and fruit, 242
    parfait, 37
Rum
    extract, 25
    pina colada pie, 79
    raspberry sherbet, 17-18, 75, 150, 243
    souffles, 61

Salads, 114
Salt, xii
    raspberry, 103
Sauces
    apple, 81
    blueberry-grape, 122, 126, 179
    creamy carob, 58, 71, 186
    as decoration, 218
    peach, 63, 118, 120
    peachy rhubarb, 162
    pears with raspberry, 19
    pineapple, 48, 55
    raspberry, 103, 117, 143, 200
    raspberry rum, 14
    raspberry with pears, 19
    ruby raspberry, 18, 19, 61, 127
    strawberry, 130, 164, 229, 230
Seeds as decoration, 215
Self-image, 1-2
Shakes. See also Milk shakes
    fruited dessert, 29
    jelly, 12
    orange, 148
Shells. See also Piecrusts
    meringue, 76
    raspberry, 164
    strawberry with raspberry sauce, 122
Sherbet(s), xi
    cantaloupe, 178
    with fruit parfaits, 243
    honeydew, 147
    orange pineapple, 70
    raspberry rum, 16-17, 75, 150, 243
Shopping tips, xii-xiii, xiv
Shortcakes
    blackberry, 187
    peach pear, 178
    skinny, 72
    strawberry, 73

Snacks, xiv-xv
    vs. big meals, 113
    calories in, 114
Snow
    grape, 159
    snow balls, 55
Sodium, xii
Sorbet(s)
    apple cider, 252
    fresh pineapple, 198
    lemon, 62
    orange, 41
    raspberry, 170
Souffle(s)
    apricot, 116
    brandy with strawberry sauce, 229
    coconut, 236
    coffee, 97
    eggnog, 250
    peach, 77
    frozen, 128
    raisin, 180
    rum, 61
    types of, 176
Soups
    blueberry-blackberry, 124
    cool strawberry, 70
    melon, 138
Sour cream, xiii
Spice(s), xiv, 23
    cake, 60
        and apple, 11
    extracts, 25-26
    popcorn, 64
    potency of, 23-24
    shopping for, 24
    whole or ground, 23-24
Squares
    banana, 32
    gingerbread, 184
    lemon, 101
Squash
    custard, 57
    pie, 247
Strawberry (Strawberries). See also
    Strawberry fan; Strawberry rose;
    Strawberry sauce
    almond rice pudding, 247
    ambrosia, 29
    availability of, 95-96

banana cream pudding, 71
banana freeze, 110
Bavarian, 198
beverages, 83
bread pudding, 80
cheese pudding, 53
cooked, 103
on cottage cheese pie, 83
as decoration, 215
in French toast, 15
frozen fluff, 40
frozen pie, 117-18
in fruit fondue, 117
in fruit kabobs, 143
in fruit mold, 181
in fruit pie, 81
in fruit pudding, 176
grape pie, 78
hulling of, 155
mango crepe stacks, 84
in melon ring, 118
in mixed fruit, 103, 161
and papaya, 108
peach pie, 111
pecan crepe rolls, 107
pudding, 253
rhubarb pie, 110
rice pudding, 119
with ricotta cheese, 242
ripeness of, 96
shells with raspberry sauce, 122
shortcake, 73
soup, 70
in summer compote, 161
in watermelon basket, 171
Strawberry fan, 215
Strawberry rose, 215
Strawberry sauce, 230
with brandy souffles, 229
in Christmas trifle, 250
in nectarine cups, 130
raspberries with, 164
Stress and exercise, 67
Substitute ingredients, 2
Sugar, ix. *See also* Honey
Sundaes, 185
cranberry-applesauce, 209
fruity, 249
Sweet potato pudding, 36
Syrups

carob, 148
as decoration, 218
maple, 28, 98, 100, 165, 243

Tangerine(s). *See also* Tangerine juice
blueberry pie, 101-102
bread pudding, 63
carob-dipped, 151
crepes, 62,
in fruit dip, 165
Tangerine juice, 46
Tapioca, xi
banana, 223
brandied peach, 188
fluffy almond, 80, 103
grape, 29
in grape-nuts cherry pudding, 116
pineapple grape, 244
as thickener, 175
Tarts
apple raisin, 199
fruit, 251
plum, 181
tropical, 185
Teas, 45, 46-47
Thickeners, 174
Tomatoes, in beverage, 39
Toppings, xi. *See also* Frosting
mock whipped cream, 9
Tortes
banana lemon, 28
cherry, 142
maple pear, 6
peachy raspberry, 105
Trifles, 176
Christmas, 250
Truffles, carob, 152

Vanilla, 25
custard, 73
ice milk, 55, 71, 72, 75, 137
poached peaches, 184
pudding, 76
very, 33, 35, 59, 76, 163, 250
Vanilla extract, 25-26
pure vs. synthetic, 26
Vitamin A, xiii
in grapefruit, 91

Vitamin C, 91
Vitamin D, xiii

Walnuts
    in baked pears, 59
    cookies, 39
    and cranberry cake, 224
    in meringue cookies, 82
    peach nut Bavarian, 13
    in prune confections, 106
Water, 45
Watermelon, 96
    in fruit kabobs, 143
    in melon compote, 125, 151
    in mixed fruit, 103
Watermelon basket, 171, 216
Whipped cream, mock, 9
Whips
    baked blueberry, 249
    baked prune, 205
    coffee, 199
    orange, 210
    orange carob, 208
    peach, 149, 189

Yogurt, xiii, xiv
    almond, 79
    blueberry with maple, 98
    fruit pie, 40
    on gingerbread, 71
    homemade skim milk, 46
    low-fat, x, 46
    mango pudding, 107
    peaches and, 186
    prune pie, 231
Yogurt fruit dip, 168